D0225664

WITHDRAWN

# How and How Much Can Intelligence Be Increased

153.9
H83d

# How and How Much Can Intelligence Be Increased

*edited by*

**Douglas K. Detterman**
*Case Western Reserve University*

**Robert J. Sternberg**
*Yale University*

 ABLEX Publishing Corporation
355 Chestnut Street
Norwood, New Jersey 07648

Copyright © 1982 by Ablex Publishing Corporation.


All rights reserved. No part of this book may be reproduced
in any form, by photostat, microfilm, retrieval system, or any other means,
without the prior permission of the publisher.

Printed in the United States of America.

**Library of Congress Cataloging in Publication Data**
 Main entry under title:

How and how much can intelligence be increased.
 Includes index.
 1. Intellect. 2. Cognition. 3. Success. I. Detterman, Douglas K. II. Sternberg,
Robert J.
BF431.H63     153.9      82-1787
ISBN 0-89391-117-8      AACR2


ABLEX Publishing Corporation
355 Chestnut Street
Norwood, New Jersey 07648

# Contents

CAT Apr 10 '84

83-5110

# PART II  MODIFYING COGNITIVE SKILLS

# PART III: DISCUSSION

# Foreword

Douglas K. Detterman

This book addresses a fundamental and important question: How and how much can intelligence be increased? The question is important from both a theoretical and applied point of view, and fundamental to human progress.

Perhaps the theoretical importance of the modification of intellectual ability is the least obvious of the justifications for this book. Psychologists, particularly American psychologists, have frequently been accused of attempting to modify processes they do not understand. Efforts to alter intelligence are seen as premature. However, knowing how and how much intelligence can be changed is important information and must be predicted by any finished theory of intelligence. Efforts to modify intellectual functioning also indicate which variables should be given importance in models of such behavior.

The practical importance of modifying intelligence is more obvious but independent of the theoretical importance. The degree to which intelligence is thought to be a biological characteristic in theoretical models has no bearing on the practical importance of its alterability. All interventions must be environmental. The development of a technology of education depends on exactly understanding how to achieve gains in intelligence.

It is easy to underestimate the fundamental nature of the question asked by this volume. However, human adaptation depends almost entirely on the discovery of new knowledge and the conveyance of that knowledge to future generations. Even small increases in intelligence could have important implications for this process. It is sometimes assumed that the progress of civilization can be credited to a few individuals who make exceptional contributions. What is often forgotten is that those contributions cannot be maintained unless the mean intelligence of the population, as a whole, is sufficient to appreciate those contributions.

Given that the individual is limited in his capacity to acquire information, there are two possibilities for future progress: First, more individuals might acquire more specialized information. No change in the capabilities of an individual would be required but the potential for progress is limited by total population, which must be finite. This seems to be the current mechanism for adaption. More people are being educated at a higher level in more specialized areas. In the world as a whole, there is a substantial reserve of talent not now being suitably used. But, if knowledge continues to expand at an exponential rate, human resources might be used up more quickly than anyone could anticipate. The progress of civilization would be seriously impaired or halted if human resources were expended entirely for the retention of old knowledge, with little or no possibility for the acquisition of new knowledge.

The second possibility is to increase the individual's capability of acquiring new information. That is what this book is about. In the long run, it is a problem fundamental to the progress of civilization. Eventually, mankind will need substantially improved intellectual abilities for continued progress.

To many, the foregoing discussion will appear to be wildly speculative and entirely lacking in substance. However, before jumping to this conclusion consider the fate of those individuals at the lower end of the distribution of intelligence. Over the last 200 years, persons of low intellectual status have had a steadily increasing difficulty in adjusting to an increasingly complex society. There seems little doubt that this trend will continue. The question is how long it can continue before we reach a state of intellectual equilibrium.

This book presents a reasonably comprehensive survey to current work on efforts to modify intelligence. It is divided into four parts. The first section is an historical introduction to such efforts. The second part presents research concerned with global attempts to modify intellectual status. These attempts have been more concerned with outcome than with process, but as the chapters in this section will show, they have taken a decidedly theoretical turn. The third part of the book presents efforts to modify specific cognitive abilities. This research area is in an embryological stage, but the results are already quite promising. The final portion of the book presents an integration of the preceding two sections.

The work presented in this book raises many more questions than it answers. Even if there is no precise answer to how and how much intelligence can be increased, at the very least the work presented here demonstrates a number of ways the question can be asked with hope of an eventual answer.

D.K.D.

# *How and How Much Can*
# *Intelligence Be Increased*

# 1

# *The Training of Intellectual Aptitude\**

RICHARD E. SNOW

*Stanford University*

Education has always been, in part, an aptitude development program. Through history, differential educability defined differential intelligence, and attempts were made to adjust education to fit intellectual differences in one way or another. But scattered theory and research also suggested that educability could be improved through direct training of intellectual abilities as aptitudes for learning. Now, cognitive instuctional psychology seems ready to produce a design for education that is both adaptive to aptitude differences and aimed at adapting aptitude differences directly. Past and present problems and prospects for theory and research in this direction are reviewed.

This volume portends a new era in educational, cognitive, and developmental psychology. It signals a challenge to a new generation of scientific psychologists to make good on a pledge enunciated most clearly two decades ago by Hunt (1961). It seeks to show how research based on today's views of intelligence and experience can be used to promote intellectual development for individuals and groups.

The challenge is not, and was not, to be taken idly. After decades of dispute, as well as passive acceptance of one or another view, many educators and psychologists believed, in 1960, that they possessed the necessary knowledge finally to show that intelligence was significantly a product of experience. Educational experiences, in turn, could be arranged to advance almost any individual's cognitive development substantially beyond what nature, home environment, or prevailing socioeconomic conditions might ordinarily dictate. But the 1960's and early 1970's was a period of trial that seemed to end in failure, and there were contro-

*Part of this chapter was prepared while the author was in residence as Fellow at the Center for Advanced Study in the Behavioral Sciences, 1979–80. He is grateful for financial support provided by the National Institute of Mental Health (2T32 MH14581-04), the Spencer Foundation, and the Personnel and Training Research Programs, Psychological Sciences Division, Office of Naval Research (Contract No. N00014-79-C-0171). The views and conclusions contained in this document are those of the author, and should not be interpreted as necessarily representing the official policies, either expressed or implied, of the Office of Naval Research, or the U.S. government. The author thanks Professors Lee J. Cronbach, Denis C. Phillips, and Robert J. Sternberg, and also Elanna Yalow and Robert Curley, for helpful criticisms of portions of the manuscript, but reserves responsibility for any errors contained herein to himself.

versies about the meaning of test results, not unlike those that had gone before (Cronbach, 1975).

Across the same decades that spawned the compensatory education movement, a new kind of cognitive psychology grew to fruition. Its outline and potential relevance to education was perceived in 1960 (see Hunt 1961; also Bruner 1960, 1966). But its development did not begin to be spliced firmly with that of educational research and development until the mid 1970's. Now, however, a field called "cognitive instructional psychology" has clearly taken shape. Central to its agenda is the issue of whether intelligence, learning ability, or some other such interpretive label for aptitude, can be directly trained.

The chapters in this book give examples of some of the first modern attempts to develop intellectual aptitude directly. This first chapter reviews some of the history of past thinking and research on this question, partly to set the stage for the rest of the book and partly to define the larger context into which present and future research on aptitude training needs to fit. It is a condensation, with some additions and changes, of parts of a larger chapter that sought to review the interrelation of intelligence and education more generally (see Snow, 1982). The present chapter first examines some aspects of the goals of education and of research in relation to the nature of aptitude for learning. Then, a brief history of past thinking about the training of aptitude is given, some categories of past research are reviewed, and some hypotheses and admonitions for the future are noted.

## EDUCATIONAL GOALS AND RESEARCH GOALS

Research aimed at training aptitude directly fits into a broader pattern of educational and research goals. These need to be distinguished, so that the place of ensuing research can be seen in the larger program.

Three themes regarding the goals of education can be discerned, with varying emphasis, in the writings of virtually all educational theorists and philosophers. First, educational institutions exist to preserve and promote the development of knowledge for its own sake. Second, educational institutions exist as selection systems, or as part of such systems, to identify and allocate talent for the societies they serve. In a democracy, a public school system may even be the institution best equipped to provide equal opportunity for talent identification and allocation to all. Third, and perhaps most importantly for the purposes of this chapter, education aims at aptitude development. Since its earliest beginnings, education has always been concerned with human preparedness for further states of life. The term "aptitude" signifies some aspect of the present state of a human being that is propaedeutic to some future achievement, whether that achievement is defined as good citizenship, vocational skill or satisfaction, higher education, or greater intelligence.

Intersecting with these three themes, one can distinguish two broad categories of educational goals (Cronbach, 1967). There are individual goals, chosen by individuals themselves for their own purposes; the elective courses available in most schools and colleges provide the most obvious examples. But there are also common goals imposed for everyone by society—the minimal expectations in reading, writing, mathematics, citizenship, and physical education are examples. What is regarded as a common goal and what is left to individual choice varies across history and locale, of course. The main concern here is with the common, aptitude development goals, for this is where research on the training of intelligence makes its primary contribution. Such research makes a secondary contribution, however, to the individual goal category and to the selection function; as it helps to show what aspects of human intellect are most amenable to modification, by what means, and for whom.

Figure 1 has been adapted from Glaser (1977) to depict schematically the components of an aptitude development system, aimed at common goals. (Glaser also showed how a multiple version of Figure 1 could provide for individually chosen, divergent goals.) The educator's primary job today is to create and maintain such a system—one that reconciles society's commitment to equal educational opportunity for all individuals with the fact that individuals differ in aptitudes relevant to learning at the start. As Cronbach (1967) and Glaser (1977) have both argued, to reach common educational goals, the instructional system must be made adaptive to the diversity of human aptitudes. It must be geared either to adapt alternative instructional treatments $(T_1, T_2, T_3)$ to compensate for persistent individual differences in prior aptitudes (A) or to train selected individual differences into irrelevance by developing the required aptitudes directly $(D_1, D_2)$. The plan in Figure 1 includes provision for both kinds of individualization since, in most educational enterprises, there must be a trade-off between the two. The educator seeks to develop skill in reading directly, for example, because the ability to read is a common educational goal itself, and also because it is an aptitude for later learning in science and social studies, to name a few other common goal areas. If some individuals require many years to develop sufficient reading ability, then the educator must adapt parallel instruction in science and social studies to fit the individual's present strengths and weaknesses, or give up these other common goals. At any time, then, there is a compromise between direct aptitude development and adaptation of instruction to circumvent existing inaptitudes. One can think of direct aptitude training as remediation or acceleration; but more is implied here. Training aims at transfer, not merely the building of competent performance on some task for its own sake. On the other hand, the adaptation of instruction seeks treatment alternatives that capitalize on what strengths the individual has at the moment, while compensating for persistent weaknesses. The outcome in either case is transferable, generalizable competence, i.e., aptitude. The credential awarded at the completion of some unit is more a promise of future performance than it is a record of past performance.

It is the realization of the sort of educational system depicted in Figure 1 that sets the purpose of much modern research in educational psychology. Aptitudes of

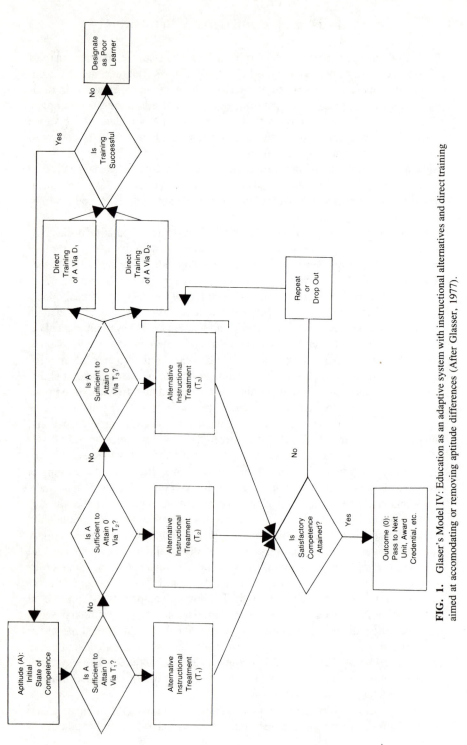

**FIG. 1.** Glaser's Model IV: Education as an adaptive system with instructional alternatives and direct training aimed at accomodating or removing aptitude differences (After Glasser, 1977).

one sort or another are defined and assessed, their relation to learning is studied, and attempts are made to determine whether identified inaptitudes can be removed directly or rendered irrelevant to learning performance by suitable adaptations of instructional method.

Any kind of individual difference in ability, personality, or motivational characteristics can serve as a source of aptitude or inaptitude for learning from instruction in some given setting, and can thus be a focus for research (see Cronbach & Snow, 1977; Snow, 1977). But the cognitive abilities usually interpreted as constituents of intelligence as aptitude for learning are of central interest. Educational psychology now recognizes intelligence as education's most important product, as well as its most important raw material. To be clear on what is meant by "intelligence" as both an aptitude and an outcome for education, however, we must demote the construct from the reified unity so often taken for granted in educational and other public discussions. Cronbach's (1977, p. 275) definition seems to do this:

> "Intelligence" is not a thing, it is a style of work. To say that one person is "more intelligent" than another means that he acts more intelligently, more of the time. "Efficiency" is a word of the same type. We cannot locate the efficiency of a factory in any one part of the operation. Rather, the purchasing division, the people who maintain the machines, and the operators, inspectors and shippers do their tasks with few errors and little lost time; efficiency is an index of how well the system functions as a whole. After Binet had observed excellent and inferior intellectual performance of children, he summed up the difference in this famous three-part description of intelligence:
>
> > the tendency to take and maintain a definite direction; the capacity to make adaptations for the purpose of attaining a desired end; the power of auto-criticism. (Translation by Terman, 1916, p. 45.)
>
> The first point has to do with accepting a task and keeping one's mind on it. The second point contrasts intelligent behavior with acting out of habit, with little analysis of the immediate situation. The third emphasizes that better performers prevent errors before they occur or catch them promptly when they are made.

The terms "intelligence," "intellectual," and the like are shorthand substitutes for this construction. The intellectual aptitudes of concern here are thus the styles of work in learning that make for successful learning outcome under given instructional conditions. There are other aptitudes for success in other pursuits, but the intellectual aptitudes of concern in this book pertain to learning ability.

A first goal for research in this direction would seem to be to define and analyze these styles of work, to understand in detail how individuals, and thus how different individuals, function psychologically to perform the kinds of tasks taken as indicators of intellectual aptitude, of learning from instruction, and of outcome from instruction. A principal question is how task characteristics moderate or modify this functioning. An increasing amount of research in cognitive instructional psychology has been aimed at this goal over the past decade (for detailed reviews of this work, see Glaser, 1978a; Glaser & Resnick, 1972; McKeachie, 1974; Resnick, 1981; Snow, Federico, & Montague, 1980; Wittrock &

Lumsdaine, 1977). Unfortunately, only in the last few years has research attention focussed directly on the kinds of task performances actually used to assess intellectual aptitude in real educational settings. Given progress in this direction, a second goal would then be research aimed at constructing and evaluating actual instructional experiences to fit the T and D requirements of Figure 1.

But work toward the second goal need not wait on the first. It can, in fact, contribute directly to the attainment of the first goal. Educational research often proceeds this way—first design an instructional treatment that works; one can later do the analytic experiments that show why it works. Theory resulting from both kinds of research should be able both to explain the chief empirical relations among intelligence, learning, and outcome indicators, and to allow the development of the kinds of instructional treatments and measures needed to realize the educational system depicted in Figure 1.

## INTELLIGENCE AND EDUCATION
## THROUGH HISTORY

It is instructive to consider some aspects of the history of ideas connecting intelligence and education. The sections below review briefly some of the historical and philosophical milestones in educational theory and research.

### Educational Philosophies

Formal education emerged as one of the earliest social institutions, seemingly in parallel with the recognition that human intellect could and should be formally cultivated. Educational theorists, from antiquity to modern times, have recognized intelligence as relevant to education. Some made distinct assumptions about individual and group differences in intelligence, and some made provision for such differences in their educational designs. Over the history, several trends seem notable.

First, throughout most of western history, human intellect has been regarded as multifaceted and educable, in either absolute or differential terms. For most early writers, observed differential educability *defined* differential intelligence. In other words, differences in intelligence were inferred from observed differences in ease of learning. Furthermore, from the Graeco-Roman philosophers to the Enlightenment, education emphasized direct training of intelligence through the discipline of mental faculties. These faculties grew strong as muscles of the mind through exercise, in the study of the classics, mathematics, and the like. There were contrary views, some with quite modern casts, but the disciplines held sway.

Second, the view that education should and could reduce intellectual differences associated with race, social class, or gender, had to wait beyond the Enlightenment to the American and French Revolutions, even though clear statements favoring equality of intelligence and education, among genders at least, had been part of several earlier philosophies. Again, some philosophies presaged the common practices by centuries.

Third, a marked change is evident in views on individuality and educability as educational history moved into progressivism in the nineteenth and twentieth centuries. The assumption of individual differences in educability resulting from prior individual differences in intelligence gave way to the assumption of mass educability without much regard to differential prior intelligence.

The shift away from mental faculties must be attributed primarily to Locke (see Garforth, 1966; Gay, 1964), who replaced the concept of innate ideas and mental disciplines with a "blank slate," on which each individual's accumulating experience was recorded. Such a view led others to an extreme form of environmentalism, wherein anyone could be molded into anything by appropriate education. But Locke also acknowledged native powers and the importance of individual differences, while withholding judgment on their origins. These were seen as potentials; they became specialized abilities and skills only through exercise in interaction with experience, and were probably limited in transferability. Locke's views have had wide and divergent effects, on up to the present (see Cleverley & Phillips, 1976). They led to the practice of direct training of sensory and perceptual skills in early progressive education and to some modern forms of individualized instruction. But they also seem close to the psychology of differential abilities advanced in the first half of this century. Following Locke, many theorists continued to write of "improving minds" or "training intellect," but such references strike one as knowingly metaphorical rather than as implications that exercise develops general mental discipline directly. In higher education, particularly, the emphasis since Locke has been on indirect training of plural abilities through didactic diversity.

Another dramatic shift is associated with Dewey (see Archambault, 1964), but it began long before. The progressive movement defined the modern elementary school and modern ideas about teacher training, early in the nineteenth century. The kindergarten was installed and special training in preschool education for mothers was advocated. The movement championed the education of the whole child through enriched sensory and perceptual experience, discovery learning, and learning-by-doing, preferably with natural objects and experiences, rather than with books. One can then trace the elaboration of one or another aspect of progressive thought on up to World War II. Human beings, particularly young children, are infinitely educable if treated humanely. Education should be child-centered, using the educational values of the child's personal and social world, including the value of active, cooperative play. Education draws out the latent creative and esthetic qualities of personality much more than it puts knowledge in. The later progressives, and particularly Dewey, sought an integration of child and curriculum as an experiential medium for mental growth. But the aim of education was to be social morality and social progress, preparation for work and life in a democracy, not mastery of subject-matter knowledge or skill for its own sake. Although new learning is interpreted and integrated in intellectual development by relating it to prior learning, interest and effort more than intelligence provide the keys.

There is a wealth of ideas in progressive theories suggesting how teachers and parents might arrange early educational experience to foster intellectual development. The theories disregard or downplay, however, the growth of individual differences in intellect and the potential effects on this growth of formal teaching of the disciplines of later education. Dewey, and other modern writers in his wake, judged particular educational exercises as they seemed to foster higher cognitive processes, broader conceptual thinking, and social skills. By emphasizing transferable knowledge and skill, rather than the immediate objectives of particular lessons, they were assuming generalizable aptitude development. But the vehicle for transfer was identical elements across experiences, since psychological experiments (Thorndike & Woodworth, 1901) had written the final epitaph of the formal discipline hypothesis. Also, all of the progressives emphasized the individuality of learners in one way or another; teachers were admonished to understand a child's individual nature. But the systematic study of intellectual differences for the purpose of adapting instruction to fit individuals was never pursued.

If one takes the primary premise of this chapter—namely, that education is an aptitude development program, that intelligence is an organization of aptitude for learning and transfer, and that instruction must be designed both to remove inaptitudes directly where possible and to adapt alternative treatments to capitalize on or to compensate for persistent aptitude differences in order to develop other aptitudes—then the line of educational theory running from the Graeco-Roman period, and particularly Quintilian (see the Butler translation, 1954, p. 265–269; also Snow, 1982), on through Locke and the Enlightenment seems the most productive. Some selections from the more recent progressive theories can also be used (e.g., Dewey's concept of education for learning-to-learn and transfer), but they must be crossed with a modern interactional (i.e., Darwinian) view of individual differences. The five themes for teachers offered by Quintilian, for example, are as relevant to educational research and practice today as they were in first century Rome:

1. Identify apparent aptitudes and inaptitudes for each learner.
2. Help to develop aptitudes by differentiating courses of instruction, allowing individual educational goals. Guide learners in choosing courses according to their aptitudes.
3. Within a course of instruction toward a common goal, seek to develop all relevant aptitudes even if some are weak at the start; adapt alternative instructional treatments to the individual's aptitude pattern, so as to remove defects and to build up strengths where they are lacking.
4. Use the individual's strengths to work on the weaknesses. Teaching that runs counter to an individual's aptitudes may actually weaken those aptitudes.

5. Even if, below a certain level of general intelligence, little can be done other than to choose goals in keeping with special aptitudes, above that general level, appropriately adapted instruction can bring initially weak aptitudes up, to equal other prior strengths.

## Scientific Beginnings

Unfortunately, early educational and psychological research did not address these hypotheses programmatically, and for the most part, still has not done so. Through the nineteenth and early twentieth century, progressivism, pragmatism, and the social reform movement in general, mixed with two different misunderstandings of Darwin's then new theory. The mixture produced a framework for education that moved away from, rather than toward the ideal of Figure 1.

On the one hand, it was believed that universal education gave all persons the opportunity to show their natural talents, regardless of family background. Higher talents were thus selected for advanced development by the formal and informal tests of education. The "survival of the fittest" interpretation of Darwin's theory seemed consistent with this view. Galton (1869) demonstrated the link to heredity. Intelligence increasingly came to be regarded as the single rank ordering of people on general mental fitness, discoverable through observed differential educational progress. As in the centuries before, educability defined intelligence.

On the other hand, the later wave of Social Darwinists turned Darwin's adaptation formula around; they saw environments as rank-orderable from good to bad on a single continuum. The aim, therefore, was to design the best possible educational environment for all children, and this aim fit perfectly with progressive theory. The way to reduce inequity was not to adapt instruction to individual differences but to find the one best instructional treatment for all. Through this whole period, the basic idea of systematic adaptive instruction was missed. (See Cronbach & Snow, 1977, pp. 6–12.)

Scientific psychology also moved in other directions at this time, due partly to other transactions between intelligence and education. Systematic measurement of individual differences had begun early in the nineteenth century. The aim was to assess precisely all the elementary reactions associated with intelligence. The work of Galton and J. McKeen Cattell is notable, but Wundt, Ebbinghaus, and other luminaries in the history of psychology also made central contributions (see Boring, 1957). Jastrow (1901) in his presidential address to the American Psychological Association summed up the hopes that this trend would illuminate the study of intelligence substantially.

But the trend was dragged to a halt by an educational study (Wissler, 1901). The detailed measurements of Galton and Cattell failed to correlate with college achievement, implying either that the measures did not represent intelligence or that the interpretation of intelligence as general learning or adaptation ability was wrong. Since academic achievements did correlate across subject-areas, it was the Galton-Cattell measures that were questioned, not the single-rank-order theory of intelligence and achievement. Spearman (1904) then identified intelligence with the central tendency apparent in intercorrelations among school achievement measures.

Meanwhile, Binet had been experimenting with some success, using measures of the more complex mental processes involved in judgment and reasoning. He was commissioned by the Paris schools to develop objective methods for distinguishing children who would be likely to profit from regular instruction from those who would not; the latter could then be removed to special schools for suitably simplified instruction. In effect, Binet was asked to study the interaction of intelligence and instructional treatment. The items found predictive of school achievement became the Binet-Simon Scale and, through translation by Terman, the Stanford Binet Intelligence Scale. The scale rapidly came into wide use in the U.S., especially in education, in the hands of clinical, counseling, and school psychologists. The use of group mental tests, validated against the Stanford-Binet, also spread rapidly following the success of Otis's Army Alpha and Beta tests during World War I. (See Linden & Linden, 1968; Jenkins & Paterson, 1961; Wolf, 1973.)

## Mental Testing in the Schools

With intelligence operationally and conceptually defined almost solely on educational criteria, and with the use of mental tests in schools proliferating rapidly, misinterpretation and misuses set in. The interpretation of intelligence as unidimensional native capacity lost sight of the fact that Binet, Terman, Otis, and their followers had put together fairly loose collections of empirically valid items, that many items reflected prior educational advantages, and that the original intent (of Binet, at least) had been to identify persons with special educational problems and needs. The tests were samples of scholastic ability, reflecting only a person's development to date of testing. To interpret them as measuring "General Intelligence" was a flagrant overgeneralization. Yet, the evidence that test score differences were associated with educational progress all along the age scale became massive. Occupational, ethnic, socioeconomic, and other group comparisons using the tests also fit with then current public attitudes. The prevailing interpretation produced the tendency to label children in schools into arbitrarily defined levels along a single rank-order continuum. Ability grouping became regular practice, while special education never really developed the truly *alternative* instructional treatments originally envisioned. Educational practice solidified into a routine that remained virtually unchanged through World War II to the early 1960's, with minor exceptions. In the elementary schools, progressive ideas seeped in, but practical economics preserved the 30-child classroom. Learners were divided into faster and slower reading groups, mathematics groups, etc., usually corresponding to measured or perceived ability levels, but not really into alternative instructional treatments adapted to different abilities while still aimed at a common goal. High schools developed the most obvious divisions based on scholastic aptitude, designated as "college preparatory," "regular," and "business" or "vocational" streams. Similar organizations could be found in the school system of England and Western Europe. But the U.S. relied much more heavily on mental tests. The tests were deemed objective and thus fair; they could replace the socioeconimic, ethnic, religious, and familial privileges and prejudices that had influenced older educational systems, detrimentally, for centuries.

## The Influence of Factor Analysis

Vernon (1951), and other British psychologists following Spearman (1923), used factor analytic studies of mental tests to evolve a hierarchical model of ability organization. Spearman's g or general intelligence was superordinate, but two clusters, called verbal-educational ability and spatial-mechanical ability, could be distinguished below it, at least in adolescence. These seemed to relate to performance in different school subjects. Beneath these were the more minor, specialized abilities. In the U.S., Thurstone (1938) and then Guilford (1967) concentrated on the special level, developing a long list of "primary" abilities, now organized into Guilford's Structure of Intellect model.

Educational practice was influenced by both these lines of work. For academic prediction and placement purposes, general ability measures yielding total IQ scores, and sometimes separating verbal and nonverbal subscores, were usually used. Attempts at developing diagnostic measures of more specific educational abilities, distinguishing vocabulary, reading comprehension, different linguistic skills, and the like, usually showed that the subdivisions were strongly correlated and thus not readily distinguishable. For counseling and guidance purposes among adolescents and adults, however, the multifactor aptitude batteries that emanated from the Thurstone-Guilford tradition were preferred because profile differences were thought to relate to success in different specialized educational programs and their associated subsequent occupations. The evidence tended to show that different abilities do correlate to some extent with success in learning different kinds of subject matter, and the patterns of correlations change over years of schooling as curricula change emphases; differential ability tests can be useful in guiding individual choices (Cronbach, 1970). For some educational and many occupational prediction purposes, however, the differential measures have done no better than a general ability measure used alone (McNemar, 1964; Ghiselli, 1966).

Many of the tests developed in factor analytic research were based on hypotheses about cognitive process differences in mental performance. For the most part, however, the process hypotheses were lost in the ensuing drive to improve the technology of testing and factor analysis. Factor theories dealt with static ability dimensions; the assumption was implicit that these were fairly stable elements of the cognitive system. Though their development could be traced along the age scale, the basic research to analyze the cognitive process and content bases of such individual differences, and the possibility of altering these directly, was not developed.

## The Influence of the Laboratory

The early studies of Binet, Wissler and Spearman seemed to equate intelligence with educational learning ability. Experimental psychologists expected, then, that mental tests should correlate with performance on the kinds of basic learning tasks they studied in the laboratory. Woodrow (1946), however, after a series of investigations, concluded that no such correlation could be found. Later studies conducted in the Thurstone tradition (Allison, 1960; Gulliksen, 1961; Stake, 1961) also failed to find substantial relationships. With the exception of a few (such as McGeogh & Irion, 1952), experimental psychologists thus largely ignored intellectual differences; learning, not intelligence, was the fundamental topic for scientific psychology. Unfortunately, research on the simple learning tasks of the laboratory had little to say to educators, beyond some suggestions about the organization of drill and practice, and the value of reinforcement. Unfortunately also, Woodrow's early work was faulty on methodological as well as substantive grounds, and the later work missed what relations existed by concentrating on special abilities, rather than a more general ability construct. What evidence there is actually supports the view that general intelligence relates to conceptual learning and that a separable rote memory ability relates to rote learning (Cronbach & Snow, 1977). Jensen's (1980) review also suggests that the characteristics of learning tasks that lead to high relations between intelligence and learning are those that also characterize school learning tasks, such as meaningfulness and complexity. Laboratory psychology had missed an important opportunity to put intelligence and learning together.

Educational psychology retained an interest in intellectual differences due to the obvious relation of general mental tests to measures of learning in school, but efforts were bifurcated (Cronbach, 1957). Experimentally-oriented research contrasted alternative instructional methods seeking general improvements without regard to individual differences; initial intellectual differences among students were covaried out of instructional studies statistically, or ignored altogether. Correlational research pursued individual prediction of achievement and factor analyses of aptitude and achievement without regard to the particular kinds of instructional programs within which students learned. Isolated evidence about the possibility of different kinds of learning abilities and disabilities being fostered by different instructional experiences, such as the classic study by Brownell and Moser (1949) did not attract concentrated research attention.

## Curriculum Reform in the 1960's

General and special abilities had thus come to be regarded as fairly fixed, stable characteristics of persons. Differential development was thought to be predetermined by heredity. Education could make use of test score information in various ways, as noted above, but efforts to develop such abilities directly were expected to be fruitless, given psychology's denial of the doctrine of formal discipline, or even of transfer beyond identical elements. Educational rhetoric in these times, as often before, still included emphasis on general intellectual development—teaching students to think, to reason, to solve problems, etc. Dewey and progressivism had changed the character of many elementary schools (Cremin, 1961). But much of educational practice, particularly in later elementary levels and beyond, emphasized knowledge and skill acquisition, where the units were facts and fairly simple procedures. Associationism in psychology reinforced this orientation in education. Instructional methods remained fairly uniform across students and subject matters.

A drastic change was then wrought by a combination of two strong forces. First, Sputnik ushered in the space era, bringing the implication that U.S. education had fallen behind in the development of scientific and mathematical talent. Scientists and mathematicians joined with educators to produce the "new curriculum" movement, which sought to correct this. "New math" and "new science" projects developed instructional materials aimed not at teaching the traditional facts and concepts but at developing aptitude. The new theory recognized that factual knowledge soon becomes obsolete, especially as technological advances accelerate. The educational requirement, then, was to equip students with the deep-structure understanding and flexible problem-solving ability they would need for later learning in a new and rapidly changing world. Teaching methods also changed to suit; the new emphasis was on the promotion of discovery learning. An associated aim was the acceleration of basic learning and the individualization of learning rate through the use of teaching machines and programmed instruction. Skinner (1954; see also Glaser, 1978b) had opened an era of research on individualization of instruction based on operant views of learning. In parallel with the new curriculum movement, research on programmed instruction sought to show that intellectual differences in learning could be minimized by such individualization.

Second, the civil rights movement and associated judicial decisions brought pressure and then federal programs to erase the educational disadvantages that stemmed from *de facto* and *de jure* inequities. Education was again seen as a principal vehicle for righting social wrongs. Headstart, Follow Through, Upward Bound, Sesame Street, and many other attempts at compensatory education aimed frankly at developing intelligence.

All this activity was fueled too, by the new awakening of psychology to the rich complexity of cognitive organization and development, and the role of experience in the production of intelligence. Hunt's (1961) early book presented the central hypothesis, and challenge for education. He combined ideas coming from research on learning-to-learn and transfer, factor analysis, Piaget's theory of development, Hebb's neuropsychological theory, and the then new work on computer simulation of cognition to conclude that:

> Intelligence . . . would appear to be a matter of the number of strategies for processing information that have been differentiated and have achieved the mobility which permits them to be available in a variety of situations (p. 354).
>
> Intelligence should be conceived as intellectual capacities based on central processes hierarchically arranged within the intrinsic portions of the cerebrum. These central processes are approximately analogous to the strategies for information processing and action with which electronic computers are programmed. With such a conception of intelligence, the assumptions that intelligence is fixed and that its development is predetermined by the genes are no longer tenable (p. 362).
>
> . . . it is no longer unreasonable to consider that it might be feasible to discover ways to govern the encounters that children have with their environments, especially during the early years of their development, to achieve a substantially faster rate of intellectual development and a substantially higher adult level of intellectual capacity (p. 363).

The challenge was accepted, and a decade of educational and psychological research, development, and field evaluations ensued, fueled by unprecedented governmental support. The goal, simply put, was to improve the generalizable intellectual, learning, and problem-solving skills of students all across the public school years, particularly in reading, mathematics, and prescience. A primary focus was to provide enriched educational opportunities to young, disadvantaged children during their preschool and early elementary school years. Gains made during these early years were expected to carry over into later grades. A comprehensive history of Project Headstart, as the focus of the movement, is available from Zigler and Valentine (1979).

### Evaluation in the 1970's

The 1960's closed in controversy. The massive Coleman (1966) study of equality of educational opportunity found that many American school districts were still largely segregated, with large regional and racial differences in school facilities, programs, and student characteristics. On average, disadvantaged, ethnic minority students scored lower on standardized ability and achievement measures than did middle-class white students; the gap increased with grade in school, and school characteristics accounted for only a small fraction of the differences in student achievement. Reviewing the storm of reanalyses, and adding data from other sources, Jencks (1972) found the Coleman conclusions supportable, with some qualifications.

Results of evaluations of compensatory education programs also began to come in, suggesting limited success, if any. An early Head Start evaluation (Cicarelli et al., 1969) compared participants and non-participants in full-year and summer programs. The children's educational performance appeared not to differ appreciably from their non-Head Start peers. The Office of Economic Opportunity conducted a national experiment on performance contracting (Ray, 1972) that seemed to end in failure, despite some limited positive effects in some locations with some children. What gains there were in various compensatory programs seemed to dissipate in subsequent years. A study reported by Weikart (1972) had randomly assigned 3- and 4-year-old underpriviledged children to either an untreated control group or to one of three enrichment programs. Treated children showed some initial gains in IQ relative to control children, but no differences were found three years after the children left the program. Similar findings came from other studies.

The Sesame Street results, also, showed that advantaged children gained as much as, and perhaps more than, disadvantaged children from viewing the programs (Cook et al., 1975). If the effect was to widen the achievement gap, despite absolute gains, were such programs justified? The issue of the relative size of the "achievement gap" between advantaged and disadvantaged children questioned the basic goals of compensatory education.

The conclusion seemed to be that, although preschool enrichment programs may produce modest, short-term increases in IQ scores, declines occur when children enter or return to regular public school. Even the modest increases might be attributable to practice on the tests, rather than to basic intellectual advancement. The issue of heredity vs. environment was again raised: How much substantive intellectual gain could be expected from compensatory education programs, if individual differences were largely genetic in origin (Jensen, 1969, 1972)?

But it was also possible to discount some negative results, to find positive results, and even to begin to identify the characteristics of successful programs (White, 1973, Zigler, 1975). In the face of the mixed findings, and the storm of public and scientific controversy, compensatory education programs were made more intense, more complex, and more experimental (Datta, 1975). The programs that followed, such as Head Start Planned Variation and Follow-Through, sought to design and compare many alternative treatments systematically, rather than to test the effectiveness of any one program against conventional practices. The effects of some programs were notable on relatively specific tests that were closely linked to program goals. Direct instruction in reading and mathematics did seem to produce improvements in the specific skills taught. Long-term growth in general intelligence or achievement, or various affective outcomes, however, were still difficult to establish, and there was the implication that the programs producing the most immediate gains in special reading and math skills were not necessarily the ones that might promote more general, transferable intellectual development of the sort required on abstract reasoning tasks (Stallings & Kaskowitz, 1974; Stallings, 1975; Kennedy, 1978; see also Snow, 1982).

Over the same years, curriculum evaluation studies of new science and new math projects, as well as direct research on discovery learning, reached no generalizable conclusion regarding the value of such instruction or the role of intelligence in it (Shulman & Keislar, 1966; Cronbach, 1977; Cronbach & Snow, 1977). The strongest implication of the results seemed to be that able students are helped to become more able by discovery methods; those less able to begin with are left behind. Research on programmed instruction also ground down to mixed reviews, as it became clear that individualization with respect to the pace of instruction alone was insufficient to overcome intellectual differences among students related to learning (Cronbach & Snow, 1977). Evaluations in all these streams of work suggested that generalizations in education are limited. Findings of positive, or negative, or no effect for a program in one school or locale say little about what might be found in another school or locale. Results vary with teachers, students, and settings, implying that complex interactions moderate most effects (Cronbach 1975; Snow, 1977).

The 1970's closed with these puzzles, and with residual hopes in some quarters and doubts in others, that intellect could in fact be directly or generally developed. The educators, left with mixed messages, continued to rely as always before on the kinds of handed-down educational practices that seemed to fit the demands of their everyday economic, social, and psychological realities.

### Modern Cognitive Psychology

Here enters the modern psychology of cognition and instruction. World War II produced experimental psychologists who had had to apply what they knew about learning to the improvement of training. Assessment of this experience showed that the traditional psychology of learning had provided some semblance of an approach to education (Miller, 1957) but was, in general, woefully inadequate (Gagné & Bolles, 1959). Research toward an instructional psychology capable of meeting the problems of educational improvement began forming (Ausubel, 1963; Gagné, 1965; Glaser, 1965, 1978a). At the same time, experimentalists had been induced by war necessities to examine the capabilities of humans as information processors (Broadbent, 1958, Sperling, 1960). The advent of information theory, cybernetics, and high speed computers also helped to launch the revolution now called cognitive psychology (Neisser, 1967; Newell & Simon, 1972). Through this development, psychology now has the opportunity to become more useful to education than it has ever been before. The theoretical machinery finally appears to be equal to the complexity of intelligence-learning relations in education, so there is new hope that such relations can be addressed, unravelled, and understood. Conferences on the coordination of cognitive theory and instruction now appear with regularity (Anderson, Spiro & Montague, 1977; Klahr, 1976; Lesgold, Pellegrino, Fokkema & Glaser, 1978), and school learning tasks have come to be seen as uniquely valuable research vehicles for the development of cognitive theory (Greeno, 1980). Though considerations regarding the role of intelligence in learning and education were not central early in this movement, they have come to the fore during its most recent years (Friedman, Das, O'Connor, 1981; Resnick, 1976; Snow, Federico, & Montague, 1980). Thus, the stage now seems finally set for the development of a cognitive psychology of intelligence and learning in education; and, the direct training of intellectual aptitudes for learning becomes a central focus for this work. Indeed, as Anderson (1976, p. 16) has proposed, ". . . we take 'understanding the nature of intelligence' to mean possession of a theory that will enable us to improve human intelligence."

## CURRENT EVIDENCE AND CONTINUING RESEARCH

It is now possible to outline the theoretical framework and current evidence that should guide continuing research. The outline brings back some old ideas that now seem translatable to fit modern theory. It also combines evidence built up from correlational and experimental research on intellectual abilities as aptitudes for learning with evidence on such aptitudes as outcomes of learning. The outline is necessarily abbreviated here; space limitations preclude elaborations.

### A Theoretical Framework for the Correlational Evidence

First, intellectual differences and learning differences correlate all along the age scale (for reviews, see Jensen, 1980; Snow, 1982). But, intelligence and learning ability cannot be simply equated; formal learning and intellectual development have to be thought of as a complex of interwoven multivariate progressions. One cannot assume that intelligence measured at one point in time merely reflects experience to that point, while intellectual growth to a later point in time is an independent variable reflecting experience in the interim. The correlation between intelligence measures at the two points would, in this view, be simply understood as the overlap of earlier intelligence with later intelligence, plus a random increment. This "overlap hypothesis" has been discredited, partly on methodological grounds. Cronbach and Snow (1977) showed that estimated true mental age in any year is positively and substantially correlated with gain in mental age in subsequent years; the increments are certainly not random.

Second, to think of this improvement as a difference in simple learning rate is theoretically superficial as well as psychometrically unworkable. "Learning rate" has to be multivariate, because a person's rate will differ for different tasks, and for different components within a task. Presumably, learning to organize the task components into a coordinated performance also has one or more rates. Equating ability with learning rate provides merely an operational definition, not a substantive explanation. And, it has already been noted that attempts to individualize instruction, based only on a notion of pace or learning rate, fail to erase individual differences. There is more to ability differences than simple rate differences.

The modern approach starts from Hunt's (1961) ideas, partly quoted earlier, and with Ferguson's (1954, 1956) early view that abilities develop as a function of learning-to-learn and transfer. These pick up some themes from Locke, but also from Dewey, that had been misunderstood or overgeneralized in the interim. They also connect back to some of Quintilian's ideas.

Ability is attained through experience over time and consolidated through exercise. Skill in one kind of task performance transfers to performances on other tasks as a function of the similarity between tasks. Abilities thus develop as transfer relations within a class of tasks. Aptitude for learning, then, is readiness to transfer prior ability to new performances on similar tasks. These abilities differentiate with age through childhood and adolescence as a result of differentiation of experience in education (Anastasi, 1970). In the new language, however, it is information processing skills and strategies rather than unspecialized "powers" or "faculties" that develop, differentiate, and transfer.

The application of information processing theory and computer simulation makes it possible to extend this approach substantially. Simon (1976) set the new stage for interpreting intelligence as complex learning and transfer by suggesting that intelligence could be

> ". . . attributed to common processes among [various more specialized] performance programs, or to . . . individual differences in the efficacy of the learning programs that assemble the performance programs" (p. 96)

In other words, there may be elementary information processes that are common to the performance programs for different tasks. These can account for some of the relations among tasks that we take as indicative of transferable ability. But, there may also be higher-order metacognitive processes that learn to assemble and control the performance programs, and these can also account for some of the transfer relations among performance tasks.

Anderson (see Anderson, Kline, & Beasley, 1980; Anderson, et al., 1981) has now provided a detailed demonstration of how nonrandom increments in such ability might be realized and represented in a computer program. The program is, in effect, a general theory of learning, where propositional networks represent factual-conceptual knowledge and production systems represent procedural knowledge. The production system model is used to show how generalizable ability might develop through exercise. The simulation assumes that a single set of learning processes underlies such development. It then provides for improvement of performance by learning, from the problems it faces, to extend or restrict the range of situations where particular productions apply and to construct new productions, which then become strengthened and integrated into the system. Thus, the theory suggests how ability arises from learning and how such ability, once developed, is involved in further learning and thus in further ability development. The reciprocity can also be expressed in Simon's language: A learning program assembles and controls performance programs, the running and evaluation of which strengthens the learning program.

The theory is not yet complete (Norman, 1980). But both Greeno (1978; 1980) and Anderson (1980) have gone on to the important step of applying this kind of theory to the analysis of learning from formal instruction. High school geometry provides the example. It is then seen that conventional texts and classroom lessons are often *incomplete* with respect to some features that the theory suggests are crucial for learning. Anderson (1980) notes that important background features of geometry problems are often left implicit in presented diagrams. He also suggests that example exercises are often insufficient to provide students with the critical juxtapositions that build up the cognitive operations needed for learning and transfer. Both Anderson and Greeno emphasize the critical importance of strategic planning, i.e., procedural knowledge. Greeno (1978) sums up his analysis with the observation that:

> "Strategic knowledge for setting goals and choosing plans is not a part of the explicit content of the course, although *it seems likely that many students acquire strategic knowledge by induction from example problems that present strategic principles implicitly.* (p. 72 emphasis added).

Both the Anderson and Greeno work prompt the hypothesis that while some students learn the implicit yet essential strategic planning knowledge by induction from examples, some do not, and the difference would be predictable from intelligence tests. Learning from instruction that is incomplete in this way requires discovery learning whether it is called "learning by discovery" or not, and the ability involved is clearly what Spearman (1932) meant by "eduction of relations": given two or more examples, produce the rule that connects them. To the extent that the examples given are also insufficient, then the ability involved is also one of "eduction of correlates", Spearman's term for producing connected examples given one example and a rule. Knowing how to produce and use the information of geometry, given that instruction is incomplete in these respects, constitutes intelligence in geometry. Knowing how to do this in school subjects generally constitutes scholastic intelligence. Learners who can elaborate their own cognitive structures and discover the necessary strategic knowledge by induction will show more facile transfer to new, different, and more difficult problems involved in learning from later instruction; this constitutes scholastic aptitude.

Thus, knowing how to assemble, control, and execute performance programs for solving problems in geometry seems to involve the essense of what we call intelligence in education. Intelligence *is* learning ability in the sense that it is the active organization of abilities needed to learn from incomplete instruction and to use what information may already be in the cognitive system, or can be induced therefrom, to help in doing this. Whether such ability transfers to task performances beyond the class of tasks represented by school learning depends on the similarity of those tasks to the tasks confronted in school. There is massive evidence to indicate that intelligence tests correlate most highly and consistently with success in school learning, somewhat less so with learning in job training situations, and much less so with indices of later job success (Ghiselli, 1966; Jensen, 1980; NcNemar, 1964; Snow, 1980).

The theoretical framework poses a reciprocal, evolutionary view of learning and intellectual organization. But, correlational and factor analytic research on mental tests has distinguised at least two major kinds of intellectual ability: crystallized intelligence (or verbal-educational ability) and fluid-analytic intelligence (Cattell, 1963, 1971; Horn, 1976, 1978; Vernon, 1951). The former is thought to be organized primarily for and by learning in the formal educational medium. The latter is conceived of as an earlier developing organization geared, perhaps, more to reasoning and problem-solving in the medium of the natural world before and outside of school, as well as within it. The two kinds of intelligence are distinguishable in adolescence and adulthood, though perhaps not in childhood. This is consistent with the transfer differentiation view of ability development (Anastasi, 1970). In any event, they are interpreted as strongly related but separable, generalized abilities.

As opposed to the rote, repetitive laboratory tasks on which traditional learning theory was based, school learning is cumulative, from week to week, month to month, and year to year. The learner is engaged in building cognitive organizations that will be helpful in learning over the long haul. Rumelhart and Norman (1976) have characterized learning from instruction as composed of three overlapping stages—accretion, restructuring, and tuning—and much the same language can be used to describe the operations of computer-based theories such as Anderson's or Greeno's, mentioned above. There is a process of fact acquisition. But the masses of loosely and simply connected knowledge must also be organized and reorganized schematically as learning proceeds. Knowledge structures must become formalized for various purposes and sharpened into useful tools of thought and further learning. Transfer among such structures can occur by identical elements, but also by analogy (Rumelhart & Norman, 1980; see also VanLehn & Brown, 1980, and Stevens & Collins, 1980). The organization thus produced integrates conceptual knowledge and procedural knowledge, and it is not hard to imagine the crystallization of such organization for educational purposes occurring over years of educational experience.

What is crystallized in this way can be called crystallized intelligence. The product is reflected in performance on scholastic ability and achievement tests all along the line, and the basic learning processes involved may not be dissimilar from those categorized by Estes (1982) as "fast" learning.

But Estes chose to form a separate category for "slow" learning, which may require a somewhat different theoretical language to explicate even if the same elementary processes are implicated. A theory such as Anderson's may also assume a single set of learning processes as the basis for developing a general ability, yet one can hypothesize two or more developmental streams, at a more molar level of description, emanating from this base. The two developmental streams can be labelled "crystallization" and "fluidation" to correspond to these two kinds of ability, respectively (see Snow, 1981). Applying again the combination of ideas from Ferguson, Simon, Anderson, and others, one can think of two constellations of ability appearing over long learning experience as a result of transfer functions.

One, crystallized intelligence, represents the organization of more formal educational experience into functional cognitive systems applicable to aid further learning in educational situations. The transfer producing this coalescence need not be only of specific knowledge but also of organized processing strategies we think of as academic learning skills that are in some sense crystallized as units for use in future learning whenever new learning conditions are similar to those in which these crystallized units have been useful in the past. Fluid ability, on the other hand, is thought of as analytic reasoning, particularly where flexible adaptation to novel situations is required and where, therefore, previously crystallized ability offers no particular advantage. There are now the beginnings of evidence that different educational environments foster these two developments differentially (Snow, 1982).

Correlational psychological evidence also suggests that a hierarchy of more specialized abilities can be differentiated beneath the general fluid and crystallized constructs, and this is consistent with the theoretical framework so far developed. Education can be seen as a medium that demands and produces certain kinds of cognitive skill organizations. Scholastic aptitude represents skill in meeting the general cognitive demands of this medium; effective performance in the medium in general and in its specialized aspects both requires and produces transferable cognitive skills. As one moves from subject to subject, from grade to grade, and from high school to college, the special messages change, sometimes gradually and sometimes abruptly, but the overall medium remains more or less the same. Thus, transfer relations operating within and between school years can produce both generalized ability tuned to the medium in general and specialized abilities tuned more specifically to the demands of special aspects of the medium we call courses. Differentiating courses of instruction helps develop differential aptitudes according to individual prior strengths, as well as individual goals.

The overall hypothesis, then, is that crystallized intelligence represents previously constructed assemblies of performance processes retrieved as a system and applied anew in instructional or other performance situations not unlike those experienced in the past, while fluid intelligence represents new assemblies, or the flexible reassembly, of performance processes needed for more extreme adaptations to novel situations. Both functions develop through exercise, and perhaps both can be understood as variations on a general production system development. But it is possible that the crystallized assemblies result from the accumulation of many "fast-process" intentional learning experiences, whereas the facility for fluid assembly and re-assembly results more from the accumulation of "slow-process," incidental learning experiences. Both kinds of intelligence will be relevant to education. Fluid ability will pertain more to learning performance with new or unusual instructional methods or content. Crystallized ability will be more relevant in the progression of familiar situations and subject-matters often characterized as conventional formal instruction. A differentiated hierarchy of specialized subabilities will also crystallize, through the same processes, as special courses of instruction define special classes of tasks and transfer relations among them.

## Expectations about Educational Treatment Effects

Continuing research in cognitive instructional psychology seeks to analyze the complex performances required in school learning and related intellectual tasks, to identify the constituent cognitive and metacognitive skills and processes. Developmental studies seek to trace the growth of these skills and processes. Both aim at promoting aptitude development through improved, direct training treatments. Hopefully, the theoretical framework sketched above can help to organize these efforts. But, evaluations of the resulting new treatments should also profit from the past research experience. That experience leads to the expectation that some aspects of aptitude will be found relatively impervious to direct training, that some treatments will be found relatively ineffective for some persons, and that different treatments may be required for different persons.

Correlational evidence from work cited in the previous section suggests that a typical correlation of aobut .50 would be expected to obtain between a measure of aptitude differences taken before instruction and a measure of achievement differences taken after instruction, in conventional educational settings. In Figure 2a, this expectation is depicted as a solid regression slope labelled $T_1$, or "conventional teaching." Note that Person X, with a high initial aptitude score is predicted to obtain a higher outcome score than is Person Y, with a relatively low initial aptitude score. The heavy dot indicates the average outcome score predicted from an average aptitude score. The dotted lines can be used to trace these predictions. A range of dashed regression slopes is also shown in Figure 2a, to suggest the range of correlations, varying between about .30 and .70, often obtained in presumably comparable, conventional instructional environments. It should be clear that some environments are better than others for Person X, and for Person Y, and some are worse than others for each person.

An important aim of research on educational treatment effects is to improve upon this state of affairs by finding or devising treatments such as $T_2$ that raise the average outcome for everyone, as in Figure 2b, or treatments such as $T_3$ that improve outcome particularly for less able students, while preserving the high achievement of more able students, as in Figure 2c. Readers can trace the dotted projection lines for Persons X and Y onto these other figures for themselves, to see the differences in predicted outcomes for different educational treatments.

Figure 2b suggests the goal of many treatment comparisons in traditional educational research, where it has often been assumed that average outcome would be influenced by treatment variables but regression slopes on aptitude would not be. The aim was to find treatments like $T_2$. The pattern in Figure 2c schematizes the goal of special education and of much research on individualized instruction, that

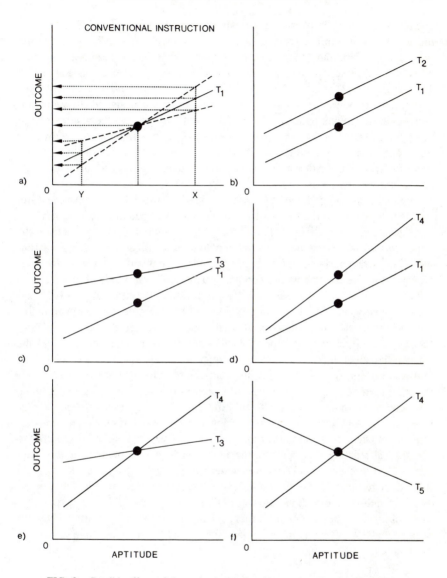

**FIG. 2.** Possible effects of alternative instructional treatments (T) on outcome averages and outcome-on-aptitude regressions. See text for discussion.

is, to find treatments like $T_3$. However, in searching for generally improved instructional methods, the result show in Figure 2d has also at times been obtained; some treatments, such as $T_4$, turn out to be particularly beneficial for more able students rather than for less able students. One could say that this is the goal of special programs for the gifted. Such a result also seems to be the most likely expectation for discovery or inductive treatments, as previously noted. This leads to the possibility of combined results such as those shown in Figure 2e; here, alternative treatments are found to produce improvements for different kinds of students. $T_4$ is best for higher aptitude students, and $T_3$ is best for lower aptitude students. This result suggests that students should be given the alternative treatment most appropriate to their initial aptitude. In the extreme, if one designed alternative instructional treatments optimally for different aptitude groups, the result pictured in Figure 2f might be expected; regression slopes approximating that shown for treatment $T_5$ have sometimes occurred, though negative slopes of this sort are more likely when personality measures, rather than cognitive ability measures, are used as aptitude.

Figures 2b through 2f depict the possible kinds of relations one can expect, regardless of what variables are entered as aptitude and outcome, on the abscissa and ordinate, respectively. Thus, the same patterns serve to define the expecatations when treatments that attempt to train intelligence directly are evaluated (i.e., when earlier and later ability scores are entered on the two axes), as when alternative treatments are compared using different kinds of aptitude and outcome measures on the two axes. Research results for either alternative treatment comparisons or direct training evaluations can therefore be examined in this way. In either case, the distance between the dots on each regression line indicates the average effect size or superiority of one treatment over another, and the nonparallelism of the regression slopes suggests the degree to which treatment effect size differs for students with different entering aptitude scores.

The patterns of Figures 2cdef are all instances of interaction between aptitude differences and instructional treatment differences (i.e., aptitude × treatment interactions, or ATI for short). It is increasingly recognized that such regression patterns often occur even when they are not sought. Evidence of ATI is required to construct alternative treatments for the adaptive educational plan pictured back in Figure 1. Hypothesized ATI patterns underly much research and development on individualized instruction and on special educational programs for gifted or retarded students. Cronbach and Snow (1977; see also Snow, 1977) have reviewed much of this literature to conclude that ATI are ubiquitous in education. They can be expected to be as likely in research on the direct training of aptitude as they are in other kinds of treatment comparisons.

### Examples of Training Treatments for
### Intellectual Aptitudes

Evaluations of treatments aimed at direct training of intellectual aptitudes fall into several categories, based on the breadth of focus of the treatment under study. Some broad programs of educational intervention have shown average positive effects (see, e.g., McKay et al., 1978; Kennedy, 1978; Snow, 1982), but these have not so far included analyses of ATI nor of particular aspects of training; as a result, one cannot develop from this work hypotheses about particular treatment effects for particular kinds of persons. Some narrow studies have assessed the effects of practice, coaching, or expectancy manipulation treatments on the aptitude tests themselves; this work has shown negligible effects with little generalizability. The best examples on which to base future research are those studies that examine carefully designed experimental treatments in an ATI framework, and assess retention and transfer as well as direct effects. Unfortunately, there are as yet few such studies.

Several examples can be pieced together briefly here to suggest the kinds of results that should be explored further in more comprehensive evaluations. Several chapters later in this book take some of these and other examples significantly further than space allows here.

There is much correlational evidence to suggest that the Raven Progressive Matrices tests reflect general or fluid-analytic ability. Linn (1970) has reviewed early evidence regarding the trainability of matrices performance. She also conducted an experiment with fourth graders to show that training designed to remove several kinds of logical errors improved performance substantially. Training effects did not generally transfer to performance on other intellectual measures, but evidence was presented to show that the patterns of performance observed on some kinds of items for some children did suggest transfer functions.

In a study of Raven performance reported by Guinagh (1971), black and white low SES third graders were trained on the kinds of concepts used in the test. Students were also divided into high and low performers on memory span ability using a digit span test. This was considered an aptitude for the training. The treatment was found to be effective for all white students, but only for black students who were high in memory span. For the black students, then, there was an interaction of initial memory ability and training on Raven concepts. The regression pattern, if drawn, would presumably look something like Figure 2d, with memory span as the abscissa, Raven performance as the ordinate, $T_4$ as the black experimental group, and $T_1$ as the black control group. A retention measure showed that gains were still evident after a one-month delay.

Another program of studies aimed at develping fluid-analytic ability among elementary students was conducted by Jacobs and his collaborators (Jacobs, 1966, 1977; Jacobs & Vanderventer, 1968, 1971a, 1971b, 1972; Jacobs & White, 1971). They investigated the effectiveness of training on the Raven and on related figural classification and reasoning tasks. Early studies demonstrated measurable but temporary improvement on the Raven, when students were trained specifically on it. Later studies aimed at training classification skills, however, showed both an increment in performance on the trained task, and transfer to related tasks, including in some cases the Raven. The effects of training were generally sustained over delays from two weeks to three months. It was also shown that the effectiveness of training was heavily dependent on the experience and skills of the trainer. Individual differences in aptitudes prior to training were not studied in a way that would allow analysis of ATI, however.

At the other end of the age scale, there have also been successful attempts to train fluid-analytic performance. An example comes from a study by Willis, Bliezner, and Baltes (1980). They trained a group of adults, with age averaging 70 years, to use verbal rule procedures in solving figural relations problems drawn from a commercially available fluid ability test. Transfer of training was assessed using a variety of fluid and crystallized ability measures after one-week, one-month and six-month delays. Compared to non-treated controls, the trained adults showed marked positive effects. These appeared to include both specific and more generalized transfer and were maintained across the six-month period of the study. As with the Jacobs project, this work has also not yet assessed ATI.

Thus, it appears that fluid-analytic performance can be directly trained among both young and old persons, and that some retention and transfer can be expected. There is some evidence that other abilities may moderate training effects; at least in the Guinagh study, training seemed to capitalize on one aptitude to develop another. There is also the implication, especially from the Willis study, that "strategic" training, as opposed to "basic skills" training, has effects. A study by Sternberg and Weil (1980) makes this point by contrasting verbal and spatial strategies for reasoning task performance among young adults. They trained college students on linear syllogisms. Those in a visualization group were instructed to represent the problems mentally in a spatial array or series; those assigned to the algorithm group were taught a simplified rule procedure based on a linguistic model previously identified. A third group was given no special training. Apparently, the algorithm training resulted in more efficient performance; it reduced response latencies relative to the visualization strategy. Based on mathematical modeling of each individual's performance, Sternberg and Weil were then able to classify subjects into four homogeneous strategy groups, depending on whether a spatial, linguistic, mixed spatial-linguistic, or algorithmic model best fit each performance. Correlations of performance with external verbal and spatial ability measures showed strikingly different patterns for groups of subjects using different strategies. Success with a linguistic strategy depended on verbal but not spatial ability, performance with a spatial strategy showed an opposite correlation pattern, and the mixed strategy gave correlations with both abilities. As expected, the simplified algorithm strategy showed reduced involvement of verbal ability, relative to the full linguistic strategy. The implication is that more than one strategy can fit a task, but that the most effective strategy for a particular person depends on that person's ability profile; effective strategies will differ from person to person and training can match or mismatch a particular person in this respect. It is therefore critical in future training research to recognize that strategic differences, between verbal, spatial, or mixed strategies for example, may reflect differences in relative strengths in analogous verbal and spatial aptitudes. Training on particular strategies will likely interact with these aptitude differences; an ATI research design must be used to detect this. Several other training studies show aspects of this phenomenon.

A study by Frandsen and Holder (1969) investigated transfer of training of spatial-visualization skills to verbal problem solving. Earlier work by Gavurin (1967) had shown the role of spatial-visualization abilities in solving symbol-manipulation problems. Thus, Frandsen and Holder hypothesized that instruction in spatial-visualization techniques should improve verbal problem-solving for those low in spatial-visualization ability, but not for those high in such ability. Students identified as either high or low on a test of space relations were pretested on verbal problems involving mental representation and manipulation of multiple pieces of information. Experimental subjects were then trained on the use of Venn diagrams, time lines, and other spatial-diagrammatic techniques of representing data. As predicted, students low in spatial ability profited from instruction and showed improved performance in verbal problem-solving. Had Frandsen and Holder plotted regression slopes for their data, with initial spatial ability on the abscissa and verbal problem-solving on the ordinate, a picture like that in Figure 2c would have been obtained; $T_3$ would represent the training result, with $T_1$ representing the control group. No aptitude posttests were administered to determine if the specific skill changes would be reflected in performance on other spatial ability tasks, nor was retention tested. It may well have been, also, that the trained spatial techniques became verbalized strategies for those students low in spatial ability initially. This early study did not include a means of diagnosing what strategies different trainees actually used.

Another series of studies has added the contrast of strategy training with direct practice, and demonstrated that training can have negative effects, depending on initial aptitude. In Salomon's (1974) research, film models of mental transformations thought to be useful in performing various spatial scanning and visualization tasks were tested against several kinds of practice conditions. The hypothesis was that the models gave low ability learners a cognitive operation to imitate. Results of several studies showed that the modeling treatment helped less able students and produced a decrement in performance for students who were high in ability initially, relative to the practice condition (i.e., something like the regression slope pattern pictured in Figure 2f was obtained, with $T_4$ representing the practice condition and $T_5$ the modeling condition).

In a recent study of this same type (Kyllonen, Lohman, & Snow, 1981), high school students were trained on a paper-folding visualization task with films demonstrating either a folding-unfolding visualization strategy or a verbal coding strategy. These conditions were compared with practice and feedback. Students initially high in spatial ability performed best on both the trained task and a visualization transfer task when given the practice-feedback condition. This treatment, in essence, permitted them to practice, in their own idiosyncratic ways, skills or strategies that were already partially developed. Performance of low spatial ability students, however, depended on the level of their verbal ability, as well as on the type of training they received. Students low in spatial ability and high in verbal ability made fewer errors on both the paper-folding and transfer tasks, if exposed to either strategy training condition; their response time was also improved, specifically by the verbal analytic training. Students low in both spatial and verbal ability were helped by the visualization training procedure, at least on transfer to the surface development task. The results were complex, but they clearly imply that strategy training alters performance, has different effects on students with different ability profiles, and may have different effects on transfer performance than on primary task performance for some students.

The training of strategic cognitive activities of learners has been a central focus of much recent research on the development of learning and memory skills. Work with retarded children and adolescents has been reviewed by Brown (1978) and Campione, Brown, and Ferrara (1982). Important advances have also been made with learning strategies for older adolescents and young adults (O'Neil, 1978; O'Neil & Spielberger, 1979). Meichenbaum (1977) has reported success in improving cognitive performance and altering emotional interference in a variety of instructional and therapeutic situations by modifying the inner speech patterns of children and adults. All this work suggests that learning and memory skills (such as self-checking, or using rehearsal, imagery, analogy or other mnemonic or heuristic strategies, or apportioning study time appropriately) can be trained, that meta-knowledge or self-awareness about one's own performance in these respects can be developed, and that transfer to different kinds of learning or problem-solving situations is possible if attention is paid in training to the generalization-transfer process.

One area of research in this direction, however, contains an example with an ATI message for future investigators similar to that of several of the example studies cited above; it also suggests that future research will need to be sensitive to the possibility that some components of performance may be modifiable by training while others are not. Ridberg, Parke, and Hetherington (1971) reported a study of modeling treatments to alter the self-checking strategies of impulsive children. Film models were prepared that verbalized or demonstrated careful checking on figural matching tasks; the aim was to increase the latencies and reduce the errors that are the twin marks of impulsivity. Treatments compared the two models with a combination of both models and a condition without models. It was found that impulsive low IQ children were prompted to take more time in answering after training with the combined verbal and demonstration model, but that impulsive high IQ children profited only from verbalization or demonstration; they were adversely affected by a combination of models. The intelligence × treatment interaction would look like Figure 2f; $T_4$ would represent the treatment using one or the other model, while $T_5$ would represent the combination treatment. It was further found that training affected only latency; it had no effect on the error component of performance.

## Implications

These example studies, and other related research, prompt a more complex view of the training of intellectual aptitudes than has been evident in much past thinking and research in education and psychology. But the research to date does lead to important implications for the future. First, it is clear that attempts to train abilities must go well beyond simply manipulating practice and feedback, or coaching, or teacher or student expectations; they must provide substantive training on the component processes and skills involved in task performance, and they msut also train directly the superordinate executive and control strategies involved in guiding performance and in generalizing and transfering trained skills to new settings. Second, even with intensive interventions of this sort, the best effects of direct training are likely to come from treatment that are also extensive, i.e., that involve long-term regularized educational programs. Third, abilities and strategies and methods of training interact. Attempts to train either component skills or metacognitive strategies must fit training methods to an assessment of prior aptitude profiles. A fourth implication appears to be that simple practice and feedback, while not effective on average, may provide the best training for learners already somewhat proficient in the ability to be trained. Training that is cognitively more intrusive is often not helpful, and sometimes actually seems to be harmful, for more able learners; such intervention may disrupt effective idiosyncratic strategies. A fifth point is that training to improve one kind of ability may work best when the treatment is designed to capitalize on some of the learner's other strengths. Finally, some aspects of intellectual aptitudes may be expected to be readily trainable and others not. Training research will need to be geared to help distinguish these categories.

## SUMMARY HYPOTHESES AND ADMONITIONS

Education is primarily an aptitude development program. It has been so viewed, with varying emphasis, throughout educational history. Intelligence is both a primary aptitude for learning in education and a primary product of learning in education. The improvement of education in this regard requires two kinds of conceptual and technical assistance from scientific psychology. One concerns the means of adapting instruction so as to optimize learning outcome for all persons, despite intellectual differences among them that may be relatively impervious to short-term change. This requires improved methods of assessing individual intellectual strengths and weaknesses, and improved methods of capitalizing on strengths to compensate for weaknesses. The second concerns the means of developing intellectual strengths directly. Both needs depend on improved content and process analyses of aptitude, learning, and instruction. Both goals are apparent in the design for adaptive education depicted in Figure 1.

In turn, scientific psychology's commerce with education can be expected to lead to improved theories of intelligence and learning. Concentration on the understanding of performance tasks that display clearly non-trivial aspects of substantive intelligence and meaningful learning provides a kind of ecological validity to theory that laboratory psychology alone could never achieve.

The history of interaction between education and the psychology of learning and intelligence shows many false starts toward an integrated theory. But a confluence of old and new ideas now provides a framework for integrated research on intelligence and learning in education, within a modern cognitive instructional psychology. This final section summarizes several aspects of the history of research on intellectual aptitudes in education to date, in the form of a list of hypotheses and admonitions for further research.

### Intelligence as Learning from Suboptimal Instruction

All instruction is incomplete in some respects for someone; and, for that person instruction can include errors of commission as well as errors of omission. It is hypothesized that the act of learning from some given instruction involves accessing, adapting, and applying whatever cognitive systems and structures one already has, and inventing new systems and structures as necessary to overcome whatever instructional impediments one meets. Intelligence as aptitude for learning appears to represent the cognitive organizational facilities involved in doing this. The degree to which individual differences in intelligence relate to learning outcome from instruction signifies the degree to which the given instruction places demands for these cognitive facilities on the persons involved. Analytic research is required to detail how prior intellectual differences are reflected as aptitude differences in meeting these demands.

### Aptitudinal Transfer

Intellectual aptitude acquired in prior learning situations transfers to learning from new instruction. Somewhere between the outmoded view of mental faculties and disciplines, and the narrow psychological theory of transfer by identical elements, there is room for the hypothesis that transfer can occur by analogy among instructional learning tasks sharing only family resemblance. What is transferred, then, may be a style of work, a mode of attack, a strategy, as much as a particular common concept, procedure, or fact. Again, individuals differ in the facility with which they do this, and research is needed to trace the details by which aptitudinal transfer, as well as the applicational transfer of common elements, is reflected in new learning.

### Aptitude Development

Over years of successful transfer, success breeds success, and the cognitive products of successful learning and transfer appear to become consolidated. Intellectual aptitude is manifested in consistent learning ability, and consistent learning is manifested in intellectual organization. But, it is possible that different kinds of learning situations breed different kinds of aptitude for further learning, as well as different kinds of inaptitude. The hypothesis that fluid-analytic and crystallized-synthetic intelligence, in particular, appear to derive from different streams of learning experience and to relate to different kinds of subsequent performances deserves longitudinal research attention. Such research will need to pay particular attention to the transfer relations among educational experiences that are hypothesized to result in ability formation and ability differentiation.

### Aptitude-Aptitude Interaction

Intellectual aptitudes are thus multivariate. These aptitudes and other "nonintellectual" aptitudes, such as anxiety, can multiply or otherwise alter the effects of one or another aptitude on learning. Aptitude profile differences seem to be associated with use of different cognitive strategies. In turn, there is evidence that learners substitute aptitudes they possess for those they lack; in other words, there sometimes appears to be an intrapersonal trade-off between strengths and weaknesses. Also, the same performance score on a complex task can be achieved using different abilities or strategies by different individuals, or by the same individual at a different point in time. Such complex interactive effects cannot be unraveled without research that produces an account of the content and process structures involved in individual differences in aptitude for learning.

### Aptitude-Treatment Interaction

There is also evidence of interaction between aptitude profiles and instructional or training treatment alternatives. The hypothesis is that treatments differ in the information processing demands they place on learners, following the implications of several of the hypotheses stated above. Process-analytic research is required to understand interactive effects of this sort. The design of instruction adapted to fit aptitude differences, that is, to capitalize on learner strengths while compensating for weaknesses, requires the ATI paradigm to test such hypotheses and to evaluate the adequacy of attempts at such instructional adaptations.

### Aptitude-Training Treatments

General intellectual aptitudes have long been regarded as impervious to change through direct training interventions, even while being susceptible to long-term development through education. Present evidence supports the hypothesis that superficial interventions based on practice, coaching, expectancy changes, and the like, have little or no effect on ability development, but that substantial educational interventions based on direct training of component skills and metacognitive strategies can sometimes have important positive effects. To the extent that further research can expose the cognitive components and metacomponents that are susceptible to training, and can suggest how effective training can be designed, adaptive instruction that develops aptitude directly may be envisioned. However, since there is also some evidence that direct training can have negative as well as positive effects, depending on student aptitude profile, the ATI paradigm is again required for training evaluation. In any event, the criterion for research of this sort is transfer to valued educational or other worldly performances, not direct training of ability itself.

### Choice of Tasks, Treatments, and Tests

If the cognitive organizational phenomena of school learning provide the primary medium in which intelligence and learning connect, then research on the connection must be based on school learning tasks. Early investigators were misled by the assumption that traditional laboratory learning tasks embodied all the essential features of learning. Also, if research is to examine the cognitive organizational phenomena connecting intelligence and school learning, then experiments must go on long enough for such phenomena to show themselves. Short experiments on school learning are useless, save for displaying the role of prior aptitude or stored knowledge in the initial steps of new learning. Accretion, restructuring, and fine tuning as processes of complex learning can be expected to materialize over weeks and months, not over minutes. This point was also missed by early investigators. The admonition applies as well to intelligence tests. Short, simple special ability tests do not necessarily embody all the features of intelligence that are essential for the study of its relation to school learning.

### Cognitive Content and Process Diagnosis

Instrumentation must be developed for such research that provides both content and process diagnoses of aptitude input, instructional or training treatment, and learning outcome. These diagnoses will need to be made sensitive to the learning-to-learn and transfer phenomena that are presumed to mediate cognitive organizational change and hence aptitude development. This is the tallest order, and thus the prime topic, for research in cognitive instructional psychology today.

### REFERENCES

Allison, R. B. *Learning parameters and human abilities.* Unpublished report, (NR 151-113) Educational Testing Service, Princeton, N.J. 1960.

Anastasi, A. On the formation of psychological traits. *American Psychologist,* 1970, *25,* 899–910.

Anderson, J. R. *Language, memory, and thought.* Hillsdale, NJ: Lawrence Erlbaum Associates, 1976.

Anderson, J. R. *A general learning theory and its application to the acquisition of proof skills in geometry.* (Tech. Rep. No. 80-1). Carnegie Mellon University, June 1980.

Anderson, J. R., Greeno, J. G. Kline, P. J., & Neeves, D. M. Acquisition of problem-solving skill. In J. R. Anderson (Ed.), *Cognitive skills and their acquisition.* Hillsdale, NJ: Lawrence Erlbaum Associates, 1981.

Anderson, J. R., Kline, P. J., & Beasley, C. M., Jr.  Complex learning processes. In R. E. Snow, P-A Federico, & W. E. Montague (Eds.), *Aptitude, learning, and instruction* (Vol 2), *Cognitive process analyses of learning and problem-solving*. Hillsdale, NJ: Lawrence Erlbaum Associates, 1980.

Anderson, R. C., Spiro, R. J., & Montague, W. F.  *Schooling and the acquisition of knowledge.* Hillsdale, NJ: Lawrence Erlbaum Associates, 1977.

Archambault, R. D.  *John Dewey on education.* Chicago, IL: University of Chicago Press, 1964.

Ausubel, D. P.  *The psychology of meaningful verbal learning.* New York: Grune & Stratton, 1963.

Boring, E. G.  *A history of experimental psychology.* New York: Appleton-Century-Crofts, 1957.

Broadbent, D. C.  *Perception and communication.* London: Pergamon Press, 1958.

Brown, A. L.  Knowing when, where, and how to remember: A problem of metacognition. In R. Glaser (Ed.), *Advances in instructional psychology* (Vol. 1) Hillsdale, NJ: Lawrence Erlbaum Associates, 1978.

Brownell, W. A., & Moser, A. G.  Meaningful versus mechanical learning: A study in grade three subtraction. *Duke University research studies in education* (No. 8). Durham, NC: Duke University Press, 1949.

Bruner, J. S.  *The process of education.* Cambridge, MA: Harvard University Press, 1960.

Bruner, J. S.  *Toward a theory of instruction.* Cambridge, MA: Belknap, 1966.

Butler, H. E. (Trans.)  *The Institutio Oratoria of Quintilian* (Vol. 1). Cambridge MA: Harvard University Press, 1954.

Campione, J., Brown, A. L., & Ferrara, R.  Experimental and clinical investigations of retarded individuals: Intelligence, learning, and transfer. In R. J. Sternberg (Ed.), *Handbook of human intelligence.* New York: Cambridge University Press, 1982.

Cattell, R. B.  Theory of fluid and crystallized intelligence: A critical experiment. *Journal of Educational Psychology,* 1963, *54,* 1–22.

Cattell, R. B.  *Abilities: Their structure, growth, and action.* Boston, MA: Houghton Mifflin, 1971.

Cicarelli, V., Cooper, W., & Granger, R.  *The impact of Head Start: An evaluation of the effects of Head Start on children's cognitive and affective development.* Westinghouse Learning Corp., 1969.

Cleverley, J., & Philips, D. C.  *From Locke to Spock.* Melbourne, Aus.: Melbourne University Press, 1976.

Coleman, J. S., Campbell, E. Q., Hobson, C. J., McPartland, J., Mood, A. M., Weinfeld, F. D., & York, R. L.  *Equality of educational opportunity.* U.S. Department of Health, Education, & Welfare, Office of Education, 1966.

Cook, T. D., Appleton, H., Connor, R. F., Shaffer, A., Tamkin, G., & Weber, S. J.  *"Sesame Street" revisited.* New York: Russell Sage Foundation, 1975.

Cremin, L. A.  *The transformation of the school: Progressivism in American education 1876–1957.* New York: Vantage, 1961.

Cronbach, L. J.  The two disciplines of scientific psychology. *American Psychologist,* 1957, *12,* 671–684.

Cronbach, L. J.  How can instruction be adapted to individual differences? In R. M. Gagné (Ed.) *Learning and individual differences.* Columbus, OH. Charles Merrill, 1967.

Cronbach, L. J.  *Essentials of psychological testing* (3rd ed.). New York: Harper, 1970.

Cronbach, L. J.  Beyond the two disciplines of scientific psychology. *American Psychologist,* 1975, *30,* 116–127.

Cronbach, L. J.  *Educational Psychology.* New York: Harcourt, Brace, Jovanovich, 1977.

Cronbach, L. J., & Snow, R. E.  *Aptitudes and instructional methods: A handbook for research on interactions.* New York: Irvington, 1977.

Datta, L.  Design of the Heat Start planned variation experiment. In A. M. Rivlin & P. M. Timpane (Eds.), *Planned variation in education: Should we give up or try harder?* The Brookings Institution, 1975.

Estes, W. K.  Learning, memory, and intelligence In R. J. Sternberg (Ed.), *Handbook of Human Intelligence.* New York: Cambridge University Press, 1982.

Ferguson, G. A. On learning and human ability. *Canadian Journal of Psychology,* 1954, *8,* 95–112.

Ferguson, G. A. On transfer and the abilities of man. *Canadian Journal of Psychology,* 1956, *10,* 121–131.

Frandsen, A. N., & Holder, J. R. Spatial visualization in solving complex problems. *Journal of Psychology,* 1969, *73,* 229–233.

Friedman, M., Das, J. P. & O'Connor, N. (Eds.), *Intelligence and learning.* New York: Plenum Press, 1981.

Gagné, R. M. *The conditions of learning.* New York: Holt, Rinehart and Winston, 1965.

Gagné, R. M., & Bolles, R. C. Review of factors in learning efficiency. In E. Galanter (Ed.), *Automatic teaching: The state of the art.* New York: Wiley, 1959.

Galton, F. *Hereditary genius: An inquiry into its laws and consequences.* London: Macmillan, 1869.

Garforth, F. W. *John Locke's Of the Conduct of the Understanding.* Classics in Education (No. 31). New York: Columbia University, Teachers College Press, 1966.

Gavurin, E. I. Anagram solving and spatial aptitude. *Journal of Psychology,* 1967, *65,* 65–68.

Gay, P. (Ed.) *John Locke on education.* Classics in education (No. 20). New York: Columbia University, Teachers College Press, 1964.

Ghiselli, E. E. *The validity of occupational aptitude tests.* New York: Wiley, 1966.

Glaser, R. (Ed.) *Training research and education.* New York: Wiley, 1965.

Glaser, R. *Adaptive education: Individual diversity and learning.* New York: Holt, Rinehart and Winston, 1977.

Glaser, R. (Ed.) *Advances in instructional psychology* (Vol. 1). Hillsdale, NJ: Lawrence Erlbaum Associates, 1978a.

Glaser, R. The contributions of B. F. Skinner to Education and some counterinfluences. In P. Suppes (Ed.), *Impact of Research on Education: Some Case Studies.* Washington, DC, National Academy of Education, 1978b.

Glaser, R., & Resnick, L. B. Instructional Psychology. *Annual Review of Psychology,* 1972, *23,* 207–276.

Greeno, J. G. A study of problem solving. In R. Glaser (Ed.), *Advances in instructional psychology:* (Vol. 1). Hillsdale, NJ: Lawrence Erlbaum Associates, 1978.

Greeno, J. G. Some examples of cognitive task analysis with instructional implications. In R. E. Snow, P-A Federico & W. E. Montague (Eds.), *Aptitude learning and instruction:* (Vol. 2), *Cognitive process analyses of learning and problem solving.* Hillsdale, NJ: Lawrence Erlbaum Associates, 1980.

Guilford, J. P. *The nature of human intelligence.* New York: McGraw-Hill, 1967.

Guinagh, B. J. Social-class differentiation in cognitive development among Black preschool children. *Child Development,* 1971, *42,* 27–36.

Gulliksen, H. O. Measurement of learning and mental abilities. *Psychometrika,* 1961, *26,* 93–107.

Horn, J. L. Human abilities: A review of research and theory in the early 1970's. *Annual Review of Psychology,* 1976, *27,* 437–485.

Horn, J. L. Human ability systems. In P. B. Baltes (Ed.), *Life-span development and behavior.* (Vol 1.) New York: Academic Press, 1978.

Hunt, J. McV. *Intelligence and experience.* New York: Ronald Press, 1961.

Jacobs, P. I. Programed progressive matrices. In *Proceedings of the 74th Annual Convention of the American Psychological Association.* New York: APA, 1966.

Jacobs, P. I. *Up the IQ: How to raise your child's intelligence.* New York: Wyden Books, 1977.

Jacobs, P. I., & Vandeventer, M. Progressive matrices: An experimental developmental, nonfactoral analysis. *Perceptual and Motor Skills,* 1968, *27,* 759–766.

Jacobs, P. I., & Vandeventer, M. The learning and transfer of double-classification skills: A replication and extension. *Journal of Experimental Child Psychology,* 1971, *12,* 240–257. (b)

Jacobs, P. I., & Vandeventer, M. Evaluating the teaching of intelligence. *Educational and Psychological Measurement,* 1972, *32,* 235–248.

Jacobs, P. I., & Vandeventer, M. Evaluating the teaching of intelligence. *Educational and Psychological Measurement,* 1972, *32,* 235–248.

Jacobs, P. I., & White, M. N. Transfer of training in double classification skills across operations in Guilford's Structure-of-Intellect model. (RB 71-64) Princeton, NJ: Educational Testing Service, 1971.

Jastrow, J. Some currents and undercurrents in psychology. *Psychological Review,* 1901, *8,* 1–26.

Jencks, C. *Inequality: A reassessment of the effect of family and schooling in America.* New York: Harper & Row, 1972.

Jenkins, J. J., & Paterson, D. G. *Studies in individual differences.* New York: Appleton-Century-Crofts, 1961.

Jensen, A. R. How much can we boost intelligence and academic achievement? *Harvard Educational Review,* 1969, *39,* 1–123.

Jensen, A. R. *Genetics and education.* London: Methuen, 1972.

Jensen, A. R. *Bias in mental testing.* New York: Free Press, 1980.

Kennedy, M. M. Findings from the Follow Through Planned Variation study. *Educational Researcher,* 1978, *7,* 3–11.

Klahr, D. (Ed.) *Cognition and instruction.* Hillsdale: NJ: Lawrence Erlbaum Associates, 1976.

Kyllonen, P. C., Lohman, D. F., & Snow, R. E. *Effects of task facets and strategy training on spatial task performance.* (Tech. Rep. No. 14) Aptitude Research Project, School of Education, Stanford University, Stanford, CA, 1981.

Lesgold, A. M., Pellegrino, J. W., Fokkema, S. D., & Glaser, R. (Eds.) *Cognitive psychology and instruction.* New York: Plenum, 1978.

Linden, K. W., & Linden, J. D. *Modern metnal measurement: A historical perspective.* Boston MA: Houghton Mifflin, 1968.

Linn, M. F. Effects of a training procedure on matrix performance and on transfer tasks. Unpublished doctroal dissertation, Stanford University, 1970.

McGeogh, J. A., & Irion, A. L. *The psychology of human learning.* Toronto: Longmans Green, 1952.

McKay, H., Sinisterra, L., McKay, A., Gomez, H., & Lloreda, P. Improving cognitive ability in chronically deprived children. *Science,* 1978, *200,* 270–278.

McKeachie, W. J. Instructional psychology. *Annual Review of Psychology,* 1974, *25,* 161–193.

McNemar, Q. Lost: Our intelligence? Why? *American Psychologist,* 1964, *19,* 871–882.

Meichenbaum, D. *Cognitive-behavior modification.* New York: Plenum, 1977.

Miller, N. E. (Ed.) *Graphic communication and the crisis in education.* Washington, D.C.: National Education Assoc., 1957.

Neisser, U. *Cognitive psychology.* New York: Appleton-Century-Crofts, 1967.

Newell, A., & Simon, H. A. *Human problem solving.* Englewood Cliffs, NJ: Prentice-Hall, 1972.

Norman, D. A. Discussion: Teaching, learning, and the representation of knowledge. In R. E. Snow, P-A Federico, & W. E. Montague (Eds.), *Aptitude, learning, and instruction:* (Vol. 2), *Cognitive process analyses of learning and problem solving.* Hillsdale, NJ: Lawrence Erlbaum Associates, 1980.

O'Neil, H. F., Jr. (Ed.) *Learning strategies.* New York: Academic Press, 1978.

O'Neil, H. F. Jr. & Spielberger, C. D. (Eds.), *Cognitive and Affective Learning Strategies.* New York: Academic Press, 1979.

Ray, H. W. Final report on the Office of Economic Opportunity experiment in educational performance contracting. Unpublished report. Columbus, OH: Battelle Laboratories, 1972.

Resnick, L. (Ed.) *The nature of intelligence.* Hillsdale, NJ: Lawrence Erlbaum Associates, 1976.

Resnick, L. B. Instructional Psychology. *Annual Review of Psychology.* 1981, *32,* 659–704.

Ridberg, E., Parke, R., & Hetherington, E. Modification of impulsive and reflective cognitive styles through observation of film mediated models, *Developmental Psychology,* 1971, *5,* 369–377.

Rumelhart, D. E., & Norman, D. A. *Accretion, tuning, and restructuring: Three modes of learning* (Report No. 7602). Center for Human Information Processing, University of California, San Diego, August 1976.

Rumelhart, D. E., & Norman, D. A. *Analogical processes in learning* (Tech. Report No. 8005). Center for Human Information Processing, University of California, San Diego, September 1980.

Salomon, G. Internalization of filmic operations in relation to individual differences. *Journal of Educational Psychology,* 1974, *66,* 499–511.

Shulman, L. S. & Keisler, E. (Eds.) *Learning by discovery.* Chicago Ill.: Rand McNally, 1966.

Simon, H. A. Identifying basic abilities underlying intelligent performance of complex tasks. In L. B. Resnick (Ed.) *The nature of intelligence.* Hillsdale, NJ: Lawrence Erlbaum Associates, 1976.

Skinner, B. F. The science of learning and the art of teaching. *Harvard Educational Review,* 1954, *24,* 86–97.

Snow, R. E. Research on aptitudes: A progress report. In L. S. Shulman (Ed.), *Review of research in education* (Vol. 4). Itasca, Il: Peacock, 1977.

Snow, R. E. Aptitude processes. In R. E. Snow, P-A Federico, & W. E. Montague (Eds.), *Aptitude, learning and instruction:* (Vol. 1), *Cognitive process analyses of aptitude.* Hillsdale, NJ: Lawrence Erlbaum Associates, 1980.

Snow, R. E. Toward a theory of aptitude for learning I. Fluid and cyrstallized abilities and their correlates. In M. Friedman, J. P. Das & N. O'Connor (Eds.), *Intelligence and learning.* New York: Plenum Press. 1981.

Snow, R. E. Intelligence and eduation. In R. J. Sternberg (Ed.), *Handbook of Human Intelligence.* New York: Cambridge University Press, 1982.

Snow, R., Federico, P-A & Montague, W. E. (Eds.), *Aptitude, learning and instruction:* (Vol. 1), Vol. 2, *Cognitive process analyses of learning and problem-solving. Cognitive process analyses of aptitude.* Hillsdale, NJ: Lawrence Erlbaum Associates, 1980.

Spearman, C. "General intelligence" objectively determined and measured. *American Journal of Psychology,* 1904, *15,* 201–293.

Spearman, C. *The nature of intelligence and the principles of cognition.* London: Macmillan, 1923.

Sperling, G. A. The information available in brief visual presentation. *Psychological Monographs,* 1960, *74,* (Whole No. 498).

Stake, R. E. Learning parameters: aptitudes, and achievement. *Psychometric Monographs,* 1961, (Whole No 9).

Stallings, J. Implementation and child effects of teaching practices in follow through classrooms. *Monographs of the Society for research in child development,* 1975, *(No. 40).*

Stallings, J., & Kaskowitz, D. Follow through classroom observation evaluation 1972–1973. SRI Project URU-7370, Stanford Research Institute, Menlo Park, CA, 1974.

Sternberg, R. J., & Weil, E. M. An aptitude-strategy interaction in linear syllogistic reasoning. *Journal of Educational Psychology,* 1980, *72,* 226–234.

Stevens, A. L., & Collins, A. Multiple conceptual models of a complex system. In R. E. Snow, P-A Federico & W. E. Montague (Eds.), *Aptitude, learning, and instruction* (Vol. 2), *Cognitive process analyses of learning and problem solving.* Hillsdale, NJ: Lawrence Erlbaum Associates, 1980.

Terman, L. M. *The measurement of intelligence.* Boston MA: Houghton Mifflin, 1916.

Thorndike, E. L., & Woodworth, R. S. The influence of improvement in one mental function upon the efficiency of other functions. *Psychological Review,* 1901, *8,* 247–261.

Thurstone, L. L. *Primary mental abilities.* Chicago IL: University of Chicago Press, 1938.

VanLehn, K., & Brown, J. S. Planning nets: A representation for formalizing analogies and semantic models of procedural skills. In R. E. Snow, P-A Federico & W. E. Montague (Eds.), *Aptitude, learning, and instruction:* (Vol. 2), *Cognitive process analyses of learning and problem solving.* Hillsdale, NJ: Lawrence Erlbaum Associates, 1980.

Vernon, P. E. *The structure of human abilities.* London: Methuen, 1951.

Weikart, D. P. Relationship of curriculum, teaching, and learning in preschool education. In J. C. Stanley (Ed.), *Preschool programs for the disadvantaged.* Baltimore, MD: Johns Hopkins University Press, 1972.

White, S. H. *Federal programs for young children: Review and recommendations*. (Vol. 1), *Goals and standards of public programs for children*. Cambridge, MA: Huron Inst., 1973.

Willis, S. L., Blieszner, R., & Baltes, P. B. Training research in aging: Modification of intellectual performance on a fluid ability component. College of Human Development, Pennsylvania State University, University Park, PA, 1980.

Wissler, C. The correlation of mental and physical tests. *Psychological Review Monograph*, 1901, *6*, (3).

Wittrock, M. C., & Lumsdaine, A. A. Instructional Psychology. *Annual Review of Psychology*, 1977, *28*, 417–459.

Wolf, T. H. *Alfred Binet*. Chicago IL: University of Chicago Press, 1973.

Woodrow, H. The ability to learn. *Psychological Review*, 1946, *53*, 147–158.

Zigler, E. Has it really been demonstrated that compensatory education is without value? *American Psychologist*, 1975, *30*, 935–937.

Zigler, E., & Valentine, J. *Project head start: A legacy of the war on poverty*. NY: The Free press, 1979.

# I

# *Modifying Intelligence*

# Introduction:
# Questions I Would Like Answered

DOUGLAS K. DETTERMAN

*Case Western Reserve University*

This portion of the book deals with efforts to modify intelligence in a global fashion. Most of the research presented here concerns efforts to raise IQ scores using extensive educational interventions in preschool children from low socioeconomic status families.

The first chapter of this section by Caruso, Taylor, and Detterman is a review of such studies to determine how social policy and research findings have interacted. This chapter has a somewhat different orientation than others contained in this volume and, therefore, requires some explanation.

Attempts to modify intelligence have a relatively long history, as the first chapter of this book shows. Have these efforts been successful? Have later studies been more successful than earlier studies? If we are developing a science of intellectual functioning then we must expect knowledge to be cumulative. If knowledge is not cumulative then we must ask why it is not. There seems to be two possibilities. All studies conducted may have been equally effective because the maximum effects they seek to produce are easily produced. A second possibility is that all of the studies may have been, on the average, equally ineffective. The chapter by Caruso, Taylor, and Detterman takes the latter position while still holding the former position as a possibility.

As a whole, the chapter argues for an integration of social policy and research. Without such an integration, progress seems unlikely. With such an integration, we would very soon have enough information to decide between the two alternatives presented above to account for lack of progress.

Integrating research with social action will not be an easy objective to obtain. A major hindrance is the general high regard given more education. It is impossible to argue that less education is better than more education. Arguments such as those presented by Caruso, Taylor, and Detterman are often interpreted as arguments for less education. However, what they and the rest of the contributiors to this volume are really arguing for it is better rather than worse education, not less than more.

The remaining two chapters of this section are reports of the most extensive, most methodologically sophisticated attempts to increase intellectual ability and subsequent school achievement yet undertaken. Future studies in this area will have to meet or exceed the standards these investigators have set if they are to make a contribution.

Ramey, MacPhee, and Yeates present data from the Abecedarian Daycare Program. Their goal is to incorporate the results of this study into a general systems model that will be theoretically useful.

The Abecedarian Project is an extensive effort at preschool intervention with children from low-income families. Subjects were randomly assigned to experimental and control conditions. Subjects in the experimental condition were given intensive educational programs which were well documented. This intervention begins as early as six weeks and is available from 7:45 a.m. to 5:30 p.m. for 50 weeks of the year. Transportation is provided.

Though in an early stage, results of this project have been quite encouraging. As will be seen from the chapter, many of the results were unanticipated and difficult to account for using traditional models. It will be years before the full implications of the Abecedarian Project are understood, but the present chapter provides a good beginning.

The last chapter in this section by Garber and Heber presents a review of the current status of the Milwaukee Project. As anyone slightly familiar with the area knows, the Milwaukee Project was the first modern attempt to conduct a methodologically sound study of the effects of early intervention. Though the results of this study will be debated for years to come, there can be no denying that it has made substantial contributions to our knowledge of how such studies must be conducted.

The Milwaukee Project was an intensive effort to prevent mental retardation. It began in the early 1960's and was based on the finding that the children of low IQ mothers show a progressive decline in IQ. The project was designed to prevent this decline by offering early education from infancy to school entry and by providing a family rehabilitation project.

Early reports of positive results gave reason for optimism. More recent results obtained after the termination of intervention are positive but less optimistic.

If there is a single theme represented in the three chapters of this section, it is that environmental effects are characterized by a high order of complexity. Each chapter takes a somewhat different view of this complexity and how it should be dealt with. Caruso, Taylor, and Detterman suggest that we will not understand the complexity of the environment until research is fully integrated into social policy making. Only then will our research methods have the power to untangle the complexities.

Ramey, MacPhee and Yeates present a system model that they hope will be capable of representing the hypothesized complexity. Garber and Heber question whether such complexity can be represented adequately in any type of model. The tone of their chapter on this issue is that of the tired campaigner made pessimistic by the magnitude of the task before them.

Besides suggesting that understanding the effects of environment on intellectual functioning will require a high level of complexity, these chapters also raise a number of questions that I would like to have answered. These questions must eventually be answered. They are centrally important to our understanding of human intelligence. They also have great social importance. Unfortunately, all of the chapters in this section do a better job of raising the questions than answering them. Of course, none was intended to do more than that.

How can environment be measured? This question has a high priority. We must have reliable measures of environmental variables related to intellectual status. Studies which have attempted to improve intellectual functioning have intervened in a global manner by doing everything the investigators thought might have the potential for increasing IQ. It is difficult to determine from such studies which part of the changed environment actually has an impact. Studies, presented in the second section of this volume, which have attempted to manipulate specific aspects of the environment often cannot be clearly related to general intellectual functioning, even though they may show substantial effects on a target behavior.

There have been surprisingly few attempts to systematically measure environmental variables. Those attempts which have been undertaken have found very small effects for those variables which have been measured, generally not amounting to more than a few percent of the total variance. Perhaps, as suggested by the chapters in this section, more complexity will have to be incorporated into these measures before they can be useful.

How much can IQ be increased? This is a question of central importance. Research to date would conservatively suggest that increases in IQ of 10 to 20 points are the maximum to be anticipated. If this upper limit merely represents our ignorance of environmental effects, or actually represents biological limitations of the organism, is a question that can only be answered by additional research.

The reason that this question is of such central importance is that any developed theory of human intelligence must be able to answer this question. A good theory of intelligence will not only tell us what intelligence is, but how and how much it can be changed. Good theories should be quantitative.

Can everyone's IQ be increased? Major efforts to increase IQ have focused on subjects thought to be at-risk for low IQ or mental retardation. These subjects are most often chosen on the basis of demographic characteristics which lead the investigator to believe that they are likely to be reared in a poor environment. Intervention efforts are viewed as an attempt to bring the environment to a level typically enjoyed by the rest of the population.

However, it is possible that similar effects could be obtained for other subjects. What would happen if similar interventions were attempted with potentially high IQ subjects? If the interventions were less effective or completely ineffective, there would be good reason to believe that the assumption on which the intervention studies reported here are based is correct. Such a finding would also provide a method for discovering which environmental differences were implicated in differences in intellectual functioning. On the other hand, if intervention was as effective or more effective for high IQ subjects, there would be extremely important implications from such a finding.

First of all, it would indicate that we have no method of appraising the quality of environment. Assessment of environments would require much more subtle methods than demographics. Secondly, it would indicate that environmental variables currently have little or no effect on an individual's IQ. This would be a most distressing finding. It would challenge many of our cherished assumptions. It would raise profound ethical questions.

For those who think this finding impossible, I would challenge them to find evidence in the literature which contradicts the possibility.

Certainly, the chapters in this section will raise many other questions for which there is no immediate answer but which eventually must be answered. Therein lies their value and our challenge.

# 2

# *Intelligence Research and Intelligent Policy**

DAVID R. CARUSO
JANINE J. TAYLOR
AND
DOUGLAS K. DETTERMAN
*Case Western Reserve University*

The relationship of research to the development of social policy is considered, using Project Head Start as an example. Before the beginning of Head Start, results of research concerning the effects of early education on intellectual development were negative. Despite the warnings of experts, Head Start was launched as a full-scale social program. Research conducted after the beginning of Head Start up to the present indicates the same things as research done before Head Start began. Nothing has been changed, despite the expenditure of $6.5 billion. Social policy must be more closely linked with social science, if either is to prosper.

To what extent does intelligence research affect social policy? In an ideal world, intelligence research should be closely linked with intelligent social welfare policy.

For our study of the relationship between policy and research, we selected Project Head Start as an example of a social program. Although we believe that examination of many other programs would lead to a similar conclusion, we selected Head Start because it is one of the best documented. We will examine the interaction of research and policy by focusing on comprehensive educational intervention research before 1965, the year in which Head Start was begun. We will then consider the rationale for initiating and continuing the Head Start program. Finally, we will consider what research from 1965 to the present tells us. We will be attempting to determine what we knew and when we knew it, and, more important, how that knowledge influenced policy decisions.

*Preparation of this manuscript was supported by Grant #5-T32-HDO7176 from the N.I.C.H.H.D. Requests for reprints may be sent to Douglas K. Detterman, Department of Psychology, Case Western Reserve University, Cleveland, Ohio 44106. We would like to thank Karen Goda for her expert editorial skills.

## RESEARCH BEFORE 1965

Prior to 1965, there was a substantial body of research on compensatory education and its effects on intellectual development. We have located 30 studies (see Table 1) published before 1965. Of those, 43% showed no effect or small effects of early education on IQ. A study was considered to show an effect if the results were statistically significant. Since the studies included are so variable in methodological adequacy, and even in what effects are designated as statistically significant, we re-evaluated some of the outcomes and concluded that by any objective criteria employed, 40 to 60% of the studies showed no effect. That range would seem to be a fair characterization of the literature. It should also be pointed out that those studies that do show effects, generally show small effects, although there are a few notable exceptions.

Even a charitable interpretation of the data would lead to the conclusion that researchers did not fully understand the variables which might produce permanent changes in intellectual functioning. Researchers were well aware of the limitations of their work. Even those who found positive effects were cautious in their interpretations. A good example is the very first study in the area by Woolley (1925), who concluded:

> Very young children may show striking increases of intelligence quotient when placed in a very superior environment. We do not know how permanent these increases are. What evidence we have shows that they tend to be maintained, though perhaps not at so high a level. Doubtless much will depend upon whether the superior environment can be maintained over a long enough period to consolidate the gains the child has made and make them a permanent part of his equipment (p. 482).

The difficulty of specifying the effects of early education on intellectual functioning was even more clearly apparent by 1940, when the *Thirty-Ninth Yearbook of the National Society for the Study of Education* presented a compilation of studies on the effect of nursery school on IQ. Except for findings by Wellman, the effects were negative and the conclusion was that there was little or no effect of nursery school on IQ.

By the late 1950's and early 1960's, the prevailing climate of opinion favored the importance of environmental factors as causative of intellectual differences. Two important works which helped produce that climate were Hunt's (1961) *Intelligence and Experience* and Bloom's (1964) *Stability and Change in Human Characteristics*. The predominant theme of both writers stressed the malleability of intelligence:

> The more recent research has demonstrated that for children growing up under adverse circumstances the I.Q. may be depressed by a significant amount and that intervention at certain points (and especially in the period from ages three to nine) can raise the I.Q. by as much as ten to fifteen points (Bloom, Davis, & Hess, 1965, p. 12).

And later in the book:

> A most striking findings is that the environment of these children causes depression of intellectual functioning, and that provision of a more adequate environment through preschool and other experiences results in considerable increase (10 to 15 points) in I.Q. and in more successful school learning. Even short-range training in perceptual skills, following directions, and other tasks has produced marked increase in intelligence test performance. Thus, levels of intellectual functioning have been found to be quite changeable for the culturally deprived and greatly affected by environmental experiences (p. 72).

Many researchers still hold that point of view. Hunt recently expressed it:

> Intelligence drops by about 50 points for children who are reared from birth in extremely monotonous and unresponsive conditions, as in some orphanages, and it can go up by 20 to 25 points—even for children of mentally retarded mothers—when children are reared in a high powered educational day-care center from a few months after birth (Pines, 1979, p. 59).

Even though there was, and still is, a good deal of optimism about the modifiability of intellectual functioning, researchers were cautious, in varying degrees, about what could actually be accomplished. They were well aware that the research issues were not finally settled. They were also well aware of the huge jump from research to successful application:

> The discovery of the ways to govern the encounters children have with their environments for this purpose would require a great deal of expensive and difficult investigation of the effects of various kinds of early experience on later intellectual capacity. Even after the discovery of the ways, if they can be found, the task of effecting the necessary changes within the culture in child-rearing practices and in educational procedures would be Herculean (Hunt, 1961, p. 363).

> Increased research is needed to determine the precise consequences of the environment for general intelligence. However, even with the relatively crude data already available, the implications for public education and social policy are fairly clear. Where significantly lower intelligence can be clearly attributed to the effects of environmental deprivations, steps must be taken to ameliorate these conditions as early in the individual's development as education and other forces can be utilized (Bloom, 1964, p. 89).

> Although as scholars and research workers we differ in our criteria of certainty, we have attempted to formulate our statements on what is known sufficiently clearly to warrant action, policy formation, or a new way of viewing a problem or task. This is a far cry from knowledge that is certain and definite (Bloom, Davis, & Hess, 1965, foreword).

Some researchers did make social policy recommendations:

> What is needed to solve our current as well as future crises in education is a system of compensatory education which can prevent or overcome earlier deficiencies in the development of each individual (Bloom et al., 1965, p. 6).

TABLE 1
Summary of Early Intervention Studies
Before 1965

| | Prior 1965 | | | | Description | | | | Pre & Post |
|---|---|---|---|---|---|---|---|---|---|
| Study | Year[a] | Age at Intervention | n[b] | | Status at Intervention | Amount of Intervention | Significance | Control Group Used? | Tests Both Used? |
| Woolley | 1925 | 2.5–5 yrs. | E 43 | C 36 | Middle to upper class IQ not cited | 7–14 mos. | + | Yes | Yes |
| Goodenough | 1928 | 2–4 yrs. | E 28 | C 28 | Cross section of SES high-normal IQ | 1 yr. | – | Yes | Yes |
| Hildreth | 1928 | Preschoolers | E 41 | E 48 | Superior homes above ave. IQ | Unclear. Not > 18 mos. and not < 4 mos. | – | Yes | Yes |
| Barrett & Koch | 1930 | 4 yrs. | E 17 | C 17 | Orphanage residents low-ave. IQ | 6–9 mos. | + | Yes | Yes |
| Kawin & Hoefer | 1931 | 2.5 yrs. | E 22 | C 22 | ? | 7 mos. | – | Yes | Yes |
| Ripin[c] | 1933 | 4–12 mos. | E 40 | C 40 | Lower class | ? | ? | Yes | Yes |
| Skeels, Updegraff, Wellman, & Williams | 1938 | 1.5–5.5 yrs. | E 40 | C 65 | Orphanage residents low-ave. to ave. IQ | > 400 days | + | Yes | Yes |
| Skeels & Dye | 1939 | 1.6 yrs. | E 13 | C 12 | Orphanage residents retarded | 2 yrs. | + | Yes | Yes |
| Skodak | 1939 | $\bar{X}$ = 3.5 yrs. | E 65 | | Lower to middle-class ave. IQ | At least 1 yr. | + | No | Yes |

| Author | Year | Age | E | C | SES/IQ | Interval | | | |
|---|---|---|---|---|---|---|---|---|---|
| Anderson | 1940 | X̄ = 3.5 yrs. | E 17 | C 17 | Non-disadvantaged above-ave. IQ | 6 mos. | – | Yes | Yes |
| Bird | 1940 | Median 4 yrs. 8 mos. | E 54 | | Cross section of SES & IQ | 4–59 wks. | – | No | Yes |
| Frandsen & Barlow | 1940 | X̄ = 3.5 yrs. | E 30 | C 28 | Lower to middle class high-ave. to above ave. IQ | Median interval 5.5 mos. | – | Yes | Yes |
| Goodenough & Maurer | 1940 | 1.5–5 yrs. | E 148 | C 166 | Above-ave. homes ave. to above-ave. IQ | 1–3 yrs. | – | Yes | Yes |
| Jones & Jorgensen | 1940 | X̄ = 2.7 yrs. | E 11 | C 11 | Above ave. in homes & IQ | X̄ = 225.2 days | – | Yes | Yes |
| Kephart | 1940 | 15–18 yrs. | E 16 | C ? | Retarded residents of institution | X̄ = 1.5 yrs. | + | Yes | Yes |
| Lamson | 1940 | Preschoolers | E 25 | C 44 | SES not cited ave. to high-ave. IQ | X̄ = 1.9 yrs. | – | Yes | No pretest |
| Olson & Hughes | 1940 | Preschoolers | E 28 | C 28 | Middle- to upper-class ave. to above ave. IQ | 1st gr. = 225 days 2nd gr. = 117 days | – | Yes | Yes |
| Pritchard, Horan & Hollingsworth | 1940 | 5–12 yrs. | E 111 | | Lower-class low-ave. to below-ave. IQ | X̄ = 2 yrs. 9 mos. | – | No | Yes |
| Reymert & Hinton | 1940 | 3–14 yrs. | E 100 | | Lower-class cross section of IQ | 4 yrs. | + | No | Yes |
| Starkweather & Roberts | 1940 | Preschoolers | E 274 | | Middle-class ave. to above-ave. IQ | 142–241 days | + | No | Yes |
| Thorndike, Flemming, Hildreth, & Stanger | 1940 | Spanning ages up to 14 yrs. | E 1167 | | Upper class above-ave. IQ | Retest after at least 2.5 yrs. | + | No | Yes |
| Voas | 1940 | Preschoolers | E 85 | C 591 | Middle class ave. to above-ave. IQ | 1–3 yrs. | – | Yes | No |

TABLE 1 (*continued*)

| | Prior 1965 | | | Description | | | | Pre & Post Tests |
| Study | Year[a] | Age at Intervention | n[b] | Status at Intervention | Amount of Intervention | Significance | Control Group Used? | Both Used? |
|---|---|---|---|---|---|---|---|---|
| Wellman | 1940 | 1.5–6 yrs. | E 686 C 34 | Middle to upper class ave. to above-ave. IQ | 1–3 yrs. | + | Yes | Yes |
| Dawe | 1942 | 5 yrs. | E 12 C 11 1 E not find a matched C. | E reside in orphanage low-ave. to below-ave. IQ | $\bar{X}$ = 50 hrs. | + | Yes | Yes |
| Schmidt | 1946 | 12–14 yrs. | E 64 C 68 | Cross section of SES retarded | 3 yrs. + 5 yrs. of follow-up | + | Yes | Yes |
| Boger | 1952 | 5–8 yrs. | E 54 C 50 | Rural children low-ave. to below-ave. IQ | 4 mos. | + | Yes | Yes |
| Mundy | 1957 | 26–28 yrs. | E 28 C 28 | Institutional residents below-ave. IQ | 1 yr. 9 mos.– 2 yrs. | + | Yes | Yes |
| Kirk | 1958 | 4 yrs. | E 40 C 38 | Institutional & foster home residents retarded | 1–3 yrs. | + | Yes | Yes |
| Brazziel & Terrell | 1962 | Preschoolers | E 26 C 66 | Lower class IQ not cited | 6 wks. | + | Yes | No pretest |
| Fouracre, Connor, & Goldberg | 1962 | Preschoolers | E 54 | SES not cited retarded | 2 yrs. | – | ? | Yes |
| Smilansky | 1964 | 5 yrs. | 306 | Lower class IQ not cited | 1 yr. | + | Yes | Yes |

Positive results: 17 out of 30 or 57%
Negative results: 13 out of 30 or 43%

[a]Year refers to the date that the research was conducted, but not necessarily the date of the reference.
[b]E = number of subjects in experimental group, C = number of subjects in control group.
[c]Due to the abstract length of Ripin's article, the lack of information prevented conclusions to be drawn. The article was kept in the Table in order to remain comprehensive in the review of the literature, but was not used in computing the percentages.

> There is an urgency about this problem and it is likely that some of the training will have to be done while the teachers are actually in the schools (Bloom et al., 1965, p. 18).

The above recommendations are almost literally reflected in the report of the panel that founded Head Start.

Given the optimistic but cautious attitude of researchers, what led to their implicit support of, or at least their lack of opposition to, the Head Start project? Apparently there are two reasons for it, each of which is difficult to document, and, therefore, extremely tentative. First, it appears that researchers had little part in the initial phases of the program, and, thus, had little opportunity to express their opinions. A second reason for implicit support seems to be that researchers naively expected that any social program begun would include a substantial research component. Researchers saw the potential for definitively answering a most important question.

An hypothesis about the initial direction of Head Start which at first seemed quite plausible was that rabid environmentalists misled government officials by selective citation of the literature. We have been unable to support that position in any way whatsoever.

## PROJECT HEAD START

There is no denying that Project Head Start began as a program to improve intellectual functioning and to increase academic achievement. There is also no denying that laymen were generally optimistic about environmental interventions and what they could be hoped to produce. A few quotes from prominent persons of the time illustrate that point quite well. Consider, for example, the following excerpt from a speech by John F. Kennedy (as cited by Jordan, 1966):

> Socioeconomic and medical evidence gathered by a panel which I appointed in 1961, however, shows a major causative role for adverse social, economic, and cultural factors. Families who are deprived of the basic necessities of life, opportunity, and motivation have a high proportion of the Nation's retarded children . . . Deprivation of a child's opportunities for learning slows development in slum and distressed areas (p. 4);

and another from a speech by Mrs. Lyndon B. Johnson (as cited by Payne et al., 1973):

> Head Start will reach out to one million young children in a grey world of poverty and neglect and lead them into the human family (p. 54).

Optimistic environmentalism was well entrenched in the public spirit of the time. Official pronouncements, however, still contained some measure of skepticism. The original impetus for Head Start came from a panel of experts who reported to the President in February, 1965 (*Recommendations for a Head Start Program by Panel of Experts,* 1972). They said it was urgent to implement the program immediately but, at the same time, they did advise caution. That caution, expressed by researchers, was, nevertheless, somewhat diluted by the perceived need for immediate social action:

> There is considerable evidence that the early years of childhood are the most critical point in the poverty cycle. During these years the creation of learning patterns, emotional development and the formation of individual expectations and aspirations take place at a very rapid pace. For the child of poverty there are clearly observable deficiencies in the processes which lay the foundation for a pattern of failure—and thus a pattern of poverty—throughout the child's entire life.
>
> Within recent years there has been experimentation and research designed to improve opportunities for the child of poverty. While much of this work is not yet complete there is adequate evidence to support the view that special programs can be devised for these four and five year olds which will improve both the child's opportunities and achievements.
>
> During the early stages of any programs . . . it would be preferable to encourage comprehensive programs for fewer children than to attempt to reach vast numbers of children with limited programs.
>
> The need for an urgency of these programs is such that they should be initiated immediately. Many programs could begin in the summer of 1965. These would help provide a more complete picture of national needs for use in future planning.
>
> Research and planning should be a key part of both local and national efforts.

Unfortunately, the recommendations urging caution and additional research were not heeded. Stevenson (cited in Miller & Dyer, 1975) describes the actual implementation of Head Start as follows:

> This massive activity was to be implemented not over the next few years as one might expect but within the next few months. In Washington the program was quickly dubbed Project Rush-Rush. Everyone rushed! In a few months curricula were improvised, teachers were trained in five day marathon sessions, aides were hastily recruited, and by early summer the first Head Start classes were in session (p. 165).

From the *Congressional Quarterly Almanac* (1965), we have the following:

> Originally aimed at enrolling 100,000 needy children from 300 communities at a cost of $17 million, Project Head Start went far beyond its goals. The summer program enrolled 561,359 children in 11,068 communities at a cost of $85,446,976 . . . (p. 410).

Why did Head Start expand so extensively and so rapidly, contrary to the recommendations of the panel of experts? The first reason seems to be that the program had lost all contact with research, and, instead, drew its scientific justification from what we call the "Joyce Brothers data base"—ideas endorsed by the public at large but not necessarily supported by research. A good example of that comes from the President's Message to Congress, 1966, made after Head Start had been in operation one year:

Few programs have had the visible success of Operation Head Start. The disadvantaged children who have benefited from this program are already entering the first grade with new confidence in themselves and greater eagerness to learn (p. 534).

A second reason seems to be that the major justification for the program had become moral indignation, not results which could be supported by research. From the *Congressional Quarterly Almanac* (1966):

"It's a point that distresses me," Kennedy said. "We're spending more than $300 million on a supersonic transport that will eventually cost over $4 billion. But we can't help 210,000 more children. We're spending $24 billion on Viet Nam . . . and we can't spend $200 million more on these children who will carry a heavy burden through life without this program. As a civilized nation we cannot be proud of this. It's an outrage (p. 233)."

Even when research began to accumulate showing that Head Start was not having the desired effect, the response was to authorize additional funds. A portion of Special Analyses, Budget of the United States (1970) declares:

The results of recent studies on the retention of developmental gains made by Head Start children have been disappointing. Consequently, increased funding is allowed in 1971 for systematic testing of a variety of approaches for preschool (p. 117).

As it became increasingly clear that Head Start was having no lasting effects on the intellectual functioning of the children enrolled in the program, administrators took the only course open to them. They changed the goals of the program. In a recent survey of Head Start program directors (Royster & Larson, 1978), self-esteem and social-skill goals were ranked as most important, while the academic skill/language cluster of curriculum goals was ranked last. Though there may be a good deal of sympathy for the new goals, they are not the ones for which the program was begun.

The pattern of funding for Project Head Start has been one of steadily increasing appropriations. Figure 1 shows the amount of money spent on the program and the number of children enrolled since Head Start's beginning. The important thing to notice is the steady rate of acceleration in funding. The 1980 appropriation for the program is $735 million. By the end of the present fiscal year, we will have spent $6.5 billion on Head Start, and that appears to be a conservative estimate.

In contrast, research—using the term very loosely—has been funded at a level so low that on the graph it would cling so close to the abscissa that we decided not to plot it. Research funding was not even included in the program until 1969. Since then, support has varied from 2.5 to 3.8% of total expenditures for the program. That small proportion, however, may represent an overestimate, since it is unclear to what extent the programs supported would be considered research.

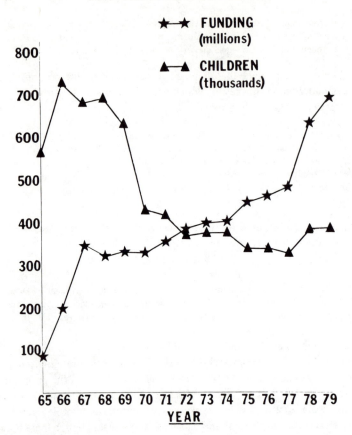

**FIG. 1.**    The number of dollars spent in millions and the number of children served in thousands for Head Start from its beginning in 1965. (Source: *Administration for Children, Youth, and Families,* D.H.E.W., September 6, 1979).

## RESEARCH AFTER 1965

If Head Start was little influenced by research, Head Start has taught us something, we should at least hope, about how to conduct early intervention. We have located 54 studies conducted after 1965 concerned with the relationship between early intervention and intellectual development. The studies are shown in Table 2. Of those studies, 49% show no or little gain in intellectual development. You will remember that 43% of the studies made before 1965 showed similar results. Evidently, little has changed.

In contrast to our view is that of Darlington, Royce, Snipper, Murray, and Lazar (1980), who have presented evidence to indicate that preschool programs positively affect special class placement and grade retention. Their data, like the data of many other studies, show that any IQ gains are largely lost. There are two possible explanations for the effects of preschool on special class placement and on grade retention. First, and most optimistically, it is possible that the initial increases in IQ from preschool programs affected placement decisions for children attending preschool programs, since those decisions are partly based on IQ. Second, it is possible that preschool programs altered social behaviors, which also affect placement decisions. In either case, the findings have no bearing on whether preschool programs affect intellectual behaviors. It is clear that they have no direct effect. The indirect effects implied by the above findings are ambiguous, since it is not at all clear whether grade retention or special class placement is a desirable outcome for children of low intellectual ability. If special class placement and grade retention accomplish their intended purposes, then control group children without preschool experiences should eventually show academic achievement superior to those having preschool experience, since they have a higher proportion of such placements.

We are left with the disappointing conclusion that research had no effect on Head Start and Head Start had no effect on research. We have examined other social programs and have come to the same conclusion: social research has little or no effect on social policy and social policy does not generate required research. It is our belief that research in the social sciences will not prosper as it has in the physical and biological sciences until the critical linkgage between policy and research is made. Another way of saying this is that social policy will not succeed until it is firmly predicated on research.

The preponderance of negative results in our area of research does not indicate that effective interventions cannot be found. What it indicates to us is that there has never been a concerted research effort to understand the development of intellectual functioning, an effort which would allow knowledge to become cumulative. Indeed, there have been successful programs.

If there is one point of agreement among scientists in the area, it is that intervention programs must begin with solid research on a small scale and allowed to grow. Even the strictest hereditarian believes that. After all, any intervention must be environmental, regardless of the source of the deficit which prompted the intervention. The point can easily be illustrated by the following quotes. Two of them are from the writings of Jensen and two from Hunt. We have found that even persons familiar with these authors' writings have a difficult time determining which statements are Jensen's and which are Hunt's (see footnote 1 for sources). Quote 1:

> People, and especially people in government, always want to do things on a large scale. That's very difficult with social problems. I believe you should have a more biological approach; you plant a seed and encourage it to develop. You kind of "grow" your institution, monitoring it all the time to make sure it is effective.

TABLE 2
Summary of Early Intervention Studies
After 1965

| After 1965 | | | | Description | | | Control | Pre & Post Tests |
| Study | Year[a] | Age at Intervention | n[b] | Status at Intervention | Amount of Intervention | Significance | Group Used? | Both Used? |
|---|---|---|---|---|---|---|---|---|
| Bereiter & Engelman (The Academic Preschool) | 1966 | 4 yrs. | E 15  C 28 | Lower class cross section of IQ | 2 yrs. | + | Yes | Yes |
| Durham Education Improvement Program | 1966–1967 | Preschoolers | Not cited | Lower class low-normal to below ave. | 8–9 mos. | + | No | Yes |
| Blatt & Garfunkel | 1967 | 3 yrs. | E 38  C 21 | Lower class low-normal IQ | 2 yrs. | – | Yes | Yes |
| Himley | 1967 | Preschoolers | E 38  C 76 | Lower-class IQ not cited | 8 wks. | – | Yes | No pretest |
| Hodges, McCandless, & Spicker (Indiana Project) | 1967 | 5 yrs. | Not cited | Lower class below ave. IQ | 1 yr. | + | Yes | Yes |
| Howard & Plant | 1967 | Preschoolers | E 33  C 33 | Lower class low-normal IQ | 8 wks. | + | ad hoc matched grp. | Yes |
| Hyman & Kliman | 1967 | Preschoolers | E 20  C 20 | Lower class IQ not cited | Not cited | – | Yes | No pretest |
| Ozer & Milgram | 1967 | Preschoolers | E 40  C presume 40 | Lower class IQ not cited | 9 mos | – | Yes | Yes |
| Sigel & McBane | 1967 | 5–5.5 yrs. | E 36  C 33 | Lower to middle class IQ not cited | Not cited | – | Yes | No pretest |

| Study | Year | Age | Class/IQ | Sample size | Duration | | | |
|---|---|---|---|---|---|---|---|---|
| Weikart (Perry Preschool Project) | 1967 | 3–4 yrs. | Lower class below-ave. IQ | Not cited | 2 yrs. | – | Yes | Yes |
| Zigler | 1967 | Preschoolers | Lower class ? | ? | 9 mos. | – | Yes | ? |
| Alexander | 1968 | Preschoolers | Lower class low-normal IQ | E 68 | 1 yr. | + | No | Yes |
| Barrett | 1968 | Preschoolers | Lower class IQ not cited | E 62 | 7 mos. | + | No | Yes |
| Bickley | 1968 | Preschoolers | Lower class IQ not cited | E 91  C 141 | 8 wks. | – | Yes | No pretest |
| Cawley | 1968 | 4.3 yrs. | Lower class below-ave. to ave. IQ | E 140 | 9 mos. | + | No | Yes |
| Faust | 1968 | Preschoolers | Lower class low-normal IQ | E 22 | 1 yr. | + | No | Yes |
| Fuschillo | 1968 | 3–3.5 yrs. | Lower class below-ave. to ave. IQ | E 36  C 63 | 2 yrs. | + | Yes | Yes |
| Karnes, Hodgins, & Teska | 1968 | 4–5 yrs. | Lower class ave. IQ | E 27  C 28 | 7 mos. | + | Yes | Yes |
| Mann & Elliott | 1968 | Preschoolers | Lower class IQ not cited | Not cited | 7 wks. | + | No | Yes |
| Rieber & Womack | 1968 | 5.6 yrs. | Lower class below-ave. IQ | E 131 | 5 wks. | + | No | Yes |
| Waller & Connors | 1968 | Preschoolers | Lower class IQ not cited | Not cited | 8 wks. | – | Yes | Yes |
| DiLorenzo | 1969 | Preschoolers | Lower to middle-class low-normal to ave. IQ | Not cited | 1 yr. | – | Yes | Yes |
| Karnes | 1969 | Preschoolers | Lower class IQ not cited | Not cited | 2 yrs. | – | No | Yes |
| Karnes, Hodgins, & Teska | 1969 | 4 yrs. | Lower class IQ not cited | Not cited | 12 wks. | + | Yes | Yes |

TABLE 2 (Continued)

| After 1965 | | | | Description | | | Control Group Used? | Pre & Post Tests Both Used? |
|---|---|---|---|---|---|---|---|---|
| Study | Year[a] | Age at Intervention | n[b] | Status at Intervention | Amount of Intervention | Significance | | |
| The Preschool Program | 1969 | 3–4 yrs. | E 600 | Lower class IQ not cited | 1–2 yrs. | + | Yes | Yes |
| Project Early Push | 1969 | 3.8–4.8 yrs. | ? | Lower class | ? | + | No | Yes |
| Gray & Klaus (The Early Training Project) | 1970 | 4 yrs. | E 38   C 41 | Lower class IQ not cited | 2–3 yrs. | + | Yes | Yes |
| Jackson | 1970 | Preschoolers | Not cited | Lower to middle-class IQ not cited | 1st grp. = 8 wks. 2nd grp. = 8 mos. | – | Yes | No pretest |
| Larsen | 1970 | Preschoolers | E 25   C 25 | Lower class IQ not cited | 8 wks. | – | Yes | Yes |
| Levensteing | 1970 | 1.7–3.6 yrs. | E 33   C 21 | Lower class low-normal IQ | 7 mos. | + | Yes | Yes |
| Lewing | 1970 | Preschoolers | E 87   C 73 | Lower class IQ not cited | 8 wks. | – | Yes | No pretest |
| White (Westinghouse-Ohio Study) | 1970 | Preschoolers | E 1,980  C 1,983 | Lower class C-higher SES IQ not cited | 1st grp. = 8 wks. 2nd grp. = 1 yr. | – | Yes | No pretest |
| Deutsch | 1971 | 3 yrs. | Not cited | Lower class low-normal IQ | 5 yrs. | – | Yes | Yes |
| Scruggs | 1971 | 4 yrs. | E 69 | C not cited | Lower class IQ not cited | + | Yes | Yes |
| Beller | 1972 | 3–6 yrs. | Not cited | Lower class IQ not cited | 2 yrs. | – | Yes | No pretest |

58

| Study | Year[a] | Age/group | E[b] | C | Population | Duration | Result | | |
|---|---|---|---|---|---|---|---|---|---|
| Braun & Caldwell | 1972 | 1st grp. < 3 yrs. 2nd grp. > 3 yrs. | E 30 | | Lower-class ave. IQ | Varied | + | No | Yes |
| Dellinger | 1972 | Preschoolers | E 51 | C 51 | Lower-class IQ not cited | 8 wks. | − | Yes | No pretest |
| Herber (The Milwaukee Project) | 1972 | 3 mos. | E 20 | C 20 | Lower-class below-ave. IQ | 5.5 yrs. | + | Yes | Yes |
| Larson | 1972 | Preschoolers | Not cited | | Lower-class IQ not cited | Not cited | − | Yes | No |
| McAfee | 1972 | 3–5 yrs. | E 32 | C 22 | Lower-class low-normal to ave. IQ | 1–2 yrs. | − | Yes | Yes |
| Schaefer & Aaronson | 1972 | 1.25 yrs. | E 31 | C 33 | Lower-class low-ave. to ave. IQ | 22 mos. | + | Yes | Yes |
| Sprigle | 1972 | Preschoolers | Not cited | | Lower-class IQ not cited | 2 yrs. | + | Yes | Yes |
| Hosey | 1973 | Preschoolers | E 23 | C 24 | Lower-class ave. IQ | 8 wks. | − | Yes | No pretest |
| Burden | 1974 | 3–5 yrs. | E 18 | C 18 | Lower-class IQ not cited | 4 mos. | − | Yes | Yes |
| Miller & Dyer | 1975 | 4 yrs. | E 214 | C 34 | Lower-class low-ave. to ave. IQ | 1 yr. | − | Yes | Yes |
| Steig, D'Annunzio, & Speilman | 1976-1977 | 3.5 yrs. | E 40 | | Cross section of SES and of IQ | ? | + | No | Yes |
| Wilkinson & Murphy | 1976 | Preschoolers | E 42 | | Lower class ? | 4 mos. | − | Yes | Yes |
| Morris & Clarizio | 1977 | 2.3–3.6 yrs. | E 12 | | Lower-class low-normal IQ | 9 mos. | + | No | Yes |
| Royster & Larson | 1978 | Preschoolers | E 656 | C 670 | Lower-class IQ not cited | Not cited | + | Yes | No pretest |

Positive results: 25 out of 49 or 51%
Negative results: 24 out of 49 or 49%

[a]Year refers to the date that the research was conducted, but not necessarily the date of the reference.
[b]E = number of subjects in experimental group, C = number of subjects in control group.

Quote 2:

> It has been claimed that . . . mammoth programs have not been adequately pinpointed to meeting specific, fine-grained cultural and cognitive needs of these children and therefore should not be expected to produce the gains that could result from more intensive and more carefully focused programs in which maximum cultural enrichment and instructional ingenuity are lavished on a small group of children by a team of experts.
>
> The scanty evidence available seems to bear this out. While massive compensatory programs have produced no appreciable gains in intelligence or achievement, the majority of small scale programs . . . have produced appreciable gains.

Quote 3:

> I am among those few who are inclined to believe that mankind has not yet developed a form of early childhood education which permits him to achieve his full genotypic potential.

Quote 4:

> . . . if the ideal of universal education is to be successfully pursued, it seems a reasonable conclusion that schools and society must provide a range of diversity of educational methods, programs, and goals, and of occupational opportunities just as wide as the range of human abilities. Accordingly, the ideal of equality of educational opportunity should not be interpreted as uniformity of facilities, instructional techniques and educational aims for all children. Diversity rather than uniformity of approaches and aims would seem to be the key to making education rewarding for children of different patterns of ability.[1]

The order of authors for the quotes is: Hunt, Jensen, Hunt, Jensen. While the above test may be entertaining, the important point is that authors with diverse opinions on other topics are in close agreement about how we should proceed.

Whether the slow, developmental approach recommended by these authors would correct the lack of linkage between research and policy is difficult to determine. The solution may be far more complicated than that. However, if a solution is not found, intelligence research will be characterized by one-shot studies, and social policy by programs that fail to fulfill their goals at immense cost to the taxpayer.

## REFERENCES

Alexander, T. Changing the mental ability of children in the city. Cited in *Review of research, 1965 to 1969 of Project Head Start* (OEO Pamphlet 6108-13), Washington, DC: Office of Economic Opportunity, June 1969.

Anderson, L. D. A longitudinal study of the effects of nursery school training on successive intelligence test ratings. In *Thirty-Ninth Yearbook of the National Society for the Study of Education* (Part II). Bloomington, IL: Public School Publishing Company, 1940.

---

[1]Quote 1: Hunt, as quoted in Pines, 1979, p. 67; Quote 2: Jensen, 1969, pp. 96–97; Quote 3: Hunt, 1969, p. 292; Quote 4: Jensen, 1969, p. 117.

Barrett, W. J. The effect of Headstart experience on deprived groups: Administrative implications. *Dissertations Abstracts International,* 1968, *28,* 3400A.

Barrett, H. E., & Koch, H. L. The effect of nursery-school training upon the mental-test performance of a group of orphanage children. *The Pedagogical Seminary and Journal of Genetic Psychology,* 1930, *37,* 102–122.

Beller, K. E. Impact of early education on disadvantaged children. Cited in U. Bronfenbrenner, *A report on longitudinal evaluations of preschool programs. Is early intervention effective?* (Vol. 2) (DHEW Publication No. (OHD) 76-30025). Washington, DC: Office of Child Development, 1974.

Bereiter, C., & Engleman, S. Teaching disadvantaged children in the preschool. Cited in J. L. Frost & G. T. Rowland, *Compensatory programming: The acid test of American education.* Dubuque, IA: W. C. Brown Co., Publishers, 1971.

Bickley, M. T. A comparison of differences in selected educational characteristics among culturally disadvantaged children who attended Project Head Start, culturally disadvantaged children who did not attend Head Start, and children who are not culturally disadvantaged as those characteristics relate to reading achievement in grade one. *Dissertation Abstracts International,* 1968, *29,* 1032A.

Bird, G. E. The effect of nursery-school attendance upon mental growth of children. In *Thirty-Ninth Yearbook of the National Society for the Study of Education* (Part II). Bloomington, IL: Public School Publishing Company, 1940.

Blatt, B., & Garfunkel, F. Educating intelligence: Determinants of school behavior of disadvantaged children. *Exceptional Children,* 1967, *33,* 601–608.

Bloom, B. S. *Stability and change in human characteristics.* New York: Wiley, 1964.

Bloom, B. S., Davis, A., & Hess, R. *Compensatory education for cultural deprivation.* New York: Holt, Rinehart and Winston, Inc., 1965.

Boger, J. H. An experimental study of the effects of perceptual training on group I.Q. test scores of elementary pupils in rural ungraded schools. *Journal of Educational Research,* 1952, 46, 43–52.

Braun, S. J., & Caldwell, B. Emotional adjustment of children in day care who enrolled prior to or after the age of 3. Cited in U. Bronfenbrenner, *A report on longitudinal evaluations of preschool programs. Is early intervention effective?* (Vol. 2) (DHEW Publication No. (OHD) 76-30025). Washington, DC: Office of Child Development, 1974.

Brazziel, W. F., & Terrell, M. An experiment in the development of readiness in a culturally disadvantaged group of first grade children. *Journal of Negro Education,* 1962, *31,* 4–7.

Burden, T. L. M. Changing parent attitudes and improving the intellectual abilities of three, four and five year old children through participation in a Home Start program. *Dissertation Abstracts International,* 1974, *34,* 7037A.

Cawley, J. F. Learning aptitudes among preschool children of different intellectual levels. *Journal of Negro Education,* 1968, *37,* 179–183.

*Congressional Quarterly Almanac* (Vol. XXI). Washington, DC: Congressional Quarterly Service, 1965.

*Congressional Quarterly Almanac* (Vol. XXII). Washington, DC: Congressional Quarterly Service, 1966.

Darlington, R. B., Royce, J. M., Snipper, A. S., Murray, H. W., & Lazar I. Preschool programs and later school competence of children from low-income families. *Science,* 1980, *208,* 202–204.

Dawe, H. C. A study of the effect of an educational program upon language development and related mental functions in young children. *Journal of Experimental Education,* 1942, *11,* 200–209.

Dellinger, H. V. A study of the effectiveness of a summer Head Start program on the achievement of first grade children. *Dissertation Abstracts International,* 1972, 32, 4832A.

Deutsch, M., et al. Regional research and resources center in early childhood: Final report (U.S. OEO). Cited in U. Bronfenbrenner, *A report on longitudinal evaluations of preschool programs. Is early intervention effective?* (Vol. 2) (DHEW Publication No. (OHD) 76-30025). Washington, DC: Office of Child Development, 1974.

DiLorenzo, L. T. Pre-kindergarten programs for educationally disadvantaged children: Final report. Cited in U. Bronfenbrenner, *A report on longitudinal evaluations of preschool programs. Is early intervention effective?* (Vol. 2) (DHEW Publication No. (OHD) 76-30025). Washington, DC: Office of Child Development, 1974.

Durham Education Improvement Program. Cited in A. R. Jensen, How much can we boost IQ and scholastic achievement? *Harvard Educational Review,* 1969, *39,* 1–123.

Faust, M. Five pilot studies: Concerned with social-emotional variables affecting behavior of children in head start. Cited in *Review of research, 1965 to 1969 of Project Head Start* (OEO Pamphlet 6108-13). Washington, DC: Office of Economic Opportunity, June 1969.

Fouracre, M., Connor, F. P., & Goldberg, I. The effects of a preschool program upon young educable mentally retarded children. Cited in S. L. Guskin & H. H. Spicker, Educational research in mental retardation. In N. R. Ellis (Ed.), *International Review of Research in Mental Retardation* (Vol. 3). New York: Academic Press, 1968.

Frandsen, A., & Barlow, F. P. Influence of the nursery school on mental growth. In *Thirty-Ninth Yearbook of the National Society for the Study of Education* (Part II). Bloomington, IL: Public School Publishing Company, 1940.

Fuschillo, J. C. Enriching the preschool experience of children from age three: The evaluation. *Children,* 1968, *5,* 140–143.

Goodenough, F. L. A preliminary report on the effect of nursery-school training upon the intelligence test scores of young children. In *Twenty-Seventh Yearbook of the National Society for the Study of Education* (Part I). Bloomington, IL: Public School Publishing Company, 1928.

Goodenough, F. L., & Maurer, K. M. The mental development of nursery-school children compared with that of non-nursery-school children. In *Thirty-Ninth Yearbook of the National Society for the Study of Education* (Part II). Bloomington, IL: Public School Publishing Company, 1940.

Gray, S. W., & Klaus, R. A. The early training project: A seventh-year report. *Child Development,* 1970, *41,* 909–924.

Heber, R., Garber, H., Harrington, S., & Hoffman, C. Rehabilitation of families at risk for mental retardation. Cited in U. Bronfenbrenner, *A report on longitudinal evaluations of preschool programs. Is early intervention effective:* (Vol. 2) (DHEW Publication No. (OHD) 76-30025). Washington, DC: Office of Child Development, 1974.

Hildreth, G. The effect of school environment upon Stanford Binet tests of young children. In *Twenty-Seventh Yearbook of the National Society for the Study of Education* (Part I). Bloomington, IL: Public School Publishing Company, 1928.

Himley, O. T. A study to determine if lasting educational and social benefits accrue to summer Head Start participants. *Dissertation Abstracts International,* 1967, *28,* 1621A.

Hodges, W. L., McCandless, B. R., & Spicker, H. H. The development and evaluation of a diagnostically based curriculum for preschool psychosocially deprived children. Cited in A. R. Jensen, How much can we boost IQ and scholastic achievement? *Harvard Educational Review,* 1969, *39,* 1–123.

Hosey, H. R. Cognitive and affective growth of elementary school students who participated in summer Head Start. *Dissertation Abstracts International,* 1973, *33,* 6591A.

Howard, J. L., & Plant, W. T. Psychometric evaluation of an operation Headstart program. *Journal of Genetic Psychology,* 1967, *111,* 281–288.

Hunt, J. McV. *Intelligence and experience.* New York: Ronald Press, 1961.

Hunt, J. McV. Has compensatory education failed? Has it been attempted ? *Harvard Educational Review,* 1969, 39, 278–300.

Hyman, I. A., & Kliman, D. S. First grade readiness of children who have had summer Head Start program. Cited in J. S. Payne, C. D. Mercer, R. A. Payne, & R. G. Davison, *Head Start: A tragicomedy with epilogue.* New York: Behavioral Publications, 1973.

Jackson, D. J. A comparison of the academic achievement in grades two and three of children who attended an eight-week and an eight-month Head Start program. *Dissertation Abstracts International,* 1970, *31,* 1512A.

Jensen, A. R. How much can we boost IQ and scholastic achievement? *Harvard Educational Review*, 1969, *39*, 1–123.

Jones, H. E., & Jorgensen, A. P. Mental growth as related to nursery-school attendance. In *Thirty-Ninth Yearbook of the National Society for the Study of Education* (Part II). Bloomington, IL: Public School Publishing Company, 1940.

Jordan, T. E. (Ed.). *Perspectives in mental retardation*. Carbondale, IL: Southern Illinois University Press, 1966.

Karnes, M. B. Research and development program on preschool disadvantaged children: Final report. Cited in U. Brofenbrenner, *A report on longitudinal evaluations of preschool programs. Is early intervention effective?* (Vol. 2) (DHEW Publication No. (OHD) 76-30025). Washington, DC: Office of Child Development, 1974.

Karnes, M. B., Hodgins, A., & Teska, J. A. An evaluation of two preschool programs for disadvantaged children: A traditional and a highly structured experimental preschool. *Exceptional Children*, 1968, *34*, 667–676.

Karnes, M. B., Hodgins, A., & Teska, J. A. The effects of short-term instruction at home by mothers of children not enrolled in preschool. Cited in U. Bronfenbrenner, *A report on longitudinal evaluations of preschool programs. Is early intervention effective?* (Vol. 2) (DHEW Publication No. (OHD) 76-30025). Washington, DC: Office of Child Development, 1974.

Karwin, E., & Hoefer, C. A comparative study of a nursery-school group vs. a non-nursery school group. Cited in F. L. Goodenough, New evidence on environmental influence on intelligence. In *Thirty-Ninth Yearbook of the National Society for the Study of Education* (Part I). Bloomington, IL: Public School Publishing Company, 1940.

Kephart, N. C. Influencing the rate of mental growth in retarded children through environmental stimulation. In *Thirty-Ninth Yearbook of the National Society for the Study of Education* (Part II). Bloomington, IL: Public School Publishing Company, 1940.

Kirk, S. A. *Early education of the mentally retarded*. Urbana, IL: University of Illinois Press, 1958.

Lamson, E. E. A follow-up study of a group of nursery-school children. In *Thirty-Ninth Yearbook of the National Society for the Study of Education* (Part II). Bloomington, IL: Public School Publishing Company, 1940.

Larsen, J. S. A study of the intelligence and school achievement of children previously enrolled in Project Head Start. *Dissertation Abstracts International*, 1970, *31*, 1014A.

Larsen, D. E. Stability of gains in intellectual functioning among white children who attended a preschool program in rural Minnesota. Cited in *Review of Head Start research since 1969 and an annotated bibliography* (DHEW Publication (OHDS) 78-31102). Washington, DC: U.S. Government Printing Office, 1977.

Levenstein, P. Cognitive growth in preschoolers through verbal interaction with mothers. *American Journal of Orthopsychiatry*, 1970, *40*, 426–432.

Lewing, H. F. An evaluation of a summer Head Start program. *Dissertation Abstracts International*, 1970, *30*, 4191A.

Mann, E. T., & Elliot, C. C. Assessment of the utility of project Head Start for the culturally deprived: An evaluation of social and psychological functioning. Cited in J. S. Payne, C. D. Mercer, R. A. Payne, & R. G. Davison, *Head Start: A tragicomedy with epilogue*. New York: Behavioral Publications, 1973.

McAfee, O. An integrated approach to early childhood education. In J. C. Stanley (Ed.), *Preschool programs for the disadvantaged: Five experimental approaches to early childhood education*. Baltimore, MD: Johns Hopkins University Press, 1972.

Miller, L. B., & Dyer, J. L. Four preschool programs: Their dimensions and effects. *Monographs of the Society for Research in Child Development*, 1975, *40*(5-6, Serial No. 162).

Morris, J. J., & Clarizio, S. Improvement in IQ of high-risk, disadvantaged preschool children enrolled in a developmental program. *Psychological Reports*, 1977, *41*, Pt. 2, 1111–1114.

Mundy, L. Environmental influence on intellectual function as measured by intelligence tests. *British Journal of Medical Psychology*, 1957, *30*, 194–201.

Olson, W. C., & Hughes, B. O.  Subsequent growth of children with and without nursery-school experience. In *Thirty-Ninth Yearbook of the National Society for the Study of Education* (Part II). Bloomington, IL: Public School Publishing Company, 1940.

Ozer, M. N., & Milgram, N. A.  The effect of a summer Head Start program: A neurological evaluation. *American Journal of Orthopsychiatry, 1967, 37,* 331–332.

Payne, J. S., Mercer, C. D., Payne, R. A., & Davison, R. G.  *Head Start: A tragicomedy with epilogue.* New York: Behavioral Publications, 1973.

Pines, M.  A head start in the nursery. *Psychology Today,* September 1979, 56–57; 59–60; 63–64; 67–68.

*Preschool Program, The* (DHEW OE 37057). Washington, DC: Department of Health, Education and Welfare, 1969.

President's Message to Congress. *Congressional Quarterly Weekly Report,* March 4, 1966 (No. 9). Washington, DC: Congressional Quarterly Service, 1966.

Pritchard, M. C., Horan, K. M., & Hollingworth, L. S.  The course of mental development in slow learners under an 'experience curriculum'. In *Thirty-Ninth Yearbook of the National Society for the Study of Education* (Part II). Bloomington, IL: Public School Publishing Company, 1940.

*Project Early Push* (DHEW OE-37055). Washington, DC: Department of Health, Education and Welfare, 1969.

*Recommendations for a Head Start Program by Panel of Experts,* February 19, 1965. Washington, DC: Department of Health, Education and Welfare (Office of Child Development), 1972.

Reymert, M. L., & Hinton, R. T.  The effect of a change to a relatively superior environment upon the I.Q.'s of 100 children. In *Thirty-Ninth Yearbook of the National Society for the Study of Education* (Part II). Bloomington, IL: Public School Publishing Company, 1940.

Rieber, M., & Womack, M.  The intelligence of preschool children as related to ethnic and demographic variables. *Exceptional Children,* 1968, *34,* 609–614.

Ripin, R.  A comparative study of the development of infants in an institution with those in homes of low socio-economic status. *Psychological Bulletin,* 1933, *30,* 680–681.

Royster, E. C., & Larson, J. C.  *Executive summary of a national survey of Head Start graduates and their peers.* Cambridge, MA: Abt Associates, Inc., 1978.

Schaefer, E. S., & Aaronson, M.  Infant education research project: Implementation and implications of a home tutoring program. In R. K. Parker (Ed.), *The preschool in action: Exploring early childhood programs.* Boston, MA: Allyn and Bacon, Inc., 1972.

Schmidt, B. G.  Changes in personal, social, and intellectual behavior of children originally classified as feebleminded. *Psychological Monographs,* 1946, *60,* 1–144.

Scruggs, A. W.  The effect of the Fall River and Lowell Head Start programs on behavioral characteristics associated with lower socio-economic class preschool children. *Dissertation Abstracts International,* 1971, *32,* 1949A.

Sigel, I. E., & McBane, B.  Cognitive competence and level of symbolization among five-year-old children. In J. Hellmuth (Ed.), *Disadvantaged Child* (Vol. 1). New York: Brunner/Mazel, 1967.

Skeels, H. M., & Dye, H. B.  A study of the effect of differential stimulation on mentally retarded children. Cited in H. M. Skeels, Some Iowa studies of the mental growth of children in relation to differentials of the environment: A summary. In *Thirty-Ninth Yearbook of the National Society for the Study of Education* (Part II). Bloomington, IL: Public School Publishing Company, 1940.

Skeels, H. M., Updegraff, R., Wellman, B. L., & Williams, H. M.  A study of environmental stimulation: An orphanage preschool project. Cited in B. L. Wellman, Iowa studies on the effects of schooling. In *Thirty-Ninth Yearbook of the National Society for the Study of Education* (Part II). Bloomington, IL: Public School Publishing Company, 1940.

Skodak, M.  Children in foster homes: A study of mental development. Cited in H. M. Skeels, Some Iowa studies of mental growth of children in relation to differentials of the environment: A summary. In *Thirty-Ninth Yearbook of the National Society for the Study of Education* (Part II). Bloomington, IL: Public School Publishing Company, 1940.

Smilansky, S. Progress report on a program to demonstrate ways of using a year of kindergarten to promote cognitive abilities, impart basic information and modify attitudes which are essential for scholastic success of culturally deprived children in their first two years of school. Cited in B. S. Bloom, A. Davis, & R. Hess (Eds.), *Compensatory education for cultural deprivation.* New York: Holt, Rinehart & Winston, 1965.

*Special Analyses, Budget of the United States.* Washington, DC: U.S. Government Printing Office, 1970.

Sprigle, H. Learning to learn program. Cited in U. Bronfenbrenner, *A report on longitudinal evaluations of preschool programs. Is early intervention effective?* (Vol. 2) (DHEW Publication No. (OHD) 76-30025). Washington, DC: Office of Child Development, 1974.

Starkweather, E. K., & Roberts, K. E. I.Q. changes occurring during nursery school attendance at the Merrill-Palmer School. In *Thirty-Ninth Yearbook of the National Society for the Study of Education* (Part II). Bloomington, IL: Public School Publishing Company, 1940.

Steig, D. R., D'Annunzio, A., & Speilman, K. Early intervention through technology. Washington, DC: Office of Child Development. (ERIC Clearing House on Early Childhood Education, Research Relating to Children, Sept. 1976–Feb. 1977, Bulletin 38)

*Thirty-Ninth Yearbook of the National Society for the Study of Education* (Parts I–II). Bloomington, IL: Public School Publishing Company, 1940.

Thorndike, R. L., Flemming, C. W., Hildreth, G., & Stanger, M. Retest changes in the I.Q. in certain superior schools. In *Thirty-Ninth Yearbook of the National Society for the Study of Education* (Part II). Bloomington, IL: Public School Publishing Company, 1940.

Voas, W. H. Does attendance at the Winnetka nursery school tend to raise I.Q.? In *Thirty-Ninth Yearbook of the National Society for the Study of Education* (Part II). Bloomington, IL: Public School Publishing Company, 1940.

Waller, D., & Connors, K. C. A follow-up study of intelligence changes in children who participated in Project Head Start. Cited in *Review of research, 1965 to 1969 of Project Head Start* (OEO Pamphlet 6108-13). Washington, DC: Office of Economic Opportunity, June 1969.

Weikart, D. P. Preschool intervention: A preliminary report of the Perry Preschool Project. Cited in J. L. Frost, & G. T. Rowland, *Compensatory programming: The acid test of American education.* Dubuque, IA: W. C. Brown Company Publishers, 1971.

Wellman, B. L. Iowa studies on the effects of schooling. In *Thirty-Ninth Yearbook of the National Society for the Study of Education* (Part II). Bloomington, IL: Public School Publishing Company, 1940.

White, S. H. The national impact study of Head Start. In J. Hellmuth (Ed.), *Disadvantaged Child. Compensatory education: A national debate* (Vol. 3). New York: Brunner/Mazel, 1970.

Wilkinson, J. E., & Murphy, H. F. Differential methods of enhancing cognitive growth in urban preschool children. *Child Care, Health and Development,* 1976, *2,* 1–11.

Woolley, H. T. The validity of standards of mental measurement in young childhood. *School and Society,* 1925, *21,* 476–482.

Zigler, E. F. *A study of culturally deprived children in kindergarten and grade one following a nine-month nursery experience: Final report.* Washington, DC: Office of Economic Opportunity, December 1967.

# 3

# Preventing Developmental Retardation: A General Systems Model*

CRAIG T. RAMEY, DAVID MACPHEE, AND KEITH OWEN YEATES
*Frank Porter Graham Child Development Center*
*University of North Carolina at Chapel Hill*

*". . . Seek simplicity and distrust it"*
Alfred North Whitehead
*The Concept of Nature*

This chapter contains a General Systems Model for developmental retardation that is the result of an eight-year, ongoing, longitudinal project aimed at preventing mild mental retardation. The proposed model is discussed and used as a heuristic device for summarizing our empirical findings related to intellectual and adaptive functioning. Key findings include: (1) evidence for primary prevention as a result of early educational intervention; (2) evidence for alteration of social characteristics of treated children; and (3) evidence for educational and employment benefits to parents of treated children. The chapter concludes with recommendations for future research.

## INTRODUCTION

Developmental retardation can be defined in terms of deficits in intellectual functioning and adaptive behavior that occur in the course of ontogeny. The developmental retardation of concern in this chapter is not caused primarily by genetic defects, teratogens, or injury, although they may be present to some degree in developmentally retarded children. Our concept of developmental retardation shares much in common with the American Association of Mental Deficiency's (Grossman, 1973) definition of psychosocial retardation, but differs in several important aspects. According to the definition adopted by the American Association of Mental Deficiency, a person is considered retarded if (1) his or her IQ score is below 70, (2) other positive indicators exist such as the presence of other retarded

---

*This research was supported, in part, by grants from the National Institute of Child Health and Human Development and the Bureau of Education for the Handicapped, Office of Education. We are indebted to Ms. Marie Butts, Ms. Pam McPherson, Ms. Nancy Daniels, and Mr. John Bernard for editorial assistance in preparing the manuscript. This chapter is reprinted with permission from J. Joffee & L. Byrd (Eds.), *Facilitating infant and early childhood development*. Hanover, NH. University Press of New England, in press.

67

family members, and (3) the individual in question has a history of maladaptive behavior in ecologically valid situations (c.f. Brooks & Baumeister, 1977). We take issue with the AAMD's definition of psychosocial retardation on two scientific points. First, an IQ of 70 as the criterion for retardation is arbitrary. Although such cutoff points must be established as administrative guidelines for therapeutic or custodial planning, they do not represent the kinds of positive diagnostic signs that should define a discrete syndrome, and, further, they imply more precision than the score warrants. Second, insisting on the presence of other retarded individuals in the family presupposes a constellation of characteristics which should be empirically determined, rather than established by a priori definition.

Our working criterion for developmental retardation is, therefore, somewhat different from that in the AAMD classification manual. We define developmental retardation as any significant impairment in ecologically valid assessments of cognitive and adaptive functioning which is known to be preventable. We think this definition is preferable for scientific purposes because (1) it avoids presently arbitrary cutoff points, (2) it focuses research attention on alterable processes governing development, (3) it does not establish by fiat what is essentially an empirical issue, and (4) it permits cultural relativism in diagnosis. However, because this proposed working definition is akin to the classification scheme currently used for placement decisions, a brief discussion of the epidemiology of psychosocial retardation is necessary to establish further the historical context of this chapter.

### Psychosocial Retardation and the Concept of Risk

Baroff (1974) reviewed the scientific literature on the epidemiology of mental retardation and concluded that approximately 89% of all retardation can be considered as mild. Although the exact percentage of mildly retarded persons in the total mentally retarded population may be debated, it seems safe to assume that the mildly retarded outnumber all other mentally retarded persons combined. Furthermore, Stein and Susser (1963) have estimated that 75% of all retarded persons have no clear-cut physiological pathology, and it seems likely that even more than 75% of the mildly retarded are free of major biological dysfunction. Thus, the largest segment of individuals classified as mentally retarded may be considered mildly impaired and without organic involvement.

If biological dysfunction is not the obvious cause of mild developmental retardation (as it almost invariably is for more severe forms), then perhaps the social ecology of the mildly retarded will provide clues to causal pathways by indicating which segments of society are most *at-risk* for the condition. By *risk,* we mean a substantiated, empirical relationship such that individuals who possess particular attributes have a greater likelihood of being classified as developmentally retarded than persons who do not possess those attributes. Risk is therefore an actuarial concept pertaining to groups with identifiable characteristics, and is probabilistic in nature.

Currently, there is general agreement that social class membership predicts psychosocial retardation. The report of a correlation between social class status and IQ, however, does not address many important issues. The most important are the accuracy of prediction for purposes of individual identification and the specification of the psychological mechanisms involved in incidence. Even though mild retardation is strongly associated with lower social class status, not all or even most lower-class individuals can be classified as mentally retarded. Begab (Note 1) has estimated that only about 10% of the poor in the United States would be considered as mentally retarded. Thus, to improve the identification process within the most at-risk population, further specification is necessary to identify which subsets of parents are more likely to give birth to a biologically intact child who at some point is classified as developmentally retarded for psychosocial reasons. One strategy to accomplish this end is to look for correlations between measures of intellectual and social adaptation *within* the lower social classes. Given that psychologists, sociologists, and educators have reported correlations between social class and many other attributes, surprisingly little is known about the correlates of IQ and other measures of social adaptation within a given social class and particularly within the lower classes.

Variables that have been related to developmental retardation (presumably of a psychosocial nature) within the lower class include: maternal IQ (Heber, Dever, & Conry, 1968; Ramey, Farran, & Campbell, 1979); family disorganization; a room ratio of two or more persons; and five or more children (Birch, Richardson, Baird, Horobin, & Illsley, 1970). Thus, at least some clues can be used to guide more refined and extensive epidemiological studies.

We know from our own early intervention work in North Carolina (e.g., Ramey & Campbell, 1979a), as well as from the research of others (e.g., Bayley, 1965; Knoblock & Pasamanick, 1953) that it is during the second year of life that social class differences become evident in cognitive functioning. Prior to 12 months of age, measurable cognitive deficits have not been reliably detected. Whether or not the failure to identify significant differences before 12 months is a function of the insensitivity of our measuring instruments is, at present, not established. Nevertheless, if early intervention is to prevent developmental retardation, then the earlier that identification can occur the better. The main task is to develop risk indicators for the prenatal or early infancy period if psychosocial retardation is to be prevented rather than remediated.

One approach to early prediction has been direct assessments of the child. However, measures of the child's performance during early infancy have not been highly predictive of the child's subsequent intellectual status. Further, high-risk indices such as the one reported by Ramey and Smith (1977) require costly interviews and family assessments, and may be limited to use in research and in predicting group rather than individual status.

Another approach to prediction has focused on assessments of the child's early environment. These measures have yielded more encouraging screening results.

Work by Elardo, Bradley, and Caldwell (1975) using the Home Observation for
the Measurement of the Environment (HOME) has indicated significant prediction of both later IQ and school achievement from assessments of the home made
during infancy. More recently, Frankenburg and his colleagues (e.g., Note 2)
have developed a brief questionnaire based on the HOME that parents can complete by themselves in settings such as waiting rooms at physicians' offices or at
social service agencies. Frankenburg's measures are highly correlated with
Caldwell's HOME scores and also predict subsequent child status. This questionnaire approach appears to be a very promising lead for screening home environments. Assessing children's home environments, however, requires that the children to be screened have contact with the agency doing the screening. Many of the
children most likely to yield positive screening results will go unseen by relevant
agencies because their families do not seek or receive services for their young children (Birch & Gussow, 1970). In order to cast the net more widely, a first-line
screening device that includes information on all children in a given geographical
area is necessary. Following the identification of high-risk children, subsequent
multiphasic screening and assessment of a more refined nature may assist families
and professionals in providing services to needy children on a more cost-effective
basis.

Recently, we have been exploring the efficacy of information available from
standard birth certificates as a possible first-line screening mechanism (Ramey,
Stedman, Borders-Patterson, & Mengel, 1978). In a retrospective study of 1,000
randomly sampled first-grade children, we found that the top six variables which
discriminated between children who were successfully achieving in school and
children who were failing were (in order of importance): (1) race, (2) having an
older sibling who had died, (3) educational level of the mother, (4) birth order, (5)
legitimacy, and (6) the month that prenatal care began. At this point, we regard
these characteristics as marker variables rather than as causal ones in the processes
of development. As marker variables, they help identify populations with elevated
risk levels, but do not necessarily indicate which psychological mechanisms require intervention.

We are now attempting to refine our first-line screening precision by
generating separate prediction equations for different racial and educational
groups (Finkelstein & Ramey, 1980; Ramey & Finkelstein, 1981). The goal of
this research is to make our prediction equations more precise and, ultimately, to
increase our initial ability to detect high-risk infants at a more reasonable cost. A
preliminary finding from our current efforts is particularly intriguing. Discrimi-
nant function equations for blacks and whites reveal different factors to be important for predicting intellectual status and/or school achievement within the two racial groups, even though the two equations are about equally discriminative for
school success or failure. For the black children in the group (N=290), the three
most important factors, in order of importance, were education of the mother,

birth order, and the month that prenatal care began. For the white children (N=631), the three most important factors were whether there were previous live births who had subsequently died, education of the mother, and maternal age. Thus, there was overlap between the two samples on only 1 of the 3 most important discriminators between school success and school failure. This would suggest that the same risk factors may enter prediction equations differently for different populations. In sum, the need for early intervention is not necessarily predicted by the same variables in different subgroups in the population.

### Form and Focus of Prevention Programs

After finding high-risk children, the next step is to have a progam to offer them. On an elementary level, the type of program that professionals offer depends on what they believe needs changing. Yet, the range of potential etiological agents of psychosocial retardation is very large (Ramey & Gallagher, 1975), and little consensus exists as to the relative importance of specific agents (Begab, 1981). Consequently, a wide range of intervention efforts have taken place. While relatively few are aimed towards mental retardation per se and even fewer are targeted specifically at prevention, the programs present a range of stances on what the best type of intervention might be; that is, what form and focus intervention efforts should take.

Intervention efforts have ranged in breadth from attempting to influence a large set of developmental domains, such as the Head Start programs (Zigler & Valentine, 1979), to programs designed primarily for one developmental process, such as the reading skills program of Wallach and Wallach (1976). Projects also have ranged in intensity from minimal to nearly full-time contact, and in scope from short-term to decade-long efforts. For example, the Ypsilanti Perry Preschool Project (Schweinhart & Weikart, Note 3) enrolled 3 to 4 year olds who spend 2½ hours per day during the school year in the program, while the Milwaukee Project (Garber & Heber, 1977) enrolled infants who spent 8 hours a day, 52 weeks a year in the program. Nevertheless, little evidence exists for the relative effectiveness of any one program or group of programs over any other (Mann, Harrell, & Hunt, 1976). The only major finding is that more structured programs seem to achieve greater gains—at least in cognitive growth—than do more play-oriented programs (Bronfenbrenner, 1975). Furthermore, while some evaluation studies find greater gains in IQ scores in more intense and lasting programs (see Stedman, Anastasiow, Dokecki, Gordon & Parker, Note 4), we do not know whether it is the *intensity* or *length* of prevention efforts that are important in producing lasting change. A definitive answer to these important issues awaits closer and continuing scientific scrutiny. We have little data, at present, to indicate that any particular intervention program is singularly more effective than others.

**Effectiveness of Prevention**

In many ways, the cost-effectiveness and manner in which intervention is implemented depend on continuing scientific inquiry into the relative efficacy of various preventive strategies. Applied scientists must be concerned with public accountability. The proof of effectiveness appears, at first glance, to be deceptively simple: decide what needs changing; implement a program; and then measure to see if the program changed the target variable(s). Unfortunately, this simplistic conception masks great complexity. First, most interventions are designed to produce changes in more than one developmental domain. Second, scientists must allow for possible unintended consequences, both positive and negative. Third, there is little consensus concerning the most effective tools for measuring development. Finally, investigators must follow their subjects longitudinally in order to determine if their program produces lasting, meaningful gains. Thus, difficulties in deciding what to measure and how to measure it, plus the need for follow-up, make proving effectiveness an arduous task.

The initial obstacle is deciding what to measure. Even this decision is problematic. In general, intervention efforts have the broad goal of improving development or preventing a decline in functioning. The word "development," though, encompasses an extensive range of possibilities such that selecting the most appropriate variables for study is quite difficult. Most studies have focused on cognitive growth, as measured by IQ tests, while other programs have preferred to use achievement tests to measure success in school. Cognitive growth and school success, though, are only two benchmarks of successful adaptation and they by no means epitomize "development." In another domain, namely adaptive behavior, one is faced with the difficulty of defining what is adaptive. While some programs have focused on school behavior, scant attention has been paid to behavior in the home or neighborhood. What is adaptive for a child in a school setting may well be maladaptive in the home or neighborhood. Measures of social adjustment have the same difficulty. Finally, little if any attention has been paid to the domains of personal adjustment, motivation, or mental health (Begab, 1981). The potential areas of change, intended or not, are numerous and some have been barely explored. Scientists must press for measurement of more than cognitive growth and move to a more balanced assessment of developmental domains.

Better assessment, however, is limited by the adequacy of the measurement tools. Unfortunately, techniques for assessment are often imprecise, invalid, or even nonexistent. In the realm of cognitive development, the IQ test has been the method of choice. Although IQ scores have been bemoaned for their unreliability, their invalidity for minority children, their lack of predictive validity, and their lack of information, among other things (Stedman et al., Note 4), they remain the psychologist's best all-around assessment instrument for general intellectual development. Substitutes have been suggested, such as measures developed from a Piagetian framework (e.g., Elkind, 1969). However, these measures have also been criticized because of their limitations in predicting success in school (Wallach & Wallach, 1976). Thus, measures of cognitive development, which are perhaps the most widely developed and used, are not fully adequate. Measures of school success, though, have not fared much better. Achievement tests often contain as many items requiring reasoning ability as they do items requiring the skill supposedly being measured (Stedman et al., Note 4). Instruments in other domains are even less adequate and too frequently are nonexistent. Attempts at measuring adaptive behavior are scarce (see Schaefer, 1981) and tools for measuring motivation or personal adjustment are practically nil. At present, the best policy may be to measure the domains of interest using the best techniques available and, if possible, to employ multiple measures of any given construct. The need for psychometrically-sound and ecologically-valid instruments for measuring development is among the most pressing today and, unfortunately, one of the most neglected.

Nevertheless, scientists need to press ahead with research, even with the problems of deciding what to measure and how to measure it. A problem that goes beyond measurement though, and that is essential to the issue of effectiveness, is the need for continuous longitudinal study. Adequate follow-up of children who have been in preventive efforts is the only effective way to investigate potentially lasting benefits (e.g., Gallagher, Ramey, Haskins, & Finkelstein, 1976). The importance of follow-up is underscored by the findings that many of the initial benefits of intervention disappear after children leave the programs (Bronfenbrenner, 1975). Furthermore, the possibility of "sleeper effects" (Kagan & Moss, 1962)—effects that become obvious only after intervention ends—requires long-term follow-up, even into adolescence and adulthood. But longitudinal study is not without hazards. Repeated measurements have long been recognized as producing, for example, regression artifacts and practice effects. In addition, the measurement of change is difficult and sometimes misleading (Cronbach & Furby, 1970). Finally, subject as well as experimenter attrition makes it difficult to maintain experimental validity or even to complete many investigations. Thus, just conducting longitudinal research is fraught with problems.

The lucky investigator is one who thinks he knows what should be measured, has several reliable and valid ways to do so, and can guarantee that his subjects will remain accessible. Unfortunately, such a bird is rare indeed. The fact is that effectiveness is difficult to prove or disprove and professionals concerned with accountability are faced with a host of obstacles. The press for increased and long-term measurement necessitates the development of more satisfactory instruments and more sophistication with valid measures of change.

## A GENERAL SYSTEMS MODEL

Although technical limitations have hampered the development of preventive programs, our limited models for general developmental processes have been an even greater hindrance. During the decade when intervention was seen as a vehicle for social change, the prevalent attitude was that children of poverty lived in an inadequate environment and that the early environment was the critical factor in later intellectual growth. These assumptions about the nature of development translated into prevention strategies that emphasized instruction in cognitive skills, with the aim of "innoculating" the child against further privation. Sameroff (1979) has noted that a medical model such as this assumes a unitary relationship between environmental deprivation (the "pathogen") and school failure (the "disease").

As a number of reports have shown (e.g., Zigler & Valentine, 1979), the intentions of earlier social policies were laudable, but rested on tenuous assumptions about the processes of development. For example, hereditarian proponents (e.g., Jensen, 1969; 1981) have attributed differences between developmentally retarded, socially disadvantaged children and middle-class children to the global wellspring of genetics without postulating either specific genetic mechanisms, or adequately acknowledging genotype-environment interactions, which are the hallmark of modern behavioral genetics (e.g., Schneirla, 1966; Gottlieb, 1976) and particularly the genetics of development (e.g., McClearn & DeFries, 1973). Environmentalists have been equally vague in identifying causal models, frequently emphasizing only one developmental domain such as language (e.g., Bernstein, 1970), mother-child interactions (e.g., Hess & Shipman, 1965), or anomie (e.g, Ogbu, 1978) as the major agent.

The skepticism about simple models of development culminated in several seminal review papers, including those by Clarke and Clarke (1976) and Sameroff (1975). Both monographs argued: (1) that development involves the action of complex regulatory processes (environmental *and* constitutional), and (2) that later outcomes have multiple causes, such that there are few isomorphic continuities in development. Additional challenges to traditional assumptions also forced researchers to consider more complex models of development. Some of the trends that have crept into current theorizing include bidirectionality of infant-caregiver effects (Bell, 1968, 1971; Harper, 1971), Bronfenbrenner's (1977) ecology of human development, and a concern for competence-related outcome measures, rather than a single criterion such as an IQ score (McClelland, 1973; Zigler & Trickett, 1978). In brief, researchers came to appreciate the complex nature of development.

The crowning blow to the Main Effects and Interactional Models of development was Sameroff's (1975) Transactional Model. In this model, Sameroff argued that the child modifies the environment at the same time the surround is acting on the child.[1] Constitutional factors are partially responsible for individual differ-

---

[1]While we recognize that Sameroff misconstrued the Interactional Model and failed to deal with some issues in the Transactional Model, it is noteworthy that his papers (Sameroff, 1975; Sameroff & Chandler, 1975) influenced the field to think in terms of multiple rather than linear causation. From a statistical or experimental design point of view, Sameroff's discussion of the Main Effects, Interactional and Transactional Models clearly is flawed. In terms of the zeitgeist, however, the Transactional Model represented a break from the past in that more complex models were seen as necessary for a complete understanding of developmental phenomena.

ences in behavior (e.g., temperamental variables such as reactivity or sociability) and for the ability to compensate following insult (see Parmelee & Michaelis, 1971; and Sameroff, 1979 for a discussion of self-righting tendencies). Environmental variables affect, among other things, the biological integrity of the organism, morphological characteristics, and what is learned. When the two—the continuum of reproductive casualty and the continuum of caretaking casualty—are interwoven in development, intellectual deficits may be amplified or reduced.

In some respects, the Transactional Model is incomplete since the intervening variables are left unspecified. For instance, the "continuum of caretaking casualty", translated into psychological variables, would go beyond social class and parental education to include patterns of dyadic interaction, modes of communication and teaching strategies. In this way, the notion of a "supportive environment" (c.f. Yarrow, Rubenstein, & Pedersen, 1973) is defined in terms of specific behaviors that can be examined for their contribution to later competencies or deficits. Ultimately, the task is to construct a model of development that (1) specifies the variables and processes constituting a supportive environment and that (2) defines the desired product of our endeavors, be it adaptation to the environment (Parmelee, Kopp & Sigman, 1976) or social competence (Zigler & Trickett, 1978). In the next section, we will discuss a variation on General Systems Theory (Bertalanffy, 1975; Miller, 1978) that attempts to do justice to the demands of this task.

### The General Systems Model

At this point, we need to introduce some of the concepts of General Systems Theory that are the core of our approach. They are as follows:

— *The emergent principle.* The developing child can be viewed as one product of a system of units that interact. According to Miller (1978), "the state of each unit is constrained by, conditioned by, or dependent upon the state of other units. The units are coupled" (p. 16). The behavior of a system *emerges* out of the interaction of the components such that there are multiple causes rather than unitary causes.

— *Levels of analysis.* Living systems have different levels of complexity and functioning, as Bronfenbrenner (1977) has pointed out. Further, complex interactions can occur *within* each level as well as *across* levels such that, for example, societal processes can influence functioning at the level of the family. Other implications might include: assessment of risk status must consider the level at which the variables operate; and intervention may have consequences across levels.

— *Range of stability.* Each variable within a system has a range of stability (Miller, 1978) that is maintained in equilibrium by transactions with the environment and the system. Any variable that forces the system beyond its range of stability is called a stress, producing strain in the system. Accord-

ing to Miller, living systems have a limited repertoire of strategies to deal
with stress, including (1) altering the system by learning new skills, (2) altering the environment, (3) withdrawing to a more favorable environment,
or (4) changing what the organism defines as stable. A corollary of the notion of equilibrium is much like Werner's (1957) orthogenetic principle:

> "a living organism maintains itself in a state of highest organization
> (and) during differentiation an organism passes from states of lower to
> higher heterogeneity" (Bertalanffy, 1975, p. 46).

When combined with self-regulatory strategies, one is then able to identify
the "competent" individual in terms of adaptive functioning and level of
organization.

— *Regulatory mechanisms.*   In the human, cybernetic processes operate to
regulate behavior. In terms of development, this means that there is constant feedback and regulation such that the child continuously adapts to the
environment. However, in cases where self-regulatory mechanisms are
unable to cope with strain on the system, disorder or maladaptive behavior
may result as in child abuse (Belsky, 1980), schizophrenia (Meehl, 1962),
or retarded growth (Tanner, 1963), unless outside resources are called
upon.

— *The active organism.*   This principle suggests that development is characterized by plasticity, since adaptation occurs in the presence of changing
demands. Furthermore, the child is seen as an active (rather than reactive)
agent, eliciting responses from the environment at the same time he or she
is adapting to its demands.

In general, Systems Theory is not a true theory as it is traditionally defined by the
ability to explain and predict. Rather, it is a perspective or paradigm (Kuhn, 1962)
in which the many components of the system interact to produce strong, *synergistic* effects. The usefulness of this approach rests in our ability to see new relationships between variables, and in the flexibility to wed different theories about component processes to each other, so as to explain behavior.

### Ontogenetic Processes

Ontogeny usually is taken to mean changes that occur over the life span of an
individual organism. In the General Systems Model, though, ontogeny can occur
at all levels of analysis (see Figure 1). Therefore, one can speak of change in the
family (as measured by marriage, child bearing, and family crises, to mention a
few), the development of neighborhoods (from the moving of neighbors to urban
decay), and the rise and fall of societies and civilizations. Implicit in this more
general use of ontogeny is the notion that the historians of different levels will be
affiliated with disciplines as diverse as developmental psychology, sociology, and
anthropology.

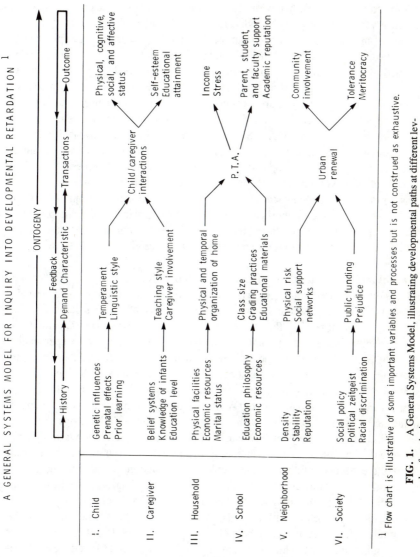

A GENERAL SYSTEMS MODEL FOR INQUIRY INTO DEVELOPMENTAL RETARDATION [1]

ONTOGENY

History → Demand Characteristic → Transactions → Outcome

Feedback

LEVELS OF ANALYSIS AND POTENTIAL LEVELS OF INTERVENTION

I. Child
Genetic influences
Prenatal effects
Prior learning
→ Temperament
Linguistic style
→ Child/caregiver interactions → Physical, cognitive, social, and affective status

II. Caregiver
Belief systems
Knowledge of infants
Education level
→ Teaching style
Caregiver involvement
→ Self-esteem
Educational attainment

III. Household
Physical facilities
Economic resources
Marital status
→ Physical and temporal organization of home
→ Income
Stress

IV. School
Education philosophy
Economic resources
→ Class size
Grading practices
Educational materials
→ P.T.A. → Parent, student, and faculty support
Academic reputation

V. Neighborhood
Density
Stability
Reputation
→ Physical risk
Social support networks
→ Urban renewal → Community involvement

VI. Society
Social policy
Political zeitgeist
Racial discrimination
→ Public funding
Prejudice
→ Tolerance
Meritocracy

[1] Flow chart is illustrative of some important variables and processes but is not construed as exhaustive.

**FIG. 1.** A General Systems Model, illustrating developmental paths at different levels of analysis.

Several terms in the General Systems Model need further clarification. By the *history* of the component, we mean the effects of previous transactions that are not manifested as observable behavior. This may be thought of as the probability of an action, given the history of the individual. History at the different levels can be thought of in terms of genotypes, teratogenic effects and learning (the child); general knowledge of child development, and attitudes and beliefs that have been inculcated by society and upbringing (the caregiver); the social status of the family; the reputation of a neighborhood; and the social policy and values advocated by a society. Historical variables are assumed to mediate or influence behavior, but they cannot be observed directly. Thus, a central issue in studying behavior is to determine how "history" (e.g., SES) is related to action (e.g., teaching strategies; language; the organization of the inanimate environment). In the domain of psychopathology, a process approach would inquire how it is that these etiological factors act on development, via their expression as concrete behaviors and actions, or *demand characteristics*. Research on risk factors in the infant, for example, has found that the mother's childhood health history is a significant predictor of her infant's postnatal condition; the process is presumed to involve the viability of the ovum as affected by diet and disease (Birth & Gussow, 1970).

*Transactions,* as used in the General Systems Model, imply an interactional process that is bidirectional. The most commonly used illustration would be interactions between the infant and caregiver. The behavior of each participant can be attributed to proximal (c.f. Patterson, 1974; Bakeman & Brown, 1977) and distal determinants. Distal determinants of interaction include general expectancies about the partner's behavior (the individual's history), as well as the demand characteristics of the partner. For instance, infant characteristics such as cuddliness (Schaffer & Emerson, 1964), temperament (Thomas, Birch, Chess, Hertzig & Korn, 1963), predominant state (Wolff, 1966), and physical attractiveness, including cry sounds (Zeskind, 1980), shape the caregiver's behavior to the infant. Similarly, the caregiver's demand characteristics include the warmth of the individual, the function of the interaction (play or caregiving) and the current mood of the mother or father. At another level, transactions between the neighborhood and society, through the mechanism of revenue sharing, would result in urban renewal. It is important to note that transactions can occur between *any* two or more levels as well as within levels. An exemplar of the former might be the role of television as a transaction between society and the child or family; the latter process might include the interaction of cognition and arousal to produce an affective state (Rothbart, 1973). The point is that a myriad of relationships between components are possible, leaving the attribution of cause in rather murky waters.

Finally, the endpoint of this stream of cause and effect would include a number of *outcome* variables that also must be measured in an ecologically valid manner. Here, the emphasis is on instruments that are appropriate to the questions being asked. In the case of developmental retardation, we would want to know about the competence of the child in a number of settings, about the ability of the child to adapt to the environment, and at another level about how supportive the environment is. These global, ill-defined terms must be translated into valid assessment instruments, in order to do justice to the complexity of development. In retrospect, it is apparent that developmental pathology can be caused by any number of factors, both within the organism (e.g., temperamental variables; limited self-righting strategies), within the dyad, and at the level of societal norms, as well as others. When these intra-, inter-, and supracomponent processes are combined, the inadequacy of simplistic models becomes all too evident.

Our conceptual model for developmental retardation contains two major process components that illustrate the interplay of ontogenetic history and transactions with the environment. These components concern the functioning of subgroups within the society (*sociocultural difference component*) and the child's contingency history (*reinforcement-motivational component*). In the past, each has been perceived as a competing explanation for developmental retardation. The General Systems Model, however, views them as complementary processes that act at somewhat different levels of analysis.

### Sociocultural Difference Component

A growing body of epidemiological literature suggests that individuals from the lower socioeconomic strata are most at risk for retarded intellectual and adaptive behavior (Ramey & Finkelstein, 1981). Poor individuals with minority group status are particularly likely to develop educational handicaps during the public school years (Ramey et al., 1978; Richardson, 1975; Mercer, 1977). We now think that the sociocultural component operates through three primary mechanisms. First, disadvantaged sociocultural subgroups may learn complex modes of intellectual and social adaptation, but learn ones *not valued* by the larger culture. Linguistic style is a good example. Baratz and Baratz (1970), for instance, argued that lower-class black dialect was equally complex as standard English, and that it was different from standard English but not inherently deficient. Second, sociocultural subgroups may learn modes of functioning *specifically disapproved* by the larger society. For instance, aggressive or assertive interactions —particularly in the school system—may be construed as disrespectful and problematic behaviors, even when there is no apparent damage. Third, the larger society may form stereotypes of sociocultural subgroups actively or unwittingly, but *systematically discriminate* with respect to intellectual and adaptive opportunities to the point of creating a self-fulfilling prophecy. A recent study by Haskins, Walden, and Ramey (Note 5) concerning ability-grouping in kindergarten and first grade illustrates this point. In assigning children to high- or low-ability groups within their classrooms, teachers reported using their own informal observations of the child's ability and teacher-made tests. None of the other factors assessed, including standardized tests, teacher recommendations, the child's interest in school work, or information about the child's home or background, were reported as influential in teachers' placement of children in ability groups. To the extent that the teacher is biased in attitudes or incorrect in assessments of children's abilities, though, the child's performance will be affected. In summarizing the results of the ability grouping study, Haskins et al. noted that:

> These teachers' beliefs about differences between students in the two (high and low) groups were clearly reflected in their instructional techniques. Thus, teachers more often kept low-group students together while sitting with them. They also used more control statements, more disciplinary statements and more positive reinforcement with low-ability groups. Finally, teachers not only engaged in more total blocks (of time) for instruction with low-ability students, they also gave them relatively more drill and less new subject matter (p. 20).

To the extent that personal bias may operate in assignment to ability groups, the structure of those groups seems likely to nuture their disadvantage through reduced exposure to new material and a social stigma that fosters a lower self-concept. This point leads us into the second major process component of our model that is important throughout the development period, especially during infancy.

### Reinforcement-Motivational Component

It is our contention that high-risk children are reared in an environment with inadequate or inappropriate contingencies (Wachs, Uzgiris, & Hunt, 1971). In turn, this has been implicated as a cause of lowered effectance motivation and reduced success in mastery situations. Further, the deficient contingency history is asserted during infancy and can be observed during the second year of life. Support for this thesis accrues from two converging lines of our research. The first aspect is a set of laboratory contingency experiments that are analogs of some components of adult-child interactions. The second line is a set of direct observations of mother-infant dyads from high-risk and general population backgrounds.

*Experimental Evidence.* Finkelstein and Ramey (1977) and Ramey and Finkelstein (1978) have reported a series of four experiments suggesting that increased amounts of response-contingent stimulation during the first year of infancy enhances subsequent learning performance when treated infants are compared to yoked controls. Ramey and Finkelstein (1978) presented a two-component model for the processes thought to underlie the strength of transfer. The components are contextual similarity between the treatment and transfer environments, and the extent to which there has been the development of an attentional strategy linking one's own responses to available external stimulation. These findings are consistent with earlier reports by Watson and Ramey (1972) and with Lewis and Goldberg's (1969) idea of a generalized expectancy for effectiveness that derives from the responsiveness of the mother to her infant's behavior.

*Observational Evidence.* For over a decade, researchers have speculated that maternal responsiveness to infants' operant behaviors (such as smiling and vocalizing) is a major determinant of the infant's subsequent cognitive and social development. Such a proposition, however, is not contradictory to Bell's (1968; 1971) notion that the infant is a determinant of parental behaviors as well. Two major types of information are relevant to caregiver-infant interactions and developmental retardation. The first type of evidence concerns the interactional differences between low-risk dyads (typically middle-class) and high-risk dyads (e.g., from poverty environments). Lewis and Wilson (1972), Ramey and Mills (Note 6), Tulkin and Kagan (1972), and others have reported social class differences in mother-child interaction during infancy (c.f. a review by Ramey, Farran, Campbell, & Finkelstein, 1978). However, it has always been unclear from comparative social class research whether the observed behavioral differences were causally related to cognitive growth, or whether they were merely correlates of social class status, of little importance to subsequent development. Therefore, a different argument is becoming increasingly influential in implicating caregiver-child interactions as causally important. This second type of evidence concerns variations in parenting style within high-risk (typically lower-class) dyads. Clarke-Stewart, VanderStoep, and Killian (1979) and Ramey, Farran, and Campbell (1979) have reported positive correlations of substantial magnitude between stimulating, interactive, and responsive behaviors, and children's cognitive development during the first three years of life within disadvantaged samples. Thus, the dimension of responsivity, viewed from a reinforcement-motivational perspective, has increased plausibility.

## Implications of the Model

There are several major implications of our model, both for normal development and for the prevention of pathology. In general, the over-riding conclusion must be that a complex process like development demands a multivariate, multilevel, interdisciplinary approach. It is worth repeating that the first principle of Systems Theory is that behavior is a product of the entire system. Components studied in isolation may yield some information about processes, but behavior cannot be explained by the action of isolated parts. For instance, some individuals assert that environmental deprivation is primarily one of an impoverished physical surround, while others counter that the social world of maternal language and teaching strategies are responsible for later deficits. From a systems perspective, though, the primary mission is to discover how these variables act in concert to produce a given outcome. A supportive social environment coupled with impoverished physical circumstances may lead a child down a different path than a child reared in a physically adequate home environment by an abusive or neglecting parent.

This brings us to a second implication of the General Systems Model: different environments may lead to qualitative or quantitative differences in outcome.

Stated differently, there may be different *paths* to the same outcome or the same process may occur but at different *levels*. In findings to be reported later in this chapter, we have found that both alternatives may occur when one group of at-risk infants is placed in an experimental daycare program and another serves as an educationally untreated control group.

A major hurdle in preventing developmental retardation is the translation of abstract and general models, such as ours, into an effective intervention strategy. Two implications of the General Systems Model speak to the design of intervention programs. The first is a corollary of the level of analysis principle: in order to prevent later pathology, we must identify components of the system where intervention *can* occur. For instance, proposed remedies for breaking the "cycle of poverty" have included preschool programs (the level of the child); a guaranteed annual income (the level of the family); urban renewal and job programs (the neighborhood); and civil rights laws that foster the establishment of a true meritocracy (the society).

The crucial question, though—and the second implication of the model—is where intervention *should* be focused. Ideally, one would want a prevention strategy that produces powerful, permanent effects with a minimum of money and effort. Invoking a cost-effectiveness criterion, we may find that some loci in the system produce greater effects than others. Furthermore, we can infer from the emergent principle that intervention at several points may produce synergistic effects (i.e., more dramatic changes than prevention aimed at isolated components). For example, Bronfenbrenner (1975) reviewed the effects of early intervention programs and concluded, among other things, that: (1) center-based programs with cognitive curricula produced greater gains than play-oriented programs, (2) parent intervention yielded benefits that extended to younger siblings, and to the attitudes and feelings of the parents, and (3) families who are under the most economic and psychological stress are the ones least likely to become involved in an intervention program.

What this suggests is that a *combination* of approaches may be the most effective. These might include quality daycare, family education, and social services that move the family into a broader social support network. The goal of prevention should be to provide a supportive environment for the child, a rearing atmosphere where the needs of the child are attended to with a maximum of flexibility and resources on the part of the caregivers. This plasticity in the behavior of the caregiver is constrained by time, economics, education and societal norms (Sameroff, 1979) so that prevention components geared to support the family may indirectly benefit the child. A major task for the future is to identify those components of a "supportive environment" that are most amenable to effective intervention.

At the core of Systems Theory is the idea of interactive influences; i.e. all properties of complex systems have multiple causes rather than single causes. Thus, intervention may initiate a series of *ripple effects* or unintended consequences, either positive or negative. One of the unfortunate byproducts of simplistic cause-effect theories of development was that evaluations of the Head Start program were cast solely in terms of intellectual gain scores. As the Lazar consortium (1978) was to discover, early interventions have a number of ripple effects including parent satisfaction and involvement, health-related benefits, a lower dropout rate in high school, and fewer cases of delinquency. On the other hand, intervention may have undesirable side effects. For example, the parents may abdicate responsibility for the child; aggressiveness in social interactions with peers may increase (Schwarz, Strickland, & Krolick, 1974); and the parent's philosophy or style of child rearing may clash with that of the intervention program. In brief, the General Systems Model cautions us to be aware of the consequences of tampering with one aspect of the system when we are most interested in its overall functioning.

Another implication of the General Systems Model is that plasticity and learning tend to strike a balance over time. While the infant is viewed as a dynamic individual, constantly adapting to changes in the environment, learning and hierarchical organization of behavior patterns are also taking place. This interplay of plasticity and learning has crucial significance for the timing of intervention and for the reversibility of its effects. Clarke and Clarke (1976), in discussing this issue, liken development to a wedge where there is "a greater potential responsiveness during early life . . . tailing off to little responsiveness in adulthood" (pp. 271–272). From a systems perspective, then, early intervention (during the period of greatest plasticity) must be coupled with continuous enrollment to ensure continuity and the learning of adaptive behavior patterns not demanded at earlier periods. Early and prolonged enrichment is even more critical in those cases where the individual's self-righting tendencies (intrinsic plasticity, if you will) or ability to learn is impaired.

One final implication of the model concerns general strategies for conducting an intervention program. Recall that equal emphasis is placed on the contribution of the infant to its own development and on the characteristics of the environment. As a consequence, the most effective prevention will capitalize on the unique capabilities of any given individual (the supportive environment theme) while emphasizing transactions that are most effective in fostering later competence. Therefore, curriculum development (what is most effective for infants in general) and research on learning styles (what is most suited to a particular infant) go hand in hand to exploit individual strengths, and overcome weaknesses. While this implication may seem so obvious as to be a time-worn adage, its full realization depends on a comprehensive knowledge of child development, a flexible and individually-tailored curriculum, an intimate acquaintance with each child's abilities, and an active program of research directed at discovering what works for given categories of child characteristics. With such a tack, we may be able to make progress in our efforts to prevent the insidious effects of development gone awry.

## THE CAROLINA ABECEDARIAN PROJECT

The Carolina Abecedarian Project is a two-pronged attack on the forces affecting the growth of high-risk children. At a *secondary level,* within the framework established in Figure 1, intervention occurs at the level of the family for both experimental and control groups. Thus, the availability of social services for the family, and medical services and nutritional supplements for the children, is common to both groups. This provision was included in order to reduce potential Hawthorne Effects in the experimental group and to ensure the delivery of a set of services already guaranteed, in principle, to all members of our society. Recent preliminary reviews of social services used by the Abecedarian families (Ramey & Dempsey, Note 7), and documented illnesses of the Abecedarian children (Ramey & Dubinsky, Note 8), revealed no substantial differences between the experimental and control group families or their children. These interventions were aimed at the socioeconomic and physical survival of our children and their families. In some sense, these services control for alternate explanations of group differences in intellectual and adaptive functioning. More importantly, we believe these services to be so vital to normal growth and development that it was ethically indefensible to withhold services from the control group.

The *primary level* of intervention is what differentiates our experimental and control groups. At this level, individual children receive direct educational programming through the mechanism of systematic, developmental daycare, as described in subsequent sections. A word of justification is in order concerning the form and focus of our preventive efforts. While parents are encouraged to be actively aware of their children's experiences, and to visit the Center and participate in its functioning, no systematic attempt is made to teach parenting skills. As in most other daycare centers, parent participation is generally sporadic.

We chose to focus our educational efforts on the child for several reasons. First, it was already clear in 1971 (when pilot work for the Project began) that at least modest cognitive success with child-centered approaches was feasible. The work of Klaus and Gray (1968), Weikart (1967), and Robinson and Robinson (1971) figured prominently in our decisions. Second, there was a growing realization that parent-focused programs were having great difficulty working successfully with the most disadvantaged or at-risk families (c.f. Bronfenbrenner, 1975; Stedman et al., Note 4). Third, daycare was rapidly growing as a social institution in this country. If we were successful, then we could anticipate more opportunities to reach other disadvantaged families through a mechanism that was, in principle, a downward extension of the public schools. Fourth, we felt that operating our own daycare facility would give us better control over the treatment process. Finally, early and continuing daycare of high quality would constitute an intensive treatment regimen for what seemed to be an intractable set of social problems faced by the families. We did not begin by assuming that daycare was the best or the most powerful treatment. Rather, it represented a prevention-oriented mechanism which looked promising and worthy of serious interdisciplinary pursuit.

## Admission of Families

The Carolina Abecedarian Project began in 1972 as an attempt to intervene with infants and children believed to be at high risk for school failure. Families were referred to the project through local hospitals, clinics, the County Department of Social Services, and other sources. Once families had been identified as potentially eligible, the nursery supervisor visited them at their home to explain the program and to determine whether the family appeared to meet selection criteria. If so, mothers were invited for an interview and psychological assessment.

During the interview, which typically occurred in the last trimester of pregnancy, demographic information about the family was obtained, and mothers were assessed with the Wechsler Adult Intelligence Scale (WAIS; Wechsler, 1955). Final determination of eligibility was made following this visit. Criteria for selection included maternal IQ, family income, parent education, intactness of family, and seven other factors that were weighted and combined to yield a single score called the High-Risk Index (see Ramey & Smith, 1977 for details). Only families at or above a predetermined cutoff score were considered eligible. Selected characteristics of all families admitted to the Experimental and Control groups are summarized in Table 1. As can be seen, well over half the families are headed by females, the average earned income is less than $1,500, and the mothers have about a tenth grade education with a mean IQ of approximately 85. Over 95% of all children in the project can be classified as Black. A recent study of 1,000 first-grade students in North Carolina indicated that race and maternal educational level (less than tenth grade) are strongly associated with school failure (Ramey, Stedman, Borders-Patterson, & Mengel, 1978). Thus, the families in the Abecedarian project appear to be at high risk for school failure and psychosocial retardation.

We admitted four cohorts of families between 1972 and 1977. The oldest children are now over seven years of age and have entered the public schools; the youngest children are approximately three years of age. Of 122 families judged to be eligible and invited to join the program, 121 families accepted the condition of random assignment to the Experimental or Control group. When these 121 families were assigned to groups, 116 or 96% accepted their group assignment. Of these 116, three children have died and one has been diagnosed as retarded due to

TABLE 1
Demographic Data by Experimental and Control Groups

| Group | N | Female-headed Family | Mean Income | Mother's Education (in years) | Mean Maternal IQ | Percent Black Families |
|---|---|---|---|---|---|---|
| Experimental | 58 | 81% | $1534 | 10.33 | 84.33 | 97% |
| Control | 54 | 63% | $1370 | 10.04 | 83.89 | 100% |
| Totals | 112 | 72% | $1455 | 10.19 | 84.22 | 98% |

organic etiology.[2] Not counting these four children, we have a base sample of 112 children and families. Of these 112 biologically normal children, including 57 Experimentals and 55 Controls, eight have dropped out of our sample as of September 1, 1978. One child was adopted out of the area, two children withdrew for personal reasons, and five moved out of the area. Thus, not counting attrition by death or biological abnormality, 93% of our sample is intact after six years. This represents a sample attrition rate of 1.18% per year. Most of the results to be reported in this chapter are derived from analyses on the first half (first two cohorts) of the sample during their first five years of development.

## The Abecedarian Daycare Program

The largest component of the Abecedarian project is the systematic, developmental, and educational daycare service that the experimental children receive. The daycare program has been developed with the hypothesis in mind that "relative inferiority in the areas of language development and motivation to learn are particularly detrimental to normal development" (Ramey & Gallagher, 1975, p. 45). The experiences of our experimental group children are planned to foster language development and to promote appropriate and adaptive social behavior. The daycare setting is operated with these goals in mind so as to provide environments that, as Harms and Cross (1978) have detailed, are: predictable and promote self-help; supportive and facilitate social-emotional adjustment; reflective of the child's age, ability, and interest; and varied in activities.

Children begin attending the center as young as 6 weeks of age; attendance must begin by age 3 months. The center operates from 7:45 a.m. to 5:30 p.m. each weekday for 50 weeks per year. Transportation to and from the center is provided for the children. The center cares for children on various parts of two floors of a four story research building. The settings for the children are structured so as to be age and developmentally appropriate. Generally, children are grouped according to age with sections for infants, toddlers, and so on. For example, prewalking infants are cared for in a two room suite, with one room for sleeping and one room for play and curriculum activities. Toys are arranged so as to be available to creeping infants. Infant seats with attractive toys suspended over them often are used for younger infants when they are not engaged in formal teaching, feeding, or changing. Prop pillows that permit free use of hands in babies unable to sit alone are also used. Teachers, throughout the day, participate actively with and talk to the infants (for more detailed descriptions of the center and the children's settings,

---

[2]In comparison to Chapel Hill and North Carolina, the infant mortality rate in our sample (25.9 per thousand) is quite high. Between 1974 and 1978, the infant mortality rate for whites in Chapel Hill was 9.3; for nonwhites in Chapel Hill it was 10.9; and for all individuals in North Carolina, the rate was 17.6 per thousand (North Carolina Vital Statistics, 1978). The infant mortality rate in the Abecedarian sample is 2.78, 2.38, and 1.47 times higher (respectively) than the figures from the general population, attesting to the high risk status of these infants.

see Ramey & Campbell, 1979a, Ramey, McGinness, Cross, Collier, & Barrie-Blackley, 1981; and Ramey & Haskins, 1981a). The goals of environments such as these, even in infancy, are to promote independence and self-help while enriching relevant developmental domains such as language and concept attainment.

An important part of the implementation of any preventive effort, of course, is the staff. In the Abecedarian Project, 12 teachers and assistants, aided by three administrative staff members, are responsible for providing the educational program for children. The typical teacher/child ratio is between 1:3 and 1:6. Teaching staff vary in their level of formal training (averaging seven years of direct experience) but all have demonstrated skill and competencies in working with young children. Staff development is a critically important and ongoing process. Of particular import is the language training program that seeks to help teachers develop childrens' communication skills through strategies based on current research in adult-child verbal interaction.

We have attempted to define an approach to language development that goes beyond linguistic forms to the development of an elaborated code. In doing so, we have agreed with a position similar to that of the Duchess in Alice in Wonderland: "Take care of the sense and the sounds will take care of themselves." The focus of our effort to date has been to promote a particular *kind* and *amount* of verbal interaction between teacher and daycare pupil. Much of our language work is derived from the frameworks developed by Tough (1976) and Blank (1973). The kind of verbal interaction encouraged is largely modeled on what a middle-class mother establishes with her child; the *amount* is higher, perhaps more like what a tutorial hour might afford. Because our daycare effort is competing with extensive experience in another type of linguistic environment (the home), we have assumed that it cannot be as casual and diluted as the normal family interaction. To foster certain types of linguistic functioning in the child's repertoire, then, we are trying to provide a large number of practice opportunities.

The language intervention approach that has been adopted rests on several assumptions:

1. The acquisition of *communicative competence* is the primary goal.
2. The notion of communicative competence is *multi-faceted,* implying competencies in at least three interrelated dimensions:
   a) social (pragmatic) competence (*language use*);
   b) representational competence (level of abstraction);
   c) linguistic competence (language structure—syntax/semantics).
3. The child acquires communication skills mainly through interaction with adults who are effective communicators, particularly in interactions in which the child is able and motivated to engage the adult in dialogue.

Thus, the language development approach is focused at the level of "critical skills" (i.e., successful communication in situations where the child really wants to communicate), with the awareness that there are specific prerequisites for success. Teachers learn to apply the approach in any potential interaction with children. In this way, they can capitalize on those situations and activities that happen to motivate individual children. In addition, teachers can use the approach in planning cohesive sequences of class activities and projects according to particular needs and constraints.

Teachers are given in-service training and consultative help in assessing children's needs, setting objectives, planning and implementing activities that will stimulate particular kinds of communication, and in evaluating their own interactions with the children. Our theoretical framework and a more detailed treatment of the language experiences can be found in a paper by Ramey, McGinness, Cross, Collier and Barrie-Blackley (1981).

Other opportunities for staff development include consultant-run workshops and the encouragement of further education in child-related areas. The goal and, we hope, the result of these opportunities is the provision of a staff who provides a variety of human contacts for the children while having gained a relatively unified and systematic approach towards the prevention of developmental retardation.

Beyond a comfortable, constructive environment and competent, creative staff, though, is the need for a curriculum that meets the needs of at-risk children. Although unstructured activities play an important role in Abecedarian daycare, standard curricula insure a continuity of intervention that spontaneous interactions cannot guarantee. The curricula used in the Abecedarian project have been developed to provide a systematic but individualized educational experience for the children. The infant curricula, which are designed to meet the goals expressed earlier, grew out of the following: (1) Piagetian developmental theory, (2) known developmental facts, (3) parental value judgments, and (4) professional value judgments. Although the curricula continue to be refined, they can be, at present, roughly divided into those for infants and toddlers (0–3 year olds) and those for young children (3–4 year olds). The division reflects both the growing efficiency of children in the use of language, and the increasing importance of peer and adult interaction in fostering adaptive social behavior.

The infant curricula that are used in the Abecedarian project are the Carolina Infant Curriculum and the Task Orientation Curriculum, developed by Sparling and Lewis (1979). These curricula consist of over 300 items in language, motor, social, and cognitive areas (see Ramey et al., 1981, for a more complete description). Each item is described in a guide sheet which sets forth a goal, the means to accomplish the goal, and the usefulness of the particular skill. Children are taught both in one-to-one interactions and, with increasing age, in small groups. Individual prescriptions of items are written for each child every two to three weeks, with a typical prescription containing two to six items. Teachers keep a developmental chart for each child to assist in providing a suitable match between child status and items selected; new items are chosen or old ones continued, based on a given child's progress. This process helps to document the variety and quality of each child's curriculum experience, while also providing a sense of continuity in the application of the curriculum. The program is formally applied up to a child's third birthday. The goal of the infant curricula is to enrich early development in several realms and to prepare the children for the more structured educational curricula they will partake of after their third year.

After the children reach 3 years of age, they begin to receive more structured educational curricula. The curricula continues to promote active child participation and independence and to provide a good deal of variety while giving the children a systematic exposure to areas such as science, math, and music. The formal cognitive curricula, which teachers can draw on as it best benefits the individual needs of a given child, include the GOAL math program (Karnes, 1973), the Peabody Early Experiences Kit (Dunn, Chun, Crowell, Dunn, Avery, & Yachel, 1976) and Bridges to Reading (Greenberg & Epstein, 1973), and for the 4-year-olds, the Wallach and Wallach (1976) reading program. The daily schedule of 3- and 4-year-olds is a mixture of structured and unstructured activities, outside and inside play, and rest times. The daily schedule also allows for the use and reinforcement of adaptive social behavior which is encouraged through the use of a program called *My Friends and Me* (Davis, 1977), a social curriculum designed to make children aware of their feelings and emotions, and of appropriate responses to these feelings. Large group, small group, and solitary activities are scheduled, with active teacher participation and an emphasis on independence and appropriate peer interaction. The children are also prepared for the transition to public school with an increasing emphasis on sustained on-task behavior and personal responsibility. The infant and early childhood curricula, in toto, provide a systematic yet individually responsive experience for at-risk children such that relevant domains of development are enriched and sustained, and so that the children are prepared to cope with the educational and social demands of public school.

### Results from the Carolina Abecedarian Project

In summarizing results from the Abecedarian Project, we will use the concept of levels of analysis and transactions of units discussed earlier and included as components in Figure 1. Specifically, we will present data from the level of the child, the caregiver, the family, the neighborhood, and society. We will also briefly summarize some data relevant to transactions of selected units.

#### Effects at the Level of the Child

*History.* The specific purpose of the Abecedarian Project was to intervene at the level of the individual or, in terms of the General Systems Model, to modify the "history" of the infant so as to sever the relationship between poverty and retarded intellectual development. Since infants were randomly assigned to the daycare and control groups, effects on other aspects of the system can be ultimately attributed to this manipulation. Changes in the development of the infant, though, can be caused by indirect influences such as the acquisition of concepts, or by direct processes involving changes in motivation or the eliciting properties ("demand characteristics") of the infant. The direct influences of daycare on cognitive and social outcomes will be considered in a later section. Now we will turn our attention to other, more subtle consequences of infant daycare.

*Demand Characteristics.* Several sources of information suggest that the Abecedarian Project has been successful in altering the demand characteristics of the child. Two studies have used behavioral ratings on the Infant Behavior Record (IBR) of the Bayley Scales of Infant Development. In a study by Ramey and Campbell (1979a), the IBR items from ratings of Cohorts 1 and 2 at 6, 12, and 18 months were factor analyzed, resulting in two factors labelled goal-directed behavior and social confidence (responsiveness to the examiner and happiness versus fearfulness). Infants attending daycare were rated as more socially confident than controls at all three ages; by 18 months, center-attending infants scored significantly higher than control children on the goal-directedness dimension. Finally, it was found that the fearfulness item showed the greatest degree of group difference at all ages, and further, that this item was uncorrelated with concurrent performance on the mental scale. Thus, daycare seems to have modified the infants' social behaviors in a manner that permits them to adjust to new situations and novel people more rapidly than infants who have not experienced our daycare.

MacPhee and Ramey (Note 9) extended these findings in their analysis of the Infant Behavior Record data for all four cohorts. Factor analysis of IBR items at 3, 6, 9, 12, 18, and 24 months revealed four factors: Task orientation (attention span and goal-directed behaviors); Cooperativeness (emotional tone, cooperativeness and response to the examiner); Activity level; and Sociability, the first two of which are similar to Ramey and Campbell's (1979a) factors. Infants attending daycare were significantly more cooperative than controls at all ages, except 9 months. Furthermore, differences in task orientation, in favor of the daycare group, emerged at 18 months ( $p < .001$) and continued to be found at 24 months ( $p < .002$). To foreshadow later discussion, a summary temperament variable—comprised of scores on all four factors—was related both to performance on the mental scales of the Bayley and to the mother's involvement with her child.

Additional support for the effects of daycare on the child's demand characteristics is furnished by Finkelstein and Wilson (note 10). Their results suggest that the daycare-attending high-risk children are as interested in peers, and are as friendly and cooperative, as more advantaged middle-class age-mates. Contrary to other research findings (e.g. Schwarz et al., 1974), daycare children were not more aggressive or more selfish as a result of having to share the teacher's attention with other children. The daycare children in the Finkelstein and Wilson study also appeared to be more willing to approach and interact with an unfamiliar adult than their home-reared middle-class peers. These findings parallel those of Ricciuti (1974), and of Kagan, Kearsley, and Zelazo (1978).

Finally, Gordon and Feagans (Note 11) have found that the patterns of language skills in these preschool children were altered by enrollment in the daycare program. Children in both high-risk groups and in a General Population Sample (GPS) drawn from local nursery schools (mainly upper middle-class) were assessed at 3½ years of age on eight psycholinguistic tasks that measured the domains of basic words, representative sentence structures, and connected discourse. Rank order analyses revealed striking consistencies in performance on the eight subtests, with GPS children's performance exceeding that of the daycare group which, in turn, was significantly greater than that of the control children in all but one instance. Gordon and Feagans concluded that the daycare intervention program facilitated children's abilities on most of the psycholinguistic tasks, especially those concerned with spatial terms, paraphrasing, and sentence comprehension. To the extent that language is used to symbolize action and to mediate interactions with the social and cognitive environment, high-risk children exposed to daycare possess a more refined strategy for dealing with and adapting to the world.

In sum, involvement in the daycare program seems to have affected the stimulus properties of the children. A profile of these children's behavior, as contrasted to that of the control group, would note that they adapt more readily to unfamiliar situations and people, that they respond more appropriately and vigorously to the demands of a task, and that they are more advanced in language development. Succinctly stated, daycare seems to have modified the demand characteristics of these infants so that they are more adept at conducting transactions with the preschool environment.

***Cognitive Outcomes.*** Figure 2 contains a plot of the Bayley Scales of Infant Devleopment administered at 12 months, the Standford-Binet (Terman & Merrill, 1973) administered at 24, 36, and 48 months, and the WPPSI administered at 60 months. These results have been reported previously by Ramey and Campbell (1981). Analyses of the results indicated a significant difference between the groups at all measurement occasions, except the 12-month assessment. Thus, the results suggest that the daycare program has been instrumental in preventing the intellectual decline observed in the control group. Another piece of evidence germane to the intellectual decline issue can be derived from the percentage of individuals in the experimental and control groups who show an educational handicap due to a cognitive deficit. For our purposes, we shall define a *cognitive educational handicap* as an IQ score less than or equal to 85. Table 2 is taken from Ramey and Haskins (1981c), and reports the percentage of experimental and control children scoring below IQ 85 at 36, 48, and 60 months for Cohorts 1 and 2 combined. As can be seen, the control group was on the average 3.54 times as likely to have low scoring children as the experimental group.

That this group of children was truly at high-risk for progressive mild mental retardation is also attested to by the performance of older siblings on standard measures of intelligence. Ramey and Campbell (1981) have reported a correla-

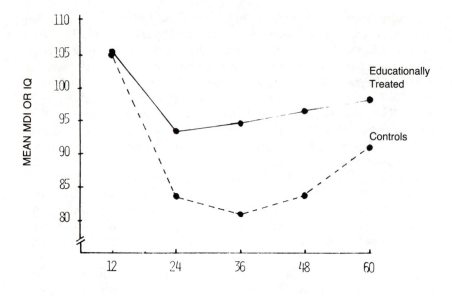

AGE AT TEST ADMINISTRATION (MONTHS)

**FIG. 2.**   Mean Bayley MDI, Stanford-Binet, and WPPSI scores at five test occasions
for the Daycare and Control groups.

TABLE 2
Percentage of Experimental and Control Children
Performing Below IQ 85 at Three Ages

|  | Age | | |
|---|---|---|---|
| Group | 36 Months | 48 Months | 60 Months |
| Experimental | 26 | 11 | 11 |
| Control | 61 | 52 | 39 |

*Note.* Averaged across the three ages, Control children are more
likely than Experimental children to score below IQ 85 by a factor of
3.54.

tion between the IQs of 41 older siblings of children in the project and their ages
(range = 57 to 220 months). Siblings were given the age-appropriate Wechsler
Scale. The mean of the IQ distribution was 87.4 with a standard deviation of 10.3.
The correlation coefficient was $r = -.45, p < .003$. This finding suggests an apparent progressive IQ decline with age in the absence of an early intervention
program.

Because measures of general intelligence do not reveal much about specific
psychological processes, we administered the McCarthy Scales of Children's

Abilities (1972) at 42 months to determine which components differentiated the treatment and control groups (Ramey & Campbell, 1979a). The educationally treated (daycare) children were superior to the educationally untreated group on the Verbal, Perceptual-Performance, Quantitative, and Memory Scales, but not on the Motor Scale. A follow-up administration of the McCarthy Scales at 54 months (Ramey & Campbell, 1979b) revealed that the Verbal, Perceptual-Performance and Quantitative Scales still differed but the Memory and Motor Scales failed to distinguish between the groups. Thus, early compensatory education appears to improve disadvantaged children's ability to attend to, comprehend, and to carry out abstract and complex tasks. Further, the effect appears broad scale rather than specific, leading us to assume that general intelligence or $g$ has been affected.

***Effects of Infant Demand Characteristics on Outcome.*** The principal message of Sameroff's (1975) Transactional Model was that linear relationships between insult to the infant and later cognitive deficits were uncommon in the normal range of environments. Two areas of inquiry from the Abecedarian Project clearly illustrate this process at work. Zeskind and Ramey (1978; 1981) have reported two analyses of the consequences of fetal malnutrition in the two high-risk groups of our project. Using the Ponderal Index (PI) as a measure of fetal growth and nutrition, infants in the daycare and control groups were classified as either malnourished or normal. Bayley mental scale scores at 3 and 18 months, and Stanford-Binet scores at 24 months (Zeskind & Ramey, 1978) and 36 months (Zeskind & Ramey, 1981) were analyzed by group (intervention group × PI status). It is clear from Figure 3 that later IQ cannot be predicted solely from the status of the organism, nor from knowing whether or not the infant attended daycare. A supportive environment (daycare) tended to ameliorate the effects of fetal malnutrition. In the unsupplemented home environment of low SES families, fetally-malnourished infants showed an even more precipitous decline in IQ than their well-nourished peers.

The synergistic effects of transactions between elements of the system are again illustrated in a recent study by MacPhee and Ramey (Note 9). As noted earlier, infants in the experimental and control groups were classified as easy or difficult in temperament, based on their scores on Bayley's Infant Behavior Record. As in the Zeskind and Ramey studies, four groups representing the two variables (intervention group × temperamental classification) were formed and examined for differences in IQ at each test occasion from 3 to 24 months. The results, shown in Figure 4, again illustrate the transactional nature of development. While infants classified as easy fared better through the first 12 months, the effects of the nonsupportive environment began to be asserted in the second year. MacPhee and Ramey concluded that temperament may represent one demand characteristic that makes the infant more or less vulnerable to the stresses of a nonsupportive environment (e.g., Garmezy, 1971).

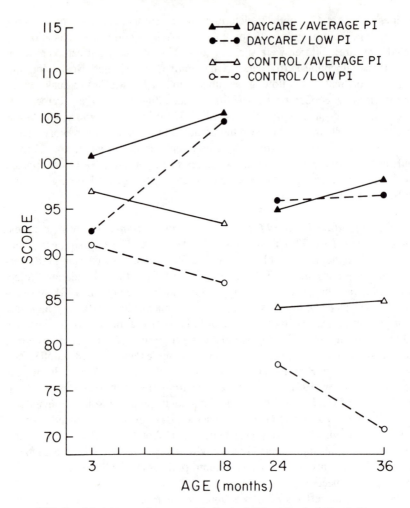

**FIG. 3.**    Mental test performance on the Bayley MDI and Stanford-Binet in Daycare and Control infants classified as fetally-malnourished or average PI.

In sum, we are suggesting that certain demand characteristics of the infant are a product of the individual's biological heritage and learning history. However, these properties of the infant are not directly related to cognitive and social outcomes. Rather, demand characteristics act upon and modify the environment, resulting in a phenotypic outcome such as IQ or maternal involvement. Some of these characteristics may buffer the child from the full effects of deprivation; characteristics such as task orientation (MacPhee & Ramey, Note 9) or activity level (Schaffer, 1966). Other behaviors such as irritability may exacerbate the effects of a stressed home environment, resulting in child abuse (Belsky, 1980). In any

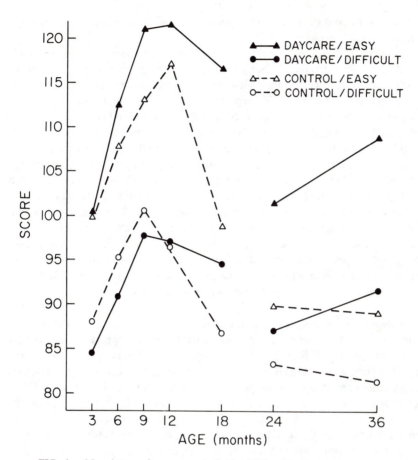

**FIG. 4.** Mental test performance on the Bayley MDI and Stanford Binet in Daycare and Control infants classified as Easy or Difficult on the Bayley Infant Behavior Record.

event, the demand characteristics of the infant are only one part—albeit an important one—of the story.

### Effects at the Level of the Caregiver

*History.* In many respects the history of the primary caregivers is the demographic and attitudinal characteristics that they possessed in the year of their children's births. These demographic characteristics have been presented in Table 1 and will not be repeated here, except to say that the mothers were from very low income families; had little formal education; were typically black and young; and had IQs which averaged in the low 80's. Almost all mothers had lived in the local community when they were children and they typically were part of a large and extended local kinship network.

Two primary measures of the mothers' attitudes were made about the time their infants were 6 months old. These measures will be conceptualized here as part of their history with respect to their views of life in general and child rearing in particular. Ramey and Mills (1977) reported analyses of the high-risk mothers' responses to Rotter's (1966) locus of control scale and to Emmerich's (1969) version of Schaefer and Bell's (1958) Parental Attitude Research Instrument (PARI). Responses of the high-risk mothers were compared to those of a randomly drawn sample of mothers from the local community with same-aged infants—referred to as the General Population Sample (GPS)—who tended to be much better educated and financially-situated. The experimental and control group mothers did not differ from one another on any of the subscales or total scores from either of these two instruments, but together they differed markedly from the GPS. Specifically, high-risk mothers perceived themselves as much more externally than internally controlled—a perception which to us seems accurate. They also reported themselves to be more authoritarian, less democratic, and less hostile and rejecting of the homemaking role than their more advantaged peers.

***Demand Characteristics.*** The initial demand characteristics of the mothers have been couched in terms of their initial speech characteristics to their 6-month-old infants (Adams & Ramey, 1980; Ramey & Mills, 1977), and by scores on a modified version of Caldwell, Heider, and Kaplan's (Note 12) Home Observation for Measurement of the Environment (HOME), which we call an Index of Functional Maternal Concern (Ramey & Farran, 1981). This index, unlike the Caldwell, Heider, and Kaplan instrument, restricts itself to overt childcare behaviors that the mother displays during a 45 minute to one hour visit to the family's home. We have found this index to correlate negatively with the mother's authoritarianism and external locus of control, and positively with her intelligence and level of education. Further, the index has been shown to be stable during the first two years of the child's life. Thus, there is reason to believe that there is substantial congruence between the mother's history as assessed at the level of attitudes and her behaviors, which we construe as demand characteristics.

With respect to speech demand characteristics, Adams and Ramey (1980) have reported a structural analysis of maternal speech to 6-month-old high-risk infants. The results from this sample were compared to those from more advantaged mothers previously reported in the psycholinguistic literature, and to other measures we have gathered concerning the risk status of the families in our sample. It was found that the proportion of imperatives, but not the amount of maternal speech, was positively correlated with our High-Risk Index and negatively correlated with maternal education and IQ. Consonant with previous findings on maternal speech to older infants, syntactic complexity was not significantly related to social risk indices. Thus, we have some evidence that the risk status of the mothers is translated into a linguistic behavioral style which is likely to affect social interchanges within the dyad.

*Outcome Characteristics.* Ramey, Farran, and Campbell (1979) have reported repeated assessments using the PARI at 6 and 18 months, and found that experimental and control group mothers were not different at either measurement occasion. At 18 months, though, the high-risk groups differed from the GPS sample in the same way that we summarized above for the six-month assessments. Therefore, at this level of analysis there is no evidence of parental attitudes being affected by daycare intervention, at least during infancy.

*Transactions Between Children and Caregivers.* Major alterations in the daily routines of families are likely to have psychological consequences. This topic is particularly controversial with respect to infant daycare. In the United States, the sanctity of the intact nuclear family as the premier rearing institution is a particularly strong ethic. Therefore, any proposed supplement or alteration in our traditional ideal is viewed with skepticism and alarm. For example, when former President Richard Nixon vetoed the Mondale-Braddamus Comprehensive Child Care Bill in 1971, one of the main reasons cited for the veto was the potentially devisive influence that expanded availability of daycare would have on families. This public policy decision was based more on appeal to common sense than on the basis of scientific evidence, which was scant in the early 1970's, with respect to daycare in this country. Further, the use of evidence concerning group rearing from other countries such as Sweden, Israel, and Russia was viewed with skepticism because of their pervasive differences in the area of family history, and the role of the state in family functioning.

At the time that the Abecedarian Project was begun, the controversy over infant daycare was in full force. We had several reasons for wanting to monitor the developing relationship between mothers and children, including the prevailing political zeitgeist; basic scientific questions concerning the role of early experience; and because of a desire to minimize potentially negative consequences to participating families. Three levels of evidence are particularly germane and will be summarized here.

The first type of evidence is derived from observations made in the children's homes using Caldwell, Heider, and Kaplan's (Note 12) Home Observation for the Measurement of the Environment (HOME), administered when the children were 6, 18, 30, and 42 months of age. The HOME measures the following dimensions of the child's home environment: (1) emotional and verbal responsivity of the mother, (2) absence of punishment, (3) physical and temporal organization of the environment, (4) provision of appropriate toys, (5) maternal involvement, and (6) opportunity for variety in daily stimulation. Neither the scale scores nor the total scores at any test occasion revealed a significant difference between the daycare and control groups, although evidence has been presented to indicate that both groups differ on all assessed dimensions as early as 6 months of age, when compared to a representative sample from the local population (Ramey, Mills, Campbell, & O'Brien, 1975).Thus, daycare does not seem to have either a positive or a negative effect on these high-risk homes as they relate directly to childrearing as assessed by the HOME.

The second type of data comes from direct observations of caregiver-child interactions assessed in a 20-minute laboratory session at 6, 18, and 30 months of age. At these ages, a representative sample of same-aged children and their mothers from the local area formed a comparison group. The laboratory sessions were conducted in a room furnished as a small living room, and a coding scheme for frequency and durations of discrete behaviors (modified from Lewis & Goldberg's, 1969, procedures) was used.

Ramey, Farran, and Campbell (1979) have presented results that indicate a great deal of similarity among all three groups at 6 months, with the only significant difference being the greater amount of talking to their infants by middle-class mothers. At 20 months, however, the middle-class mothers not only talked more to their toddlers but interacted more with them as well. The interaction patterns of the daycare and control groups did not differ significantly from one another on a factor that Farran and Ramey (1980) have labeled *dyadic involvement*. O'Connell and Farran (Note 13), in a more refined analysis of the videotapes from the 20-month interaction session, found that experimental group infants were communicating to their mothers at a significantly higher level than the control infants. Further, infants attending daycare were communicating at a level equal to middle-class infants on what O'Connell and Farran call "requesting" behaviors. Thus, there appears to be some evidence that the daycare children are presenting different "demand characteristics" when in interaction with their mothers, and this, in turn, may affect the quality of the mother-child interactions over time.

Some further evidence for this change in "demand characteristics" is derived from observations of mothers and children conducted in the laboratory when the children were 36 months of age. These interactions have been coded with the Reciprocal Control System developed by Farran & Haskins (Note 14). Comparisons of the dyadic interactions using conditional probabilities have been made between the experimental and control groups combined and middle-class mother-child dyads (Farran & Haskins, 1980). Preliminary comparisons of the experimental and control groups suggested that daycare may have had the effect of modifying the child's behavior in social interactions with his mother. Experimental children were four times as likely to attempt to modify their mothers' behavior (e.g., asking mothers to watch their activity, read them a book, or join them in a tea party) compared to control children. Moreover, the mutual play activities lasted twice as long for experimental dyads, leading one to the speculation that with the child's increasing skills, play becomes more enjoyable to the mother. Thus, the evidence from this level of analysis not only indicates that there are no negative effects on the dyad's behavior, but may also portend a slightly positive effect mediated by the altered demand characteristics of the child, plausibly attributable to the behaviors encouraged within the daycare center.

The third type of data about caregiver-child interactions derives from direct observations involving the child, his mother, and the child's daycare teachers. The central issue here is whether the mothers' saliency for her child, as Kagan, Kearsley and Zelazo (1978) have termed it, has been replaced by that of the child's teachers in the daycare center. Because of our experimental design, this issue is germane only to our experimental group dyads. Farran and Ramey (1977) pursued the issue of saliency of mothers and teachers within a social preference paradigm in which the child, mother, and the child's daycare teacher were simultaneously present in a small playroom. Observations of behaviors were made during a 12-minute free play period and also during a 2-minute period when the infant was given a problem (getting a cookie out of a locked clear plastic container) that he could not solve by himself. Results indicated a uniform preference for proximity to the mother in this situation. In addition, the children were much more likely to solicit help from the mother in solving the problem. Thus, children overwhelmingly preferred to be near and to interact with their mothers rather than their teachers, indicating that the attachment bond to the mother had indeed been formed. Moreover, they perceived their mothers as a provider of help when faced with a mildly difficult, ecologically valid problem. Therefore, our working assumption at this point is that while the concern over daycare and its relation to the disadvantaged family is well intended, the evidence from our own work suggests that it is not necessarily detrimental to mother-child relationships and may be, in fact, mildly positive and mediated by the increased competence of treated children.

### Effects of Maternal Demand Characteristics on Infant Outcome

Fortunately, one of the dividends of the General Systems Model is that new relationships between variables can be spelled out and investigated. In this section, we are interested in the possible relationship between aspects of the parent, such as attitudes, perceptions of the infant, and demand characteristics, and the child's cognitive and social development. While a cause-and-effect linkage between the two has been implicit in some theories of child development (e.g., Schaefer, 1981; Baumrind & Black, 1967), little research has been done to verify that such a path exists, much less explicate the processes involved. Some findings from the Abecedarian Project are germane at this point, although the connections we are exploring are acknowledged to be tenuous.

Newman and Ramey (Note 15) investigated the relationships between child self-concept, maternal attitudes, maternal self-esteem, and child outcome as assessed by the Peabody Individual Achievement Test (PIAT), and by the Wechsler Intelligence Scale (WPPSI) administered during kindergarten or first grade. The high-risk group (daycare and control sample combined) did not differ from GPS children on the self-concept scale (Cicarelli, Note 16). However, GPS and high-risk mothers both differed in their perceptions of their children's temperament using Buss and Plomins' (1975) Inventory. High-risk children were rated as more impulsive and less sociable by their mothers. Furthermore, one of the three PARI factors (democratic attitudes) was correlated with the WPPSI, while maternal self-esteem and perceptions of the child related to both cognitive measures. While the correlations do not account for more than 25% of the variance in any one correlation—suggesting that other processes are mediating or supplementing the effects of parental characteristics—it is important that the processes underlying these findings be examined more closely.

In a study involving only children in the high-risk control group, Ramey and Brownlee (Note 17) studied variables that might increase the precision of early identification of at-risk children. Predictor variables included maternal attitudes assessed when the infants were 6 months old (the PARI and Rotter's Internal-External locus of control scale), maternal IQ (the WAIS), infant temperament at 6 months (the IBR), measures of the home environment at 6 months (the HOME), and the amount of time the child spent outside the home in the care of others during the first six months. Three of the variables showed significant prediction of 24-month infant Stanford-Binet IQ. The three variables included temperament, time outside the home in the care of others in the first six months of infancy, and the democratic attitudes factor of the PARI. Ramey and Brownlee concluded that the lack of a well-defined philosophy of childbearing, as exemplified by low scores on the PARI, may translate into inconsistent actions which would leave already-stressed mothers ill-equipped to deal with an irritable child or a chaotic setting. If so this would suggest another transactional process that ultimately may affect the outcome of the infant.

***Intervention effects on relationships among variables.*** Early intervention may affect development in at least two basic ways. First, it may affect the frequency or type of behaviors that are presumed or posited to be part of a causal chain, ultimately linked to measures of child outcome. Generally, the form of analysis at this level is a group comparison of the presence or amount of selected variables as a function of differential treatment.

There is a second and perhaps more subtle influence that early intervention may exert. Early intervention may affect the relationships among variables in a causal network. Recall from the General Systems Model that behavior *emerges* out of the interaction of components of a system such that there are multiple causes of a given outcome. By simultaneously modifying several of these processes, intensive intervention may alter traditionally reported relationships among constellations of parent-child variables. Several pieces of empirical data have given us some tantalizing leads on this topic. Because we don't, as yet, have a unified, detailed, a priori theory of the specific psychological mechanisms likely to be altered as a function of the form and focus of preventive intervention strategies, we will have to make this point by example. We will limit ourselves to two illustrations.

One of psychology's time-honored empirical findings is that the intellectual status of parents is moderately and positively predictive of the intellectual status of their offspring. Generally, the magnitude of parent-child IQ correlations for intelligence averages about .5. Major controversy has existed, and still exists, concerning the meaning of this relationship. Jensen (1981) has argued, for example, that this relationship is best accounted for by genetic inheritance. Others have argued that it represents the shared environments that parents and children typically inhabit. Because experimental tests of either of these positions (or alternative positions) have been virtually impossible to conduct in the past for ethical reasons, the nature-nurture controversy has generated more heat than light.

Because the random assignment to treatment groups in our intervention program is a powerful design feature ensuring, within the limits of sampling theory, initial group equivalence, it has allowed us to pursue this issue without some of the confounding influences characteristic of most earlier studies. We think this is true because our cognitive curriculum is individually prescribed, based on the child's developmental status and is delivered independently of the child's parents. Thus, there is at least an attenuation of the usual genotype-environment correlation that typically confounds consanguinity studies. Therefore, Ramey and Haskins (1981b; 1981c) have presented parent-child IQ correlations based upon assessments when the children were 3, 4, and 5 years of age. In the control group, each of these correlations is statistically significant and not different from the expected coefficient of .5. Thus, our findings for the control group replicate those already in the literature. The correlations in the experimental group are quite different, however. None of the three coefficients are statistically significant and, with one exception of a nonsignificant .34 correlation at 48 months, they are remarkably close to 0. At age 3, the correlation coefficient is -.05, and at age 5, the correlation is .14. Thus, the relationship between such a basic psychological construct as parent-child intellectual resemblance has apparently been significantly altered as a byproduct of manipulating other units within the system.

Another example of the alteration among relationships is derived from a paper by Ramey and Campbell (1981). In that report, backwards elimination multiple regression equations were used to predict WPPSI IQ scores at 60 months of age separately for the experimental and control groups. The potential contributors to the prediction equation included maternal age, years of schooling completed by mothers when children were 54 months of age, the family's High-Risk Index Score at the time of the child's birth, family yearly income from the year that the children were 54 months, maternal scores on the PARI authoritarian, hostility, and democratic attitude factors ascertained when the child was 18 months, and the mother's IQ. Of this set of potential predictors of the 60-month WPPSI IQ, four variables remained significant for the control group yielding an $R^2$ of .57 or 57% of the variance in the IQ scores. Significant variables, in order of importance were: (1) maternal IQ, (2) HOME total score at 54 months, (3) PARI Hostility-Rejection from 18 months, and (4) PARI authoritarianism assessed at 18 months.

For the daycare treated group, only the HOME score at 54 months entered significantly into the equation, resulting in an $R^2$ of .38. Thus, as with the earlier and simpler bivariate correlations concerning parent-child IQ similarity, this more complicated model of developmental forces, as represented by different regression equations, indicates a modification among relationships as a function of preventive intervention. In summary, it appears that the emergent principle from our General Systems Theory model is supported empirically by our data.

### Effects at the Level of the Family

The relationship between caregiver characteristics and household characteristics are obviously intertwined and somewhat redundant. The choice of what data to include at the caregiver level of analysis has a direct bearing on what is presented at the family level. Thus, we are aware that initial demographic and psychological attributes such as parental intelligence, attitudes, and the quality of the home as assessed by Caldwell, Heider, and Kaplan's Inventory could be justified as measures pertaining to this level. Given that they have already been presented and constitute a "history" section, we will present only two types of data at this level. These can be construed both as demand characteristics of the household and as outcome measures that illustrate the effects of preventive intervention at the family level.

Maternal interviews conducted when the children were 54 months old have revealed what we consider to be some potentially very important changes in the life circumstances of 27 mothers in our experimental group, relative to 23 control group mothers. These changes concern the potential availability of intellectual, financial, and role-model resources that may ultimately but indirectly affect child progress. With respect to formal education, Ramey, Dorval and Baker-Ward (in press) have reported that mothers of the daycare children have significantly more formal education by the time their children are 54 months old (11.9 years) than the mothers of the control children (10.3 years), although the groups were educationally equivalent in the year of the children's births (10.30 and 10.12 years for the experimental and control groups, respectively). This means that daycare for the children of high-risk mothers has apparently allowed more of them to continue their education. Given that education of the mother again has been validated as a major predictor of children's intellectual and adaptive behavior in first grade in North Carolina (Ramey, Stedman, Borders-Patterson & Mengel, 1978; Finkelstein & Ramey, 1980), this educational differential linked to early daycare intervention may bode well for the experimental group's performance in public school.

When data from the 54-month maternal interview was coded with respect to maternal employment, another striking finding was noted. We classified maternal

TABLE 3
Employment Status of Experimental and Control Group
Mothers When Their Children Were 54 Months Old

| | Group Assignment | |
| | Daycare Group Mothers (N=25) | Control Group Mothers (N=21) |
| --- | --- | --- |
| Unemployed or Unskilled | 37% | 65% |
| Semiskilled or Skilled | 55% | 26% |

$X^2 = 4.54, p < .05$

occupation into: (1) unemployed or unskilled, (2) semiskilled or skilled, or (3) student. Table 3 contains the percentages of both the experimental and control group mothers who fall into each of these categories at 54 months, excluding students. A Chi-Square test was completed for the two groups concerning employment. The Chi-Square was significant ($\chi^2 = 4.54$, p < .05) indicating that more of the control group mothers were unskilled and/or unemployed and conversely that more of the daycare mothers held semiskilled or skilled jobs. This finding is consistent with the educational advancement just reported and adds optimism to the prediction of the children's subsequent performance in school. We hypothesize that because education and employment represent structural and permanent changes in the families, they may continue to draw the more accomplished high-risk families closer to the resources enjoyed by the mainstream of American Society.

## Effects on the Neighborhood

We have chosen to investigate neighborhood influences on development beginning when children are in their kindergarten year of public school. From each public school classroom in which one or more of our high-risk children are placed, we randomly draw an equal number of same-sexed children. Typically, any given classroom contains only one of our children, although occasionally, school district lines and available classrooms result in more than one high-risk child in a given classroom. As part of our school-aged assessments, we gather information about neighborhood composition and social functioning through parental interviews and naturalistic observations. Preliminary data from these observations, which are under the direction of Dr. Ron Haskins and Dr. Neal Finkelstein, has recently been reported in a chapter by Ramey and Haskins (1981a). The naturalistic observation data were derived from 16 5-year-old experimental and control children and 12 middle-income children from the GPS sample. Children from low-income families were dropped from the GPS sample for the analysis to be reported. On each of three days, four 10-minute blocks of observational data were obtained for each child. Approximately 30 pre-determined behavioral categories were scored including talking, playing, attempting to modify or change another person's behavior, crying, striking, and so on.

The results revealed very low levels of aggression both in the neighborhoods of high-risk and middle-income children; more talk by and toward middle-income children; and more higher-order play (coordinate play) involving explicit rules or games. Thus, these results suggest that there may be differences in the neighborhood social experiences of children from low-income and middle-income families. However, not enough data have been gathered to be reported with great confidence, because most of the children are not yet old enough. These preliminary data are reported to typify a style of inquiry and a level of analysis rather than for their substance. Results at this level await more complete data collection and analysis.

### Effects at the Level of Society

The data germane to this level of analysis are not yet ready for dissemination because the Abecedarian Project is too far from completion. However, two generic types of analyses are anticipated and we will mention them briefly. The first type will involve a more thorough comparison of the fate of the high-risk families relative to that of peers from the local community (society in microcosm). This is similar in form to that reported earlier by Ramey, Farran, and Campbell (1979) but expanded to include larger networks of variables. Thus, we have planned a series of analyses based on children's intellectual and adaptive performance through the early elementary school years, with performance at the end of third grade as our criterion. Because most of our children are not yet that old, the analyses cannot be conducted.

A second type of analysis for determining the effects on society must also await the passage of time. However, a brief mention of our general plan may be of interest. We plan an economic cost-benefit analysis of the effects of prevention similar to the one recently and successfully reported by Schweinhart and Weikart (Note 3). We propose to examine employment histories, special educational placements, health system use-patterns, grade retention, and other relevant variables to determine what, if any, return on the financial investment of preventive services is reaped by the taxpayer. Even preliminary analyses, however, are at least several years in the future.

### SUMMARY

Having reviewed the empirical data from the Abecedarian Project in relation to the General Systems Model, we now want to return to a consideration of the model and its implications for further research. Specifically, we will organize our thinking around the main constructs of the model, namely: the emergent principle; levels of analysis; range of stability; regulatory mechanisms; and the concept of an active organism. We will conclude our summary with a brief discussion of ontogenetic processes.

## The Emergent Principle

Development is multiply determined by transactions among many variables. To understand the development of real children, we must go beyond typical laboratory experiments which investigate whether given variables *can* have an influence on developmental outcome and determine if that variable is typically active in ecologically important ways (McCall, 1977). It is unlikely that an adequate understanding of developmental retardation will emerge from theoretical systems that stress the primacy of single factors. As our data illustrate, the associative paths of active variables are complex and dynamic. For example, the provision of daycare has affected children's cognitive, linguistic, social, and affective development. It is also implicated in changes in parental education and income which are time-honored predictors of child performance in school. Thus, developmental daycare has at least partially restructured the network of influences which impinge upon the child's daily life. The synergistic outcomes of transacting units are not easy to anticipate. Gestalt principles of perception indicate that the whole is greater than the sum of the parts. If this is true of a psychological process like perception, can it be any less true of the more complicated social mechanisms implicated in developmental retardation? The central issue is whether the system is too complex to permit adequate prediction and ultimate therapeutic control. We find optimism and direction by fixing the criterion performance (developmental retardation) and examining the forces that are related to it.

A corollary of the emergent principle is that unintended consequences, or ripple effects, will result from changes in the system. Several of our findings suggest that such processes have indeed occurred. The most notable example is that the mothers of children in daycare have been able to continue with their education, the implication being that the Abecedarian Project was indirectly able to foster a supportive home environment. We envision additional studies that would focus on such ripple effects as the health of the children, aggressiveness with peers, and changes in the attitudes and socioeconomic status of the family. By ferreting out positive and negative unintended consequences, we will be better able to determine the cost-effectiveness of our own program, and forewarn other intervention efforts about the pitfalls of modifying a dynamic system.

## Levels of Analysis

Bronfenbrenner's (1977) concept of the ecology of human development argues that effects on development spring from a hierarchy of embedded levels. Our lev-

els of analysis borrow heavily from this concept and so needs little further explica-
tion. There are three implications of this idea that merit a parting comment. First,
a condition like developmental retardation that is caused by processes occurring
within and between levels demands a concerted, multidisciplinary approach. We
know from our own work that clear contributions to preventing mild mental retardation can be made by disciplines as diverse as bacteriology and anthropology.
The level of analysis and the questions being asked will determine the choice of
disciplinary approach. Second, prevention efforts can be targeted at any one level,
or at a combination of levels. Previous research (Bronfenbrenner, 1975) would
suggest that a combination of approaches would be the most effective, although
this is an empirical issue. Finally, the design of future programs—and analysis of
the data that result—must take the level of analysis into account. As Miller (1978)
has pointed out, misleading conclusions about causation can result unless consideration is given to analyses of the data at the appropriate level. Echoing
Bronfenbrenner (1977), perhaps the most useful function of this concept is that it
makes us aware of the intricacies of developmental processes.

### Range of Stability

In a living system, each unit is assumed to operate within a given range of stability. Furthermore, this range of stability is a function of inherent constraints
(e.g., the genotype of the child; the income of the family), as well as learned behavior patterns that allow the organism to adapt to changing circumstances. An
older child or one reared in an enriched environment should have a range of stability that exceeds that of a young or deprived child. At another level of analysis, a
well-to-do family living in a stable, friendly atmosphere should be more able to
cope with stress than a poor family living in a fragmented, tough neighborhood. In
general, the more isolated the component of the system is from other elements,
and the fewer strategies and resources it has at its disposal, the more it is at-risk for
pathology and dysfunction.

The Abecedarian Project was designed with a range of stability principle in
mind, although we didn't call it that in 1971. Specifically, a High-Risk Index was
used to identify infants at-risk for mild mental retardation. This Index (see Ramey
& Smith, 1977) contains variables related to sibling status, parental intelligence,
and family resources. Implicit in the notion of a threshold score on this scale is that
it is a point where the range of stability for the family has been exceeded such that
the development of the child is imperiled. Thus, risk status can be construed as a
measure of the limits of stability.

Intervention programs based on the concept of risk status can also be couched
in terms of the range of stability. The Abecedarian Project was designed with two
goals in mind: (1) to teach the child those skills that are prerequisite to success in
society in general and the schools in particular, and (2) to insure that the family
had at least the minimal resources of nutrition, medical care, and social services

for the child. In the first case, our goal was to teach the children how to *adapt* to stress, instead of succumbing to a fate of retardation and further poverty, or redefining the "range of stability" (e.g., lowered expectations and self-concept). It is too early to tell whether or not we have been completely successful in achieving this aim, but the IQ results (Ramey & Haskins, 1981b; 1981c; Ramey & Campbell, 1979a) and the data on self-concept (Newman & Ramey, Note 15) are encouraging. As far as stress on the family is concerned, the daycare program seems to have given the family a chance to marshal its resources and to remain within a range of stability (Ramey, Dorval & Baker-Ward, in press). This may be due to the combined effects of support services and the freedom from full-time child care that permitted a return to work or school. While information on this outcome of daycare is sparse, the Abecedarian Project seems to have been successful in assisting the family, as well as the child.

In sum, the range of stability is a concept that was used by the Abecedarian Project to *identify* infants at-risk and to *teach* these children how to adapt to stress. Broadly conceived, the goal of the intervention program was to expand the range of stability of the child by fostering adaptive skills and, secondarily, to alleviate some of the stress on the family through social services and time away from caregiving.

### Regulatory Mechanisms

The regulation of behavior and devleopment is a concept that is simple to convey yet difficult to study. Perhaps one reason for this is that continuous adaptation to the environment (or to a genotypic "blueprint"—see Tanner, 1963) makes intuitive sense. In order to study cybernetic processes, though, one must examine a system gone awry, as is the case with deprivation or prenatal insult, or study behavior at a molecular level. Two examples from the Abecedarian Project will serve to illustrate regulatory processes in development and behavior.

Effectance motivation is a term that has been used to explain an organism's efforts to affect and master the environment (White, 1959). Research on effectance motivation suggests that exposure to an unresponsive environment can have adverse effects on development, while experience with response-controlled stimuli can facilitate social and intellectual growth (Seligman & Maier, 1967; Wachs, Uzgiris & Hunt, 1971). Thus, effectance motivation is a product of previous experience and, in turn, serves to structure and guide succeeding transactions with the environment. As such, it can be thought of as a mechanism that regulates development through feedback and change.

Finkelstein and Ramey (1977), in a series of three experiments, attempted to tease out the process by which experience with controllable stimulation influences effectance motivation. They concluded that changes in attention to response performance may be the mediating variable. In other words, infants who transferred training to later trials had learned self-monitoring strategies such that "infants who received prior experience learning to control stimulation were subsequently better able to determine the relation between their behaviors and environmental events'' (p. 818). In a related vein, two studies of attentional strategies revealed significant differences between the Abecedarian daycare and control groups. MacPhee and Ramey (Note 9) studied infants through the second year and found significant differences in task orientation by 18 months. Finkelstein, Gallagher, and Farran (1980), studying 3- and 4-year-olds in both high-risk groups and in the GPS sample, found significant differences 'between the daycare and control groups in auditory perception and language ability. Both groups, however, fared less well than more advantaged children in attention to complex or demanding stimuli. Thus, there is some evidence for the effects of a responsive environment (daycare) on attention deployment, but the results are not conclusive.

At a more molecular level, studies of social interactions have found that behavior is the product of mutual regulation between the actors, whether the dyad consists of peers (Patterson, 1974) or caregiver and infant (Fogel, 1977; Bakeman & Brown, 1977). Bell (1968, 1971) has termed this process bidirectionality of effects, stating that an individual's behavior in an interactive setting is *co-determined* by both partners. A study from the Abecedarian Project illustrates this regulatory mechanism. As mentioned in previous sections, Farran and Haskins (1980) studied mother-child dyads from the high-risk and GPS samples. Important to the present discussion is their finding that, although the *quantity* of interaction differed between groups, the interactive *processes* of turn-taking did not. Although the overall duration of mutual play, for example, was longer in the GPS sample, the use of behaviors that modified ongoing activity did not differ.

In summary, we have argued that certain processes regulate development and behavior. While out list certainly is short and incomplete, this does not imply that regulatory mechanisms are unimportant. To the contrary, it is our fervent hope that more attention is directed to the study of these processes. For instance, there is a need for more information on how motivation (to control) fuels ability (to adapt). There is a need to find out which regulatory mechanisms do not develop or are interfered with in children reared in poverty. While this lament is nothing new, it is worth repeating that effective prevention of psychosocial retardation will occur only when the relevant developmental processes are understood.

### The Active Organism

One of the principles of General Systems Theory is that the organism is active rather than reactive. While this is really nothing more than a philosophical assertion, there is some evidence to support it. The burgeoning literature on early competencies, reviewed by Appleton, Clifton, and Goldberg (1975), suggests that neonates come equipped with the means to elicit responses from the environment. Similarly, research on caregiver-infant interactions has found that even young infants actively modify the course of a social exchange (cf. Bell & Harper, 1977; Lewis & Rosenblum, 1974).

The primary implication of this principle is that an active organism constantly adapts to the environment while modifying it (Sameroff, 1975). In a nonsupportive environment, we might expect the most active infants to be less vulnerable to deprivation (Schaffer, 1966). Even so, as research on learned helplessness (Seligman & Maier, 1967) and effectance motivation (Finkelstein & Ramey, 1977) has shown, an active organism reared in an unresponsive or non-contingent environment may be adversely affected. Evidence for both hypotheses can be found in the MacPhee and Ramey (Note 9) paper in which it was found that: (1) daycare caused a change in the infant's demand characteristics, (2) infants classified as easy (more cooperative, task oriented, sociable, and moderately active) fared better in low-income homes than difficult infants, and (3) without the benefit of daycare, the IQ scores of difficult *and* easy infants declined. The moral of this principle seems to be that acting upon the environment may incur some benefits, perhaps through increased stimulation, but it does not insure adequate development.

## Ontogenetic Processes

The Abecedarian Project was specifically designed to alter the course of development in children of low-income families. Several general comments about our success in this endeavor can be made at this point.

*Transactional Processes.* The General Systems Model views an outcome as the product of interactions among many variables. Coupled with Sameroff's (1975) Transactional Model, this would lead us to conclude that development is not simply the result of a poor environment, nor of an inferior or dysfunctional organism. Rather, each can be viewed as multivariate or multilevel components that constantly modify each other. A number of results from the Abecedarian Project demonstrate that there is no such equation as "Child History = Child Outcome," nor "Caregiver History = Child Outcome," nor "Family Characteristics = Child Outcome." The results from the fetal malnutrition research (Zeskind & Ramey, 1978; 1981) and the infant temperament research (MacPhee & Ramey, Note 9) show that child IQ scores are jointly determined by infant variables and by the presence or absence of a supportive environment. Ramey and Haskins (1981b; 1981c) reached the same conclusion when they found that child-mother IQ correlations in the control group were correctly predicted by a polygenetic model of intelligence, but were not significantly different from zero in the daycare group. Clearly, when asking whether organismic *or* environmental variables determine developmental outcome, one can only reply, "Neither of the above . . . both do."

*Paths Versus Levels.* One intriguing and important justification for a process approach to development is that a given outcome may be the product of different paths or different levels of functioning. During the 1960's, the prevailing attitude was that low-income children needed *more* education and *more* environmental stimulation to overcome the effects of their "impoverished" surroundings (cf. Zigler & Valentine, 1979). Research on maternal teaching styles (Hess & Shipman, 1966; 1968), dialect (Baratz & Baratz, 1970), and the characteristics of the home environment (Wachs, Uzgiris & Hunt, 1971) gradually led to the realization that there is a sociocultural *difference* between members of different socioeconomic strata. Therefore, different paths, as well as levels of development, may be followed.

Some findings from the Abecedarian Project illustrate this concept. Ramey and Campbell (1981) regressed a number of predictor variables onto 60-month WPPSI IQ scores and found that different predictors entered the daycare and control group equations. In addition, recall that there were absolute differences in IQ at this age, suggesting that different paths were taken to different end points. The Farran and Haskins (1980) paper suggests that the same processes of dyadic interaction can occur concurrent with differences in the amount of mutual activity. We would hope that more investigators pursue such a course, whether it involves the longitudinal study of developmental processes or the more immediate determinants of behavior.

**Plasticity.** Plasticity in development can be defined as the ability to be molded or changed by circumstances. Several processes may act to constrain the plasticity of development, including learning and genetic limitations, such that there is a range of reaction for a given phenotype (cf. Waddington, 1962). The plasticity of development has several crucial implications for intervention programs, most notably for when intervention begins (*timing*) and for the prognosis once intervention ceases (*reversibility*). Results from the Abecedarian Project suggest that intervention should be implemented before 18 months of age, if one is to *prevent* (as opposed to ameliorate) developmental retardation. Analyses of our IQ data typically find no differences between groups through 12 months (Figure 2); by 18 months, though, the paths diverge as the control group begins to decline in performance. It could be the case that infant development to this point is so preprogrammed or canalized (Waddington, 1962) that change due to environmental press is not feasible. Rather than "blaming the infant" for not being responsive to daycare, we could ask whether the IQ tests being used are truly sensitive to group differences. In fact, the Bayley Scales are heavily weighted with motor items, while the Abecedarian curriculum has focused on linguistic, cognitive and social development. In reality, some combination of canalization (cf. Gesell & Thompson, 1934) and test limitations may explain our findings more accurately. In any event, further research on the malleability of early development (and ways to accurately measure it) will be needed before a definitive conclusion on the timing of intervention can be reached.

We can only speculate at this point about the prognosis for the Abecedarian children, once they have completed the preschool program. Results through 42 months on the McCarthy Scales (Ramey & Campbell, 1979) and through 60 months on the Stanford-Binet (Ramey & Haskins, 1981c) are encouraging but, as of yet, tell us little about their progress in school. Although there is a great deal of plasticity even at this age (e.g., Bronfenbrenner, 1975; Clarke & Clarke, 1976; Kagan, Klein, Finley, Rogoff, & Nolan, 1979), we hope that by providing the children with the cognitive and social skills needed for competing in school, we have been able to give them a chance of success in later life.

## CONCLUSION

The final issues on which we would like to comment have less to do with scientific questions than with ones of ethical responsibility. As scientists, we cannot let ourselves lose sight of the fact that we are dealing with human participants. While we make the assumption that intervention efforts are potentially worthwhile, the fact remains that our knowledge is limited. The range of possible effects of intervention efforts is immense, and some outcomes may fail to be beneficial for those involved. In many ways, intervention programs carry along with them sets of cultural and social values, usually implicit, that may be at odds with the values of program participants. To paraphrase Harriet Rheingold (1976) and Edward Zigler (in press), we must be careful.

The state of limited knowledge presents several difficulties. The foremost of these is the possible unintended negative consequences of intervention. In preventive efforts, children are necessarily selected as being at-risk for developmental retardation. The long-term effects that the label *at-risk* might have on a child's development are unclear but potentially harmful (Mercer, 1977). While more recent findings have indicated that daycare programs may not be harmful and may even be beneficial (Etaugh, 1980; Belsky & Steinberg, 1978), most of that research has focused on high-quality, experimental-type programs. Little is known about the effects of lesser quality programs.

Of course, unintended positive consequences can also occur. Gilmer, Miller, and Gray (1970), for example, found that the addition of parent participation in their preschool program apparently produced benefits for the younger siblings of the participating child, a phenomenon now termed *vertical diffusion*. An unexpected finding of the Abecedarian Project is that mothers of children in the experimental program are more likely to find productive employment and to resume their schooling than mothers of children in the control group. If programs have positive consequences, however, the scientist faces another dilemma. That is, if preventive efforts work, then the continued random assignment of children into experimental and control groups must be questioned. As Hunt (Note 18) has so cogently noted, the needs of science and the demands of social responsibility can quickly come into conflict. The potential for negative and positive consequences of preventive efforts, then, is a two-edged sword.

An even larger set of ethical questions arises when one examines the social and cultural implications of intervention efforts. While intervention programs are not forced upon unwilling participants, programs still almost inevitably introduce a strong influence into a child's home and general enviroment and have implicit sets of values that may conflict with those within the home. While the influence of these conflicts on the results of any given effort is an important question (Stedman et al., Note 4), perhaps a larger question surrounds the ethical implications of introducing implicit cultural and social values to relatively unsuspecting families. The influence of large-scale, intense, preventive efforts may be an invasion of privacy that is relatively unwarranted, given our present state of knowledge (Wallach & Wallach, 1976). As responsible social agents, applied scientists cannot lay claim to the proposition that science is a value-free enterprise. Sensitivity toward and respect for the children and their families is a necessity.

### Directions for the Future

It is obvious that the issues involved in preventing developmental retardation are numerous and important. They deserve and must receive thoughtful scrutiny. We think that among the many unresolved issues in preventing developmental retardation, four are particularly important and deserve high places on our research agendas. First, there is a need for more effective and efficient means of identifying high-risk children. Second, there is a need for continuing research into the cost-effectiveness of program variables such as intensity, duration, age of entry, and format. Third, there is a need for more sophisticated measurements of adaptive behaviors. Finally, there is a need for long-term follow-up of treated children to determine the full impact of preventive efforts. It is our hope that General Systems Theory will guide our interdisciplinary, longitudinal inquiry along the winding empirical paths to greater knowledge about preventing development gone awry.

### REFERENCE NOTES

1. Begab, M. *Issues in the prevention of psychosocial retardation.* Paper presented at a colloquium at the University of North Carolina Mental Retardation Center on Issues in the Prevention of Psychosocial Retardation, Chapel Hill, December, 1978.
2. Frankenburg, W. K., Coons, C. E., van Doorninck, W. J., Goldstein, E. A., Berrenberg, J., & Moriarty, K. R. *Evaluation of the home environment using a self-administered questionnaire.* Paper presented at the biennial meeting of the Society for Research in Child Development, New Orleans, LA, March 1977.
3. Schweinhart, L., & Weikart, D. P. Perry Preschool effects nine years later: What do they mean? Paper presented at a conference on the Prevention of Retarded Development in Psychosocially Disadvantaged Children, Madison, WI, July 1978.
4. Stedman, D. J., Anastasiow, N. J., Dokecki, P. R., Gordon, I. J., & Parker, R. K. *How can effective early intervention programs be delivered to potentially retarded children?* A report for the Office of the Secretary of the Department of Health, Education and Welfare, October 1972.
5. Haskins, R., Walden, T., & Ramey, C. T. *The effects of ability grouping on teacher and student behavior.* Unpublished manuscript, University of North Carolina, 1980.

6. Ramey, C. T., & Mills, P. J. *Mother-infant interaction patterns as a function of rearing conditions.* Paper presented at the biennial meeting of the Society for Research in Child Development, Denver, March 1975.
7. Ramey, C. T., & Dempsey, H. *Social services received by cohorts I and II.* Unpublished document, University of North Carolina, 1979.
8. Ramey, C. T., & Dubinsky, S. *Incidence of illness by cohort.* Unpublished document, University of North Carolina, 1979.
9. MacPhee, D., & Ramey, C. T. *Infant temperament as a catalyst and consequence of development in two caregiving environments.* Unpublished manuscript, University of North Carolina, 1980.
10. Finkelstein, N. W., & Wilson, K. *The influence of daycare on social behaviors towards peers and adults.* Symposium paper presented at the biennial meeting of the Society for Research in Child Development, New Orleans, LA, March 1977.
11. Gordon, A. M., & Feagans, L. *Assessing the effects of systematic daycare on the language development of high-risk children.* Paper presented at the biennial meeting of the Society for Research in Child Development, New Orleans, LA, March 1977.
12. Caldwell, B., Heider, J., & Kaplan, B. *The inventory of home stimulation.* Paper presented at the annual meeting of the American Psychological Association, New York, September 1966.
13. O'Connell, J., & Farran, D. C. *The effects of daycare intervention on the use of intentional communicative behaviors in socioeconomically depressed infants.* Paper presented at the Sixth Biennial Southeastern Conference on Human Development, Alexandria, VA, April 1980.
14. Farran, D. C., & Haskins, R. *Reciprocal control in social interactions of mothers and three-year-old children.* Paper presented at the biennial meeting of the Society for Research in Child Development, New Orleans, LA, March 1977.
15. Newman, L., & Ramey, C. T. *Maternal attitudes and child development in high-risk families.* Paper presented at the annual meeting of the American Psychological Association, New York, August 1979.
16. Cicarelli, V. G. *The Purdue self-concept scale for preschool children: Norms-technical manual.* Prepared for the Office of Child Development, pursuant to Contract 50037.
17. Ramey, C. T., & Brownlee, J. R. *Improving the identification of high-risk infants.* Paper presented at the Gatlinburg Conference on Research in Mental Retardation, Gatlinburg, TN, May 1980.
18. Hunt, J. McV. *Concepts and factors important for infant education.* Colloquium presentation at the University of North Carolina, Chapel Hill, NC, April 1980.

## REFERENCES

Adams, J., & Ramey, C. T. Structural aspects of maternal speech to infants reared in poverty. *Child Development,* 1980, *51,* 1280–1284.
Appleton, T., Clifton, R., & Goldberg, S. The development of behavioral competence in infancy. In F. D. Horowitz (Ed.), *Review of child development research* (Vol. 4). Chicago, IL: University of Chicago Press, 1975.
Bakeman, R., & Brown, J. V. Behavioral dialogues: An approach to the assessment of mother-infant interaction. *Child Development,* 1977, *48,* 195–203.
Baratz, S. S., & Baratz, J. C. Early childhood intervention: The social science base of institutional racism. *Harvard Educational Review,* 1970, *40,* 29–50.
Baroff, G. S. *Mental retardation: Nature, cause, and management.* Washington, DC: Hemisphere Publishing Corp., 1974.
Baumrind, D., & Black, A. E. Socialization patterns associated with dimensions of competence in preschool boys and girls. *Child Development,* 1967, *38,* 291–327.

Bayley, N. Comparisons of mental and motor test scores for ages 1–15 months by sex, birth order, race, geographic location, and education of parents. *Child Development*, 1965, *36*, 379–412.

Begab, M. (Ed.) *Psychosocial influences and retarded performance: Strategies for improving social competence* (Vol. 2). Baltimore, MD: University Park Press, 1981.

Bell, R. Q. A reinterpretation of the direction of effects in studies of socialization. *Psychological Review*, 1968, *75*, 81–95.

Bell, R. Q. Stimulus control of parent or caretaker behavior by offspring. *Developmental Psychology*, 1971, *4*, 63–72.

Bell, R. Q., & Harper, L. V. *Child effects on adults*. Hillsdale, NJ: Lawrence Erlbaum Associates, 1977.

Belsky, J. Child maltreatment: An ecological integration. *American Psychologist*, 1980, *35*, 320–335.

Belsky, J., & Steinberg, L. D. The effects of daycare: A critical review. *Child Development*, 1978, *49*, 929–949.

Bernstein, B. B. *Primary socialization, language and education*. London: Routledge & K. Paul, 1970.

Bertalanffy, L. V. *Perspectives on general system theory*. New York: George Braziller, 1975.

Birch, H. G., & Gussow, J. D. *Disadvantaged children: Health, nutrition, and school failure*. New York: Grune & Stratton, 1970.

Birch, H. G., Richardson, S. A., Baird, D., Horobin, G., & Illsley, R. *Mental subnormality in the community: A clinical and epidemiologic study*. Baltimore, MD: The Williams & Wilkins Co., 1970.

Blank, M. *Teaching learning in the preschool: A dialogue approach*. Columbus, OH: Charles E. Merrill Publishing, 1973.

Bronfenbrenner, U. Is early intervention effective? In M. Guttentag & E. L. Struening (Eds.), *Handbook of evaluation research* (Vol. 2). Beverly Hills, CA: Sage Publications, 1975.

Bronfenbrenner, U. Toward an experimental ecology of human development. *American Psychologist*, 1977, *32*, 513–531.

Brooks, P. H., & Baumeister, A. A. A plea for consideration of ecological validity in the experimental psychology of mental retardation. *American Journal of Mental Deficiency*, 1977, *81*, 407–416.

Buss, A. H., & Plomin, R. *A temperament theory of personality development*. New York: Wiley, 1975.

Clarke, A. M., & Clarke, A. D. B. *Early experience: Myth and evidence*. London: Open Books, 1976.

Clarke-Stewart, A. K., VanderStoep, L. P., & Killian, G. A. Analysis and replication of mother-child relations at two years of age. *Child Development*, 1979, *50*, 777–793.

Cronbach, L. J., & Furby, L. How should we measure "change"—or should we? *Psychological Bulletin*, 1970, *74*, 68–80.

Davis, D. E. *My friends and me*. Circle Pines, MN: American Guidance Service, 1977.

Denenberg, V. In L. A. Bond & J. M. Joffe (Eds.), *Facilitating infant and early childhood development*, in press.

Dunn, L. M., Chun, L. T., Crowell, D. C., Dunn, L. G., Avery, L. G., & Yachel, E. R. *Peabody Early Education Kit*. Circle Pines, MN: American Guidance Service, 1976.

Elardo, R., Bradley, R., & Caldwell, B. The relation of infants' home environments to mental test performance from six to thirty-six months: A longitudinal analysis. *Child Development*, 1975, *46*, 71–76.

Elkind, D. Piagetian and psychometric conceptions of intelligence. *Harvard Educational Review*, 1969, *39*, 319–337.

Emmerich, W. The parental role: A functional cognitive approach. *Monographs of the Society for Research in Child Development*, 1969, *34*, (Whole No. 8).

Etaugh, C. Effects of nonmaternal care on children: Research evidence and popular views. *American Psychologist*, 1980, *35*, 309–319.

Farran, D. C., & Haskins, R. T.  Reciprocal influence in the social interactions of mothers and three-year-old children from different socioeconomic backgrounds. *Child Development*, 1980, *51*, 780–791.

Farran, D. C., & Ramey, C. T.  Infant daycare and attachment behaviors towards mothers and teachers. *Child Development*, 1977, *48*, 1112–1116.

Farran, D. C., & Ramey, C. T.  Social class differences in dyadic involvement during infancy. *Child Development*, 1980, *51*, 254–257.

Finkelstein, N. W., Gallagher, J. J., & Farran, D. C.  Attentiveness and responsiveness to auditory stimuli of children at risk for mental retardation. *American Journal of Mental Deficiency*, 1980, *85*, 135–144.

Finkelstein, N. W., & Ramey, C. T.  Learning to control the environment in infancy. *Child Development*, 1977, *48*, 806–819.

Finkelstein, N. W., & Ramey, C. T.  Information from birth certificate data as a risk index for school failure. *American Journal of Mental Deficiency*, 1980, *84*, 546–552.

Fogel, A.  Temporal organization in mother-infant face-to-face interaction. In H. R. Schaffer (Ed.), *Studies in mother-infant interaction*. New York: Academic Press, 1977.

Gallagher, J. J., Ramey, C. T., Haskins, R., & Finkelstein, N. W.  The use of longitudinal research in the study of child development. In T. Tjossem (Ed.), *Intervention strategies for high-risk infants and young children*. Baltimore, MD: University Park Press, 1976.

Garber, H., & Heber, F. R.  The Milwaukee Project: Indications of the effectiveness of early intervention in preventing mental retardation. In P. Mittler (Ed.), *Research to practice in mental retardation: Care and intervention*. (Vol. 1). Baltimore, MD: University Park Press, 1977.

Garmezy, N.  Vulnerability research and the issue of primary prevention. *American Journal of Orthopsychiatry*, 1971, *41*, 101–116.

Gesell, A. L., & Thompson, H.  *Infant behavior: Its genesis and growth*. New York: McGraw-Hill, 1934.

Gilmer, B., Miller, J. O., & Gray, S.  *Intervention with mothers and young children: A study of intrafamily effects*. Nashville, TN: DARCEE Papers and Reports, 1970, *4*(11).

Gottlieb, G.  Conceptions of prenatal development. *Psychological Review*, 1976, *83*, 215–234.

Greenberg, P., & Epstein, B.  *Bridges to reading*. Morristown, NJ: General Learning Corp., 1973.

Grossman, H. J. (Ed.)  *Manual on terminology and classification in mental retardation*, 1973 Revision. American Association on Mental Deficiency. Special Publication Series No. 2, 1973.

Harms, T., & Cross, L.  *Environmental provisions in daycare*. Chapel Hill, NC: DayCare Training and Technical Assistance system, 1978.

Harper, L. V.  The young as a source of stimuli controlling caretaker behavior. *Developmental Psychology*, 1971, *4*, 73–88.

Heber, F. R., Dever, R. B., & Conry, J.  The influence of environmental and genetic variables on intellectual development. In H. Prehm, L. A. Hamerlynck, & J. E. Crosson (Eds.), *Behavioral research in mental retardation*. Eugene, OR: University of Oregon, 1968.

Hess, R. D., & Shipman, V. C.  Early experience and the socialization of cognitive modes in children. *Child Development*, 1965, *34*, 869–886.

Hess, R. D., & Shipman, V. C.  Maternal influences upon early learning: The cognitive environment of urban preschool children. In R. D. Hess & R. M. Bear (Eds.), *Early education*. Chicago, IL: Aldine, 1966.

Hess, R. D., & Shipman, V. C.  Maternal attitudes toward the school and the role of the pupil: Some social class comparisons. In A. H. Passow (Ed.), *Developing programs for the educationally disadvantaged*. New York: Teachers College, Columbia University, 1968.

Jensen, A. R.  How much can we boost IQ and scholastic achievement? *Harvard Educational Review*, 1969, *39*, 1–123.

Jensen, A. R.  Raising the IQ: The Ramey and Haskins study. *Intelligence 6*, (3) to appear.

*Kagan, J., Kearsley, R. B., & Zelazo, P. R.  Infancy: Its place in human development*. Cambridge, MA: Harvard University Press, 1978.

Kagan, J., Klein, R. E., Finley, G. E., Rogoff, B., & Nolan, E. A cross-cultural study of cognitive development. *Monographs of the Society for Research in Child Development,* 1979, *44* (Whole No. 180).

Kagan, J., & Moss, H. A. *From birth to maturity.* New York: Wiley, 1962.

Karnes, M. B. *GOAL Program: Mathematical concepts.* Springfield, MA: Melton-Bradley, 1973.

Klaus, R., & Gray, S. The early training project for disadvantaged children: A report after five years. *Monographs of the Society for Research in Child Development,* 1968, *33* (Whole No. 120).

Knobloch, H., & Pasamanick, B. Further observation on the behavioral development of Negro children. *Journal of Genetic Psychology,* 1953, *83,* 137–157.

Kuhn, T. S. *The structure of scientific revolutions.* Chicago, IL: University of Chicago Press, 1962.

Lazar, I., & Darlington, R. (Eds.). *Lasting effects after preschool.* Final report, HEW Grant 90C-1311 to the Education Commission of the States, 1978.

Lewis, M., & Goldberg, S. Perceptual-cognitive development in infancy: A generalized expectancy model as a function of mother-infant interaction. *Merrill-Palmer Quarterly,* 1969, *15,* 81–100.

Lewis, M., & Rosenblum, L. A. (Eds.). *The effect of the infant on its caregiver.* New York: Wiley, 1974.

Lewis, M., & Wilson, C. D. Infant development in lower-class American families. *Human Development,* 1972, *15,* 112–127.

Mann, A., Harrell, A., & Hunt, M., Jr. *A review of Head Start research since 1969.* Washington DC: Social Research Group, George Washington University, 1976.

McCall, R. B. Challenges to a science of developmental psychology. *Child Development,* 1977, *48,* 333–344.

McCarthy, D. *McCarthy Scales of Children's Abilities.* New York: Psychological Corp, 1972.

McClearn, G., & De Fries, J. *Introduction to behavioral genetics.* San Francisco, CA: W. H. Freeman, Co., 1973.

McClelland, D. C. Testing for competence rather than for "intelligence". *American Psychologist,* 1973, *28,* 1–14.

Meehl, P. E. Schizotaxia, schizotypy, schizophrenia. *American Psychologist,* 1962, *17,* 827–838.

Mercer, J. R. Cultural diversity, mental retardation and assessment: The case for non-labeling. In P. Mittler (Ed.), *Research to practice in mental retardation: Care and intervention* (Vol. 1). Baltimore, MD: University Park Press, 1977.

Miller, J. G. *Living systems.* New York: McGraw-Hill, 1978.

Ogbu, J. V. *Minority education and caste: The American system in cross-cultural perspective.* New York: Academic Press, 1978.

Parmelee, A. H., Kopp, C. B., & Sigman, M. Selection of developmental assessment techniques for infants at risk. *Merrill-Palmer Quarterly,* 1976, *22,* 177–199.

Parmelee, A. H., & Michaelis, R. Neurological examination of the newborn. In J. Hellmuth (Ed.), *Exceptional infant; Studies in abnormalities* (Vol. 2). New York: Brunner/Mazel, 1971.

Patterson, G. R. A basis for identifying stimuli which control behaviors in natural settings. *Child Development,* 1974, *45,* 900–911.

Ramey, C. T., & Campbell, F. A. Compensatory education for disadvantaged children. *School Review,* 1979, *82,* 171–189. (a)

Ramey, C. T., & Campbell, F. A. Early childhood education for psychosocially disadvantaged children: The effects on psychological processes. *American Journal of Mental Deficiency,* 1979, *83,* 645–648. (b)

Ramey, C. T., & Campbell, F. A. Educational intervention for children at risk for mild retardation: A longitudinal analysis. In P. Mittler (Ed.), *Frontiers of knowledge in mental retardation: Volume I.* Baltimore, MD: University Park Press, 1981. 47–57.

Ramey, C. T., Dorval, B., & Baker-Ward, L. Group daycare and socially disadvantaged families: Effects on the child and the family. In S. Kilmer (Ed.), *Advances in early education and daycare.* Greenwich, CT: JAI Press, in press.

Ramey, C. T., & Farran, D. C. Functional concern of mothers for their infants. *Infant Mental Health Journal*, 1981, *1*, 48–55.

Ramey, C. T., Farran, D. C., & Campbell, F. A. Predicting IQ from mother-infant interactions. *Child Development*, 1979, *50*, 804–814.

Ramey, C. T., Farran, D. C., Campbell, F. A., & Finkelstein, N. W. Observations of mother-infant interactions: Implications for development. In F. D. Minifie & L. L. Lloyd (Eds.), *Community and cognitive abilities: Early behavioral assessment*. Baltimore, MD: University Park Press, 1978.

Ramey, C. T., & Finkelstein, N. W. Contingent stimulation and infant competence. *Journal of Pediatric Psychology*, 1978, *3*, 89–96.

Ramey, C. T., & Finkelstein, N. W. Psychosocial mental retardation: A biological and social coalescence. In M. Begab (Ed.), *Psychosocial influences and retarded performance: Strategies for improving social competence* (Vol. 1). Baltimore, MD: University Park Press, 1981.

Ramey, C. T., & Gallagher, J. J. The nature of cultural deprivation: Theoretical issues and suggested research strategies. *North Carolina Journal of Mental Health*, 1975, *7*, 41–47.

Ramey, C. T., & Haskins, R. The causes and treatment of school failure: Insights from the Carolina Abecedarian Project. In M. Begab, H. Garber, & H. C. Haywood (Eds.), *Causes and prevention of retarded development in psychosocially disadvantaged children*. Baltimore, MD: University Park Press, 1981, (a)

Ramey, C. T., & Haskins, R. The modification of intelligence through early experience. *Intelligence*, 1981, *5*, 5–19 (b)

Ramey, C. T., & Haskins, R. Early education, intellectual development, and school performance: A reply to Arthur Jensen and J. McV. Hunt. *Intelligence*, 1981, *5*, 41–48. (c)

Ramey, C. T., McGinness, G. D., Cross, L., Collier, A. M., & Barrie-Blackley, S. The Abecedarian approach to social competence: Cognitive and linguistic intervention for disadvantaged preschoolers. In K. Borman (Ed.), *Socialization of the child in a changing society*. Elmsford, NY: Pergamon Press, 1981.

Ramey, C. T., & Mills, P. J. Social and intellectual consequences of daycare for high-risk infants. In R. Webb (Ed.), *Social development in childhood: Daycare programs and research*. Baltimore, MD: Johns Hopkins University Press, 1977.

Ramey, C. T., Mills, P., Campbell, F. A., & O'Brien, C. Infants' home environments: A comparison of high-risk families and families from the general population. *American Journal of Mental Deficiency*, 1975, *80*, 40–42.

Ramey, C. T., & Smith, B. Assessing the intellectual consequences of early intervention with high-risk infants. *American Journal of Mental Deficiency*, 1977, *81*, 318–324.

Ramey, C. T., Stedman, D. S., Borders-Patterson, A., & Mengel, W. Predicting school failure from information available at birth. *American Journal of Mental Deficiency*, 1978, *82*, 525–534.

Rheingold, H. L. Discussant's comments. In T. Tjossem (Ed.), *Intervention strategies for high-risk infants and young children*. Baltimore, MD: University Park Press, 1976.

Richardson, S. A. Reaction to mental subnormality. In M. J. Begab, & S. A. Richardson (Eds.), *The mentally retarded and society: A social science perspective*. Baltimore, MD: Unviersity Park Press, 1975.

Ricciuti, H. Fear and development of social attachments in the first year of life. In M. Lewis & L. A. Rosenblum (Eds.), *The origin of human behavior: Fear*. New York: Wiley, 1974.

Robinson, H., & Robinson, N. Longitudinal development of very young children in a comprehensive daycare program: The first two years. *Child Development*, 1971, *42*, 1673–1683.

Rothbart, M. K. Laughter in young children. *Psychological Bulletin*, 1973, *80*, 247–256.

Rotter, J. B. Generalized expectancies of internal versus external control of reinforcement. *Psychological Monographs*, 1966, *80*, (Whole No. 609).

Sameroff, A. J. Early influences on development: Fact or fancy? *Merrill-Palmer Quarterly*, 1975, *21*, 267–294.

Sameroff, A. J. The etiology of cognitive competence: A systems perspective. In R. B. Kearsley & I.

E. Siegel (Eds.), *Infants at risk: Assessment of cognitive functioning*. Hillsdale, NJ: Lawrence Erlbaum Associates, 1979.

Sameroff, A. J., & Chandler, M. J. Reproductive risk and the continuum of caretaking casualty. In F. D. Horowitz (Ed.), *Review of child development research* (Vol. 4). Chicago, IL: University of Chicago Press, 1975.

Schaefer, E. S. Development of adaptive behavior: Conceptual models and family correlates. In M. Begab, H. Barger, & H. C. Haywood (Eds.), *Prevention of retarded development in psychosocially disadvantaged children*. Baltimore, MD: University Park Press, 1981.

Schaefer, E. S., & Bell, R. Q. Development of a parent attitude research instrument. *Child Development*, 1958, *29*, 339–361.

Schaffer, H. R. Activity level as a constitutional determinant of infantile reaction to deprivation. *Child Development*, 1966, *37*, 595–602.

Schaffer, H. R., & Emerson, P. E. Patterns of response to physical contact in early human development. *Journal of Child Psychology and Psychiatry*, 1964, *5*, 1–13.

Schneirla, T. C. Behavior development and comparative psychology. *Quarterly Review of Biology*, 1966, *41*, 283–302.

Schwarz, J. C., Strickland, R. G., & Krolick, G. Infant day care: Behavioral effects at preschool age. *Developmental Psychology*, 1974, *10*, 502–506.

Seligman, M. E. P., & Maier, S. F. Failure to escape traumatic shock. *Journal of Experimental Psychology*, 1967, *74*, 1–9.

Sparling, J. J., & Lewis, I. S. *Learningames for the first three years: A guide to parent-child play*. New York: Walker and Co., 1979.

Stein, Z., & Susser, M. The social distribution of mental retardation. *American Journal of Mental Deficiency*, 1963, *67*, 811–821.

Tanner, J. M. The regulation of human growth. *Child Development*, 1963, *34*, 817–847.

Terman, L. M., & Merrill, M. A. *The Stanford-Binet Intelligence Scale*. New York: Houghton Mifflin Co., 1973.

Thomas, A., Birch, H. G., Chess, S., Hertzig, M. E., & Korn, S. *Behavioral individuality in early childhood*. New York: New York University Press, 1963.

Tough, J. *Listening to children talking*. London: Ward Lock Educational, 1976.

Tulkin, S., & Kagan, J. Mother-child interaction in the first year of life. *Child Development*, 1972, *43*, 31–41.

Wachs, T., Uzgiris, I., & Hunt, J. Cognitive development in infants of different age levels and from different environmental backgrounds: An exploratory investigation. *Merrill-Palmer Quarterly*, 1971, *17*, 283–317.

Waddington, C. H. *New patterns in genetics and development*. New York: Columbia University Press, 1962.

Wallach, M. A., & Wallach, L. *Teaching all children to read*. Chicago, IL: University of Chicago Press, 1976.

Watson, J. S., & Ramey, C. T. Reactions to response contingent stimulation early in infancy. *Merrill-Palmer Quarterly*, 1972, *18*, 219–227.

Wechsler, D. *Wechsler Adult Intelligence Scale*. New York: The Psychological Corporation, 1955.

Weikart, D. P. (Ed.). *Preschool Intervention: Preliminary report of the Perry Preschool Project*. Ann Arbor, MI: Campus Publishers, 1967.

Werner, H. *Comparative psychology of mental development*. New York: International University Press, 1957.

White, R. W. Motivation reconsidered: The concept of competence. *Psychological Review*, 1959, *66*, 297–333.

Wolff, P. H. The causes, controls, and organization of behavior in the neonate. *Psychological Issues*, 1966, *5* (No. 1).

Yarrow, L., Rubenstein, J., & Pedersen, F. *Infant and environment: Early cognitive and motivational development*. New York: Halsted, 1973.

Zeskind, P. S. Adult responses to cries of low-risk and high-risk infants. *Infant Behavior and Development,* 1980, *3,* 167–177.

Zeskind, P. S., & Ramey, C. T. Fetal malnutrition: An experimental study of its consequences on infants in two caregiving environments. *Child Development,* 1978, *49,* 1155–1162.

Zeskind, P. S., & Ramey, C. T. Preventing intellectual and interactional sequelae of fetal malnutrition: A longitudinal, transactional and synergistic approach to development. *Child Development,* 1981, *52,* 213–218.

Zigler, E. In L. A. Bond & J. M. Joffe (Eds.), *Facilitating infant and early childhood development,* in press.

Zigler, E., & Trickett, P. K. IQ, social competence and evaluation of early childhood intervention programs. *American Psychologist, 1978, 33,* 789–798.

Zigler, E., & Valentine, J. (Eds.). *Project Head Start: A legacy of the War on Poverty.* New York: Free Press, 1979.

# 4

# *Modification of Predicted Cognitive Development In High-Risk Children Through Early Intervention**

Howard Garber and Rick Heber
*University of Wisconsin*

The children of 40 seriously disadvantaged families were identified and closely followed for 10 years through and after a comprehensive treatment program called the Milwaukee Project. A differential of 20 points in Wechsler IQ found at the end of a preschool program was maintained at the end of fourth grade, indicating that a treatment program for high-risk children can prevent mental retardation. Reexamination of early intellectual, language and problem-solving data suggested sources of influence on IQ performance in addition to the educational treatment program including the mother, siblings, and the child himself. A wide range of within group variation suggests caution in treatment and evaluation of the efficacy of such programs.

The objective of this paper is threefold. First, to review the basis for the hypothesis of our early intervention program (Heber & Garber, 1975) and its general findings to date (Garber & Heber, 1980); second, to suggest the source of other major influences that operate to modify performance levels; third, to show that the range of individual variation in children of severely disadvantaged families is a factor underestimated and is perhaps a far more viable component of the inefficacy of such ventures than has been appreciated heretofore.

Specifically, we are interested in the prevention of mental retardation—a certain kind of mental retardation—a mild form, sometimes called *cultural-familial* or *sociocultural* mental retardation. It has been in many ways at the heart of the social issue about the origins of intelligence. Mild mental retardation refers to individual IQ test performance in the range of 50 to 80, but is more closely defined as the 50–70 range and referred to today as *psychosocial retardation* (Grossman, 1973). We refer to this as cultural-familial retardation because its prevalence is to excess and is most closely associated with seriously disadvantaged subpopulation groups and in those families, especially, where at least one parent and often a sib-

*This research supported in part by Grant 16-P-56811/5-14 from the Social and Rehabilitation Service of the Department of Health, Education and Welfare.

ling are mentally retarded. There is of course some arbitrariness to definition, but the major problem for this category of retardation has been to determine the source of the retardation. Though this category of retardation is the largest—some 3/4 of all individuals ever identified as retarded—it is unlike the lower IQ group of retarded (generally below 50 IQ), the other 25%, where a specific etiologic referent for retardation can be ascertained. In the larger group, although still containing a wide range of individuals, there is no obvious expression of pathology (as in the lower group) which, together with its mildness, has made this form of retardation so resistant to preventive efforts. Such hypotheses as nature-nurture, social deprivation, critical periods, and so on, have been invoked as explanation, but in point of fact up until the middle 1960s, most hypotheses about this category of human behavior were without a substantive empirical base.

Our research effort, known as the Milwaukee Project, attempted to determine whether it is possible to mitigate or prevent predicted intellectual deficits in the offspring of seriously disadvantaged high-risk families by including the low IQ ($\leq 75$) mother in a rehabilitation program and her newborn child (3 months of age) in an early education program. This research differs from other compensatory programs in that its focus was the subject who, in the epidemiological sense, was at the highest risk for mental retardation. In fact, because of severe disadvantagement and a mother whose IQ was below 75, the risk factor for such children ranged as high as 14 times that for a similar child whose mother had an IQ of 100 or more. Second, intervention began in very early infancy and was continuous until school entry. Third, it included components of the family in a rehabilitation program to prevent mental retardation.

In the early 1960s, a field laboratory was established in an inner city area of Milwaukee, identified by U.S. Census Bureau data as the most impoverished, and by public school data which showed this same area contained 33% of the EMR students for the city, but had less than 5% of the population. This area, formed by contiguous census tracts, was surveyed by door-to-door interviews of families with a newborn child and one other child of at least 6 years of age. These extensive survey data from several hundred families ultimately indicated that certain identifiable families produced retarded children at a disproportionate rate from their neighbors. Specifically, we found that the offspring of seriously disadvantaged mothers with IQs below 80 showed a different pattern of intellectual development than did children of above 80 IQ mothers. The children of below 80 IQ mothers undergo a marked decline in IQ performance which begins before school and continues until their mean IQ at maturity (14–16 years of age and beyond) is in the retarded range. This lower mean IQ is accompanied by an increased incidence of below 80 IQs, on the order of 70 to 80%. In contrast, the children of their inner-city neighbor's families, where the maternal IQ was above 80, maintained IQ levels in the normal range. We hypothesized that mitigating negative environmental influences, obviously one being the mother's influence, would permit normal intellectual development. In effect, we intervened into the lives of these families when the child was very young and before he began the highly probable decline in IQ performance, in order to prevent that decline.

We selected a sample of 40 seriously disadvantaged families from this same general area. The families were identified by low maternal IQ of ≤75 (full scale WAIS), all had newborn children within 3 to 6 months of age and with no obvious pathology. Half of these families were assigned Control status; the other half were introduced to a comprehensive program of rehabilitation for the mothers and an education program for the children. The rehabilitation program for the mothers included job training, home management, and remedial education and took place mainly during the first 2 years of the overall program. The preschool program began for each child between 3 and 6 months and continued until 6 years or first grade entry. The program, especially from 2 years on, was a structured educational program with major emphasis on problem-solving and language skills. A full day year-round program included small group directed instruction, large group activities, and even time for choosing activities in a free-flow environment. A teaching staff, mainly paraprofessional, was responsible for each child and for small groups (three to four). The teacher utilized an open-ended questioning approach to teaching, trying to expand beyond the immediate. Two certified teachers were introduced late in the program for teaching reading and mathematics.

The differential development between the children in the Experimental education program and the nontreated Controls has been marked. On the Gesell Developmental Schedules administered between 6 months and 24 months of age, there was a significant difference in the growth of the two groups in favor of the Experimental group. Although growth was reasonably comparable up to 14 months, the Experimental group accelerated and showed rapid developmental growth from there on, while the Control group began to decline. By 22 months of age, the Experimental group was more than 5 months above average in development and the Control group nearly one month below average. Beginning at 2 years of age and continuing until 6 years, the children were tested with the Stanford-Binet (Form L-M) which showed a sustained significant differential in IQ performance in favor of the Experimental group throughout the course of the preschool program. The order of the differential was about 25 IQ points (120 for the Experimental group and 94 for the Control group). Both groups remained fairly stable after some rise for the Experimental and some additional decline for the Control group between 2 and 3 years of age. The differential IQ status of the two groups indicated that treatment was successful in preventing mental retardation in the Experimental group as compared to the untreated Control group, at least until the age of public school entry (72 months).

In addition to the IQ data, we administered numerous other measures of development, which are extremely important in that they both support and extend the differential in intellectual development revealed by the Stanford-Binet IQ data.

We tested the children on a number of experimental learning tasks including a color-form and a probability-matching problem. In these tasks, we could ask questions about the manner of the child's responding—not simply whether or not he responded. Moreover, these tasks gave us a measure of the development of the learning process in a way that increased our understanding of how certain characteristics of early behaviors either facilitate or interfere with cognitive performance. These learning measures were administered each year beginning at 2½ and continuing to the age of 7½ years.

On these learning tasks, the Experimental children began much earlier, as a group, to "work" the problem and showed successively more developmentally sophisticated patterns of responding. On color-form matching, for example, the Experimental children showed an earlier and progressively stronger tendency to prefer dimensionally. The Control children, on the other hand, showed a far greater tendency to perseverative responding, relative insensitivity to reinforcement, and slow growth of strategy-hypothesis behavior.

In spite of the apparent simpleness of the task requirements, there is provided an opportunity to rather powerfully demonstrate the association of early intellectual development with the ability to impose order on the environment. This ability is basic to intellectual development and appears to be a major benefit of early cognitive stimulation, i.e., when we consider the marked difference in approach to problem-solving between Experimental and Control children. Thus, style or strategy responding does develop in the early years and influences later learning. For the Control children, it should interfere with later learning, whereas the style of the Experimental children should facilitate problem-solving.

In addition, extensive data were collected on the children's language behavior. By 22 months of age, the Experimental children's language performance was 6 months ahead of the Control children on the language schedule of the Gesell. Between 18 and 30 months, the Experimental children showed language growth in free speech communication not attained by the Controls on gross features until 36 months. On tests of imitation and comprehension, the Experimental children between 36 and 72 months showed positive language growth superior to the Control children of 1 to 2 full years. Thus, a 6-months superiority in language ability that emerged for the Experimental group in the second year of life increased in subsequent years to a difference of 2 years. These later differences were based on our analysis of the more elaborate and deeper patterns of language behavior which required cognitive skills, such as short-term memory and the comprehension of unique syntactic and semantic structures.

As a group, the Experimental children showed an aptitude for language substantially greater than that of their counterparts in the Control group. The readiness with which they grasped and acquired new linguistic structures appeared to be a manifestation of their readiness to learn structure in general and suggested enhanced awareness of their surroundings and of their ability to express themselves in relation to these surroundings. Perhaps more important, they entered school with the language skills and aptitudes needed for further learning.

We carefully examined the mother-child interaction by using some of the techniques of Hess and Shipman (e.g., 1968). These data showed that mothers, who are themselves poor in cognitive abilities, transfer these skills directly and indirectly to their children. It is the mother's linguistic and her regulatory behavior which induce and shape the information processing strategies and style in her child—and these can act to either enhance or limit further intellectual growth.

In the mother-child interaction, most sophisticated behavior, such as the initiation of problem-solving behavior by verbal clues and verbal prods, or the organization of tasks with respect to goals in problem-solving situations, is done by the mother. But, in the case of these low IQ, low verbal skill mothers, the interaction was more physical, less organized, and less direction was given to the child. Yet, though the mothers in both the Experimental and Control groups were comparable in that neither made spontaneous offerings of help, the Experimental dyads transmitted significantly more information than the Control dyads. How this was possible—even though there was no significant difference between Experimental and Control mothers' teaching ability—can be attributed to the significant difference in quality of the verbal behavior of the children. The Experimental children supplied more information verbally and initiated more verbal communication than in the Control dyads. The children in the Experimental dyads took responsibility for guiding the flow of information, providing most of the verbal information and direction. Thus, in response to the "solicitations" of their children, the Experimental mothers became more responsive, less physical, more verbal, and even offered more verbal reinforcement in helping their children. The Experimental mothers modeled some of their children's behavior and, in effect, responded to the child who became the "educational engineer" in the dyad, structuring the interaction session either by their questioning or by teaching the mother.

The educational treatment program markedly changed the Experimental children's approach to problem-solving: we administered several problem tasks to both the mother and child including the Sigel Sorting Task, the Matching Familiar Figures Test, the Kansas Reflectivity-Impulsivity Scale, and the Embedded Figures Test. The Control mothers and Control children both tended to use strictly relational sorting, which requires a minimal analysis of a stimulus display, and also found difficulty in verbalizing the type of sorting they had done. The Experimental children, unlike their mothers or the Controls', tended to analyze stimulus arrays in a much more thorough manner before responding and tended to use a strategy behavior in how they approached the problem. For example, they were more field independent: they were able to ignore misleading cues and analyze the stimulus display more efficiently by using sorts based on categorization and description. In the Control dyads, the children tended to perseverative behavior with idle stacking and unstacking of blocks. Control mothers often lost interest, but when they gave directions, they were more often means oriented without reference to a final goal, as in the command "Put that over here." This behavior probably would have characterized the Experimental dyads, had it not been for the ability of the Experimental children to successfully structure a learning situation for their mothers to facilitate her performance on their behalf.

After a period of over four years, since the end of the preschool program, we still had contact with more than three quarters of the original families (Experimental $N = 17$; Control $N = 17$). Across the first four grades of school, the Experimental children are significantly superior to the Control group on total reading ($p < .06$) and total mathematics ($p < .01$) as measured by standard scores on the Metropolitan Achievement Test. The Experimental group's language-related subtest performance more consistently showed significant differences over the Control group across the four grades on the nine subtests of the MAT than performance on mathematics subtests.

When standard scores are converted to percentile and grade equivalent scores, there is a significant decline for both groups from first through fourth grade. Although the Experimental group remains superior to the Control group throughout the first four grades, the performance of both groups falls below national norms as they progress through the grades. For the first year, the distribution of the Experimental children as a group approximated the national profile on the MAT; while the Control group was already depressed. The performance of the Experimental group since then has further declined, first to the lower level of the city, and then to the still lower one of the inner-city schools, and the magnitude of differences between groups decreases.

Notwithstanding the differential performance between the Experimental and Control children on school achievement, which is generally poor when judged by grade level standards, it is, however, possible to differentiate between the groups by consideration of two additional factors. First, the Control children have been placed in special classes or given special help at twice the rate of the Experimental children. Second, the incidence of social behavior problems has occurred at a greater rate for the Experimental children than for the Control children. Reports of extensive disruption in classroom behavior, together with a poor quality educational environment, are interfering with the development of appropriate educational skills. For the Experimentals, however, there is a much greater MAT/IQ performance discrepancy than for the Control group.

As part of the follow-up evaluation of the children, we administered the WISC at roughly one-year intervals through the fourth grade. The data are presented in Figure 1. The WISC differential in favor of the Experimental group at 120 mos. is on the order of 20 points (mean $= 104.2$, $SD = 11.5$ range $= 93$-$138$ vs. mean $= 86.3$, $SD = 9.8$, range $= 72$-$106$) and suggests the extent to which the gains of intervention will be maintained over time. An examination of the distribution of within group performance revealed that no Experimental children tested below IQ 85, while for the Control group, 60% have scores more than one standard deviation *below* the mean ($\leq 85$), and half of these are below IQ 80. These data indicate a substantial difference in the intellectual strength of the two groups, in favor of the treated group. The Experimental group of children are not

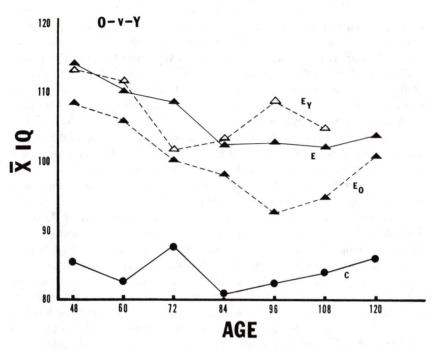

**FIG. 1.** Comparison of Treated Experimental Older and Younger Siblings on Wechsler IQ Tests and The Total Experimental and Control Group From Preschool Through 4th Grade.

without their problems in terms of support from the school and their homes as well as their own social behaviors in school, but there certainly remains a considerable indication of hope for their future because of the difference in the level and quality of their performance compared to the Control group.

In this perhaps all too brief summary and overview of the results of treating a group of children at high risk for mental retardation, we have mainly featured those statistically treated measures which indicated significant performance differences across time between the groups. They are the measures by which the efficacy of the intervention is most directly indicated.

There were, however, a number of additional indications of the effects of the treatment program which could be inferred as indirect and suggest additional sources of influence on intellectual development. The mechanism by which these sources produce their effect is not readily apparent, i.e., as compared to the effect of direct teaching in the educational program. In other words, after examining the data from the 10-year longitudinal study and asking if mental retardation had been prevented, we asked how else the intelligence of the children had been modified, i.e., beyond the obvious effect of the educational treatment program.

Other sources of influence were operating to modify performance levels which we were able to infer from the data in analyses subsequent to the main hypotheses.

These data suggested to us that intellectual performance on IQ tests can be modified by a complex of factors that may not be either easily manipulated or measured. The enhancement of the learning environment by an inspired, self-confident mother and the reciprocal relationship between stimulating supporting siblings are not easily assessed and are not typically manipulated variables in treatment; but some of our data does offer some room for speculation based on changes in IQ performance at different points in time.

At the beginning of the Milwaukee family program, each mother in the Experimental family began a program of vocational training and remedial education at the same time her infant was entered into the infant stimulation component of the preschool program. Subsequent to this initial input phase of the program (which lasted the better part of 2 years), five additional siblings were accepted into the program. In the Fig. 2, we have illustrated the mean performance of the older, first-entered siblings; the mean performance of the younger, subsequently entered siblings in comparison to the mean performance of the total group including the older but not the younger sibling. These data are the mean performance on the Gesell Developmental Schedules, administered at successive 4-month intervals, beginning at 6 months of age. The data are mean deviation in months from the age month's norm at which time the Schedules were administered. Between 6 and 14 months, the siblings, older and younger, are quite comparable, but between 14 and 18 months, they sharply diverge. The older siblings are above the mean overall group performance, while the younger siblings are well below that and their older sibling. The older siblings show a much faster rate of development between 14 and 22 months than their younger siblings. The younger siblings are obviously benefiting from the treatment program as they are 3 months ahead of normal by 22 months, but their older siblings are more than 6 months ahead. At this same point, the Control children are more than 1½ months below normal. In part, we believe the enhancement of the older siblings can be attributed to the overlap of the mother in the maternal rehabilitation program with her child in the infant stimulation program; a benefit, if you will, not enjoyed by the younger sibling. Other influences, of course, may be operating that have contributed to the increased performance level of the older siblings. For example, the second or younger sibling may not receive the same level of maternal enthusiasm that the first or prior born child enjoys; also, the mother's pregnancy with the younger sibling may have somehow heightened her interest in the program and her positive influence on the child, or some unrecognized feature of the program may even have changed. The latter, we believe, is the least likely. Subsequent to the infancy period, the IQ performance of the younger siblings is the same, even superior to their older siblings, which supports for us that there was an additional influence affecting the older Experimental sibling child between 1 year and 2 years that is "momentarily" additive.

We inferred additional support for this "momentary" changing effect of the treated mother from testings of all the untreated siblings of both groups. That the

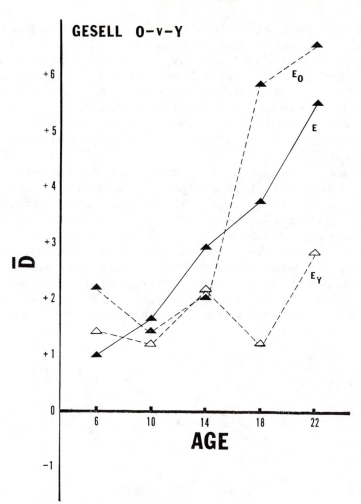

**FIG. 2.**   Mean Deviation Gesell Schedule Performance Comparison of Treated Older and Younger Experimental Siblings and Total Experimental Group

mother's influence may well have acted to positively heighten the performance of her children is suggested by the apparent change in mean IQ of the untreated siblings of the Experimental families. We sampled untreated siblings' IQ performance of both the Experimental and Control family off and on over a period of 6 years. We separated sibling IQs obtained during the time of the maternal rehabilitation program and compared it to samplings made some 4 years later. We found, that during the time the mother was directly involved in the rehabilitation treatment program, the mean IQ performance of the untreated siblings was positively elevated on the order of 7 to 10 points, especially for the children between 6 and

12 years of age. The testings made nearly 4 years after the maternal program show same-aged siblings to have a lower performance level. No such difference is revealed in examination of the Control group siblings. From the first to second testing of the Control siblings, there is almost no difference. The heightened effect for the Experimental siblings does not endure, but it certainly points, on the one hand, to the additional benefit to the family of the mother in treatment and perhaps, as well, to the sensitivity of the siblings to respond. Why the elevated performance does not remain and, of course, how it comes about would be quite valuable to explore.

What does remain, however, is a substantial difference overall between the untreated Experimental and Control siblings. The majority of the sampled IQs were obtained near the end of the program, while we still had active contact with the families. In the next figure, we have illustrated the mean intellectual performance of the siblings with increasing age. The data are essentially composed of two to three IQ test measures on some 150 different siblings. As can be seen, both groups begin the characteristic decline for such disadvantaged populations, but whereas the Control group continues this decline beyond 84 months to the lower 70s, the Experimental group discontinues the decline and remains in the mid 80s. The untreated Control group siblings' pattern of intellectual performance coin-

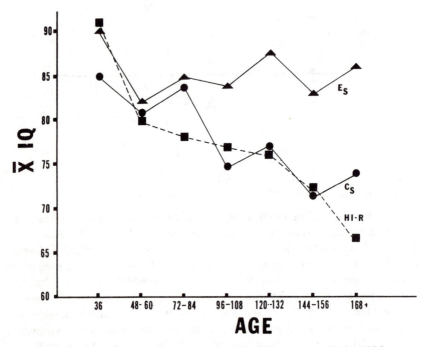

**FIG. 3.** Comparison of Untreated Experimental and Control Group Siblings' IQ Performance with a High-Risk Contrast Group

cides with the declining IQ of our original survey high-risk sample upon which the hypothesis of performance for untreated samples was predicated.

Support for a general effect of enhanced intellectual performance for the family is suggested not only by the difference in the pattern of intellectual performance between the groups, but also by the difference in the incidence of IQs ≤80 between the untreated siblings of both groups. At 6 years of age, the rates are comparable, 32% vs. 30%, but beyond 12 years of age, the Control group siblings' rate has risen to 70%, whereas the Experimental group siblings show about the same rate—35%—as they do at 6. To us, this was further evidence for the pervasiveness of the intervention program's effect, in that it has contributed to the discontinuation of declining IQ in the offspring of these families, with mean IQ remaining fairly stable in the mid 80s.

There is also evidence that such beneficial effects may be diffusing through the family, not only from the mother but through the target child himself to other siblings. In the following figure, we have illustrated the mean IQ performance of the siblings of both the Experimental and Control target children as a function of the ordinal position of the sibling to the target child. In this figure, we can see that, although there is a similar decline in the IQ performance of siblings as we move from the position of first younger to first older and beyond, the effect of the treated child is to brake the trend to declining IQ of their siblings with increasing age, which is characteristic of this population in general and replicated by the performance of the Control siblings. In other words, although both groups decline in IQ, at least initially, the Control siblings continue the decline in mean IQ as they move through the ordinal position of the untreated targeted child. Where the child has been treated, the siblings' IQ decline is discontinued, and it appears to be the result of an effect diffusing from the treated child. This could be referred to as vertical diffusion (Gray, 1980). At the fourth ordinal position removed from the target child, there is over a 16 point difference in sibling IQ in favor of the Experimental siblings.

An additional source of influence that serves as a modifier of intellectual performance is the child himself. Certainly, the performance of the Experimental and Control children discussed earlier is evidence that a range of differences exist "even" within this group of disadvantaged children. In an article in *Science,* Zigler (1967) clarified anew that there exist two distinct groups of mentally retarded: a group with organic etiology and the lowest functioning with IQs below 50; and a second moderate and mild group with no obvious pathology with IQs 50 to about 80.* As important as this clarification was to the field, it has left the misleading impression for many that the mild group is homogeneous within and that any of the subject characteristics, such as low IQ, poor, disadvantaged, etc., adequately describe all who either fall into or are at risk to fall into this range. Obviously, there is not room here to discuss this issue, but for the moment, suffice it to

---

*AAMD cutoff is defined as IQ 70; Grossman, 1973.

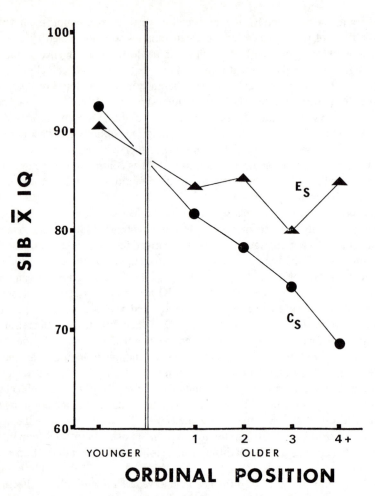

**FIG. 4.**   Comparison of Untreated Experimental and Control Group Siblings' IQ Performance  as  a  Function  of  Their  Ordinal  Position  to  the  Target  Child

say that the range of differences, i.e., individual variation, that exists for such
children is considerable and that its underestimation has misled attempts to re-
solve the problems of these children and in turn raised many false hopes. As we
indicated earlier, many of the Controls and a few Experimentals tended to response stereotypy which persisted beyond earliest childhood and showed passive,
unenthusiastic behavior in problem-solving situations. We interpreted this idiosyncratic behavior which persists in an antagonistic fashion beyond the preschool
years as one that interferes with learning and successful performance in school. In
addition, upon examination of IQ performance over time, some children showed

changes with relatively large swings, up and down, in IQ performance over a relatively short time span. Because of such differences within group between children in their performance, it became quite clear to us that the prevention of mental retardation must much more carefully delineate subject selection and coordinate that with treatment. It would appear that neither are all of these children doomed to fail in life any more than are they all capable of being helped to perform at normal and above IQs.

Predicting intelligence levels from early IQ scores has a notoriously poor record (Bayley, 1966), even when developmental experiences are considered normal (Brody & Brody, 1976). Yet, many developmental psychologists—especially present-day early interventionists—have argued the movement of IQ scores on the order of a half-dozen points. Not only has Thorndike (1978) argued that the Stanford-Binet shows a 4.7 "natural" drop over time, McCall et al. (1973) have suggested swings of 25 to 40 points as not unreasonable over the early developmental life span. Therefore, considering the range of differences that exists within the sample of the seriously disadvantaged at-risk child who is developing in a unique environment to which he is obviously quite sensitive, we should be committed to discussing not the IQ levels achieved by such groups of children, but the probability of a level being achieved and how that may vary given certain factors of risk—socioeconomic, educational, economic, medical, etc., and what *percentage* of the treated group succeeds as compared to the untreated group. These risk factors can be derived from child measures, but in fact in the more mild, less obvious child disabilities, risk is better determined from family characteristics (Heber & Garber, 1980), and, perhaps more specifically, the mother.

Obviously, a major source of influence, and probably the major source, is the mother. It is very important to realize that differences we see in children are in many ways differences reflecting differences in mothers. In other words, although most research has tended to group mothers as poor or low IQ, it has not adequately differentiated among these types of mothers with respect to their style of interaction with their children or the process by which they manage their family. The extent to which this knowledge is limited is a measure of the extent to which the efficacy of the treatment for such families is compromised. The inadequate assessment of such mothers, as to the many other characteristics of their life, has allowed for the continued underestimation of both the importance of and the mechanism for the mother's influence on the cognitive development of the child of the seriously disadvantaged family, who is therefore at high risk for mental retardation.

We reexamined each family according to a series of indices which we hoped would differentiate among high-risk families in a way that would help us understand whether the program had differentially benefited some as a function of their family. The original selection criterion for these families insured that they all shared the common key indicator variables of low IQ, low socioeconomic and educational level, residential area, etc. We assessed all of the families on a high-risk index derived from several presently being used, which included assessments of the mother's age at child birth, maternal literacy, average spacing between children, and evaluation of the quality of the home. Some values are arbitrary and all are somewhat interdependent.

We separated these high-risk families into lower and higher high risk, and compared the children on a general IQ (McCall et al., 1973) derived from the WPPSI and WISC tests administered in preschool and through the fourth grade. There appears to be about a 10–12 point advantage in mean IQ for the Experimental group children who come from *low* high-risk homes, as compared to the higher risk families. In preschool, the low high-risk group of Control children were 12 points higher than the high high-risk group of Control children, but the difference is only about 5 points once in school. Interestingly, the difference of 5 points between the low and high Control children is due to a mean loss of 7 points by the low-risk children, while the already low-scoring, higher risk children stay about the same. Again, given the nature of the measure and problem of justifying the assignment values, it would appear that fundamental to the efficacy of intervention (if measured by the performance of the children) is the quality of the home, for that persists beyond intervention.

Earlier in our discussion, we noted that the Experimental children were not without their problems. We were referring to reports of misconduct in school for the older siblings from first grade on. The younger Experimental siblings were admitted into the program later and followed their older siblings through the experimental program. The older Experimental siblings were held in the program until first grade entry; the younger Experimental siblings were entered into kindergarten (as were all the Control children). Their behavior is different. In the figure (Figure 1) of intellectual performance comparing Experimental and Control groups, we have also included the mean IQ performance of the older siblings. The younger siblings' data are incomplete at 120 months. Between 48 and 72 months, both older and younger siblings declined in similar fashion, but whereas the first grade entering older siblings continued to decline until the end of second grade where they begin to improve, the younger siblings begin to improve between kindergarten and first grade. The Control children also show recovery to the decline in performance, shown upon entering school, earlier than the older Experimental siblings and at least more obviously than the improvement in level shown by the total Experimental group. This has suggested to us that kindergarten can be an especially useful experience in which to encourage school-appropriate behavior and to allay whatever childhood anxieties there may be about school. Its immediate benefit was to facilitate social performance in school by helping the children to adjust. Although not clearly differentiable, both the younger Experimental siblings and the Controls tended to have a lower rate of misconduct. In defense of the older Experimental children, reported misconducts were verbal confrontations which were not acceptable as "typical" by the teachers for such children.

An additional source of influence that we would be remiss to ignore is the health status of the child. In general, we quite conscientiously assisted the Experimental families in seeking appropriate health care for their children as needed. Medical evaluations, however, have shown no significant substantive differences between the Experimental and Control children's physical development.

Another related source of influence which could be interpreted as biological status is based on Epstein's (1974) findings of biennial changes in mental test data. These changes indicate four, perhaps five, correlated brain and mind growth spurts (3–10 months, 2–4 years, 6–8 years, 10–13 years, and possibly 14–17 years). The growth spurt is indicated by fairly sharp changes in individual variation. We found some evidence for this spurt by examining the changes in the standard deviation of the Wechsler IQ data. Between 48 and 72 months, the mean standard deviation for the Experimental group's mean Wechsler performance is 7.2; the mean standard deviation between 84 and 108 months is 11.5. According to Epstein's notion of *phrenoblysis* (correlated brain and mind growth spurts), the Experimental children conform to a nonspurt or nongrowth phase, and to a growth phase. The process seems delayed in the Control group. Epstein argues that when standard deviations decrease sharply, the reduced variability is an indication of a nongrowth phase. The obvious change is a decreased standard deviation for the Control group beginning at 72 months and maintained until 96 months. The mean standard deviation is 11.8 for 48 to 60 months, 9.4 from 72 to 96 months, and 10.8 to 120 months. The Control children appear to be delayed as much as 2 years, according to these calculations. This delay is on the same order as their language performance in comparison to the Experimental group. If these data indeed fit with Epstein's other findings, they have major implications for education in that novel intellectual inputs to children are more effective during brain growth spurts than during the between phases. Indeed, Epstein (1978) notes that Head Start's difficulties may be related to the fact that the majority of the programming occurs during a nongrowth phase, i.e., 4 to 6 years, and therefore the effectiveness of its treatment is prematurely blunted.

By noting the changes in IQ performance at different points in time during the Experimental program, we have tried to suggest that there are many sources of influence, and each seems to be able to play the performance levels up or down with some ease. The reliance on IQ score taken at a single point in time as a predictive index or as the end-all measure of efficacy can be misleading, for good or bad, given this kind of "moveability." As we consider our own data and the comments we have made in speculating upon apparent sources of influence on IQ peformance, together with the apparent *ease* of finding gains that seems to us to be a legitimate interpretation of the effects of early intervention studies in general (see Palmer, 1980) and the reanalysis of the Fels growth study data (McCall, Appelbaum, & Hogarty, 1973) which shows large individual swings in performance over time, it certainly would appear that movement of IQ performance levels is not very difficult to accomplish. Therefore, since most behavioral scientists seem to prefer the availability of such instruments, it behooves us to be much more concerned about the nature of such ease of movement, i.e., whether it is due to the responsiveness of the individual being tested to some environmental source of treatment or to the sensitivities of the test. It should be a fundamental to understand not only why peformance levels change but what causes them to have (or not have) an enduring quality over time. The most obvious explanation is that IQ performance is not a function of some one single source of influence, but rather a complex of forces that are interactive. We need to move beyond the simplistic notions of the prepotence of either genetic inheritance or optimal environments and recognize the tremendous range of individual variation all along the normal (50 to 150) scale of intelligence estimates. At any moment in one's life, an inspired, encouraging mother, cooperative sibling(s), or a supportive school environment can support a behavior system appropriate to the academic demands of school. These forces interact, however, and in the case of the low SES child born into a family headed by a low IQ, low verbal skilled mother where the health of family life is constantly violated by crises, the developing behavior system may be quite antagonistic to successful academic performance—e.g., insensitivity to reinforcement leading to perseverative behavior, use of primitive strategy behaviors, limited development of language skills, and social incompetencies (but these are quite possibly evidence of poor behavior, not necessarily poor potential).

We have speculated upon several sources of influence on early IQ performance in addition to one's given potential, but which are just as important: his peculiar learning habits and his language skills which are his tools to work the world and, as well, his environment and what it offers in support. His environment, unfortunately, can include a low IQ, low verbal skill mother and father, and the unique psychological environment they create, the reciprocal relationship among siblings who are suffering from their own problems of development, a school experience which is not adequate, a relationship with teachers with negative attitudes, and peers who suffer similarly. Therefore, we need to argue on behalf of children. They are the victims in major part of their environment and yet too easily are they given the onus for demonstrating success while given fragmented and limited help to do otherwise. Though we do not think that the problem of the excess prevalence of low IQs among disadvantaged population subgroups has been resolved, there has been a turning of the corner in our understanding of the need to appreciate how a complex of interacting variables can influence *individual* cognitive growth. To the extent we further delineate these variables and come to understand how they operate, we can then control and manipulate them to improve the intellectual status of all children at all levels. And, after all, isn't that what it's all about?

## REFERENCES

Bayley, N. Development of mental abilities. In P. Mussen (Ed.), *Carmichael's Manual of Child Psychology* (3rd ed., Vol. 1). New York: Basic Books, 1966.

Brody, E., & Brody, N. *Intelligence: Nature, determinants, and consequences*. New York: Academic Press, 1976.

Epstein, H. Phrenoblysis: Special brain and mind growth periods. II. Human mental development. *Developmental Psychology*, 1974, *7*(3), 217–224.

Epstein, H. *Education and the brain*. Chicago: University of Chicago Press, 1978.

Garber, H., & Heber, R. The efficacy of early intervention with family rehabilitation. In M. J. Begab, H. C. Haywood, & H. L. Garber (Eds.), *Psychosocial influences in retarded performance. Volume II: Strategies for improving competence*. Baltimore: University Park Press, 1981.

Gray, S. A fifteen year follow-up of the participants in the early training project. In M. J. Begab, H. C. Haywood, & H. L. Garber (Eds.), *Psychosocial influences in retarded performance. Volume II: Strategies for improving competence*. Baltimore: University Park Press, 1981.

Grossman, H. (Ed.). *Manual on terminology and classification in mental retardation*. Washington, DC: American Association on Mental Deficiency, 1973.

Heber, R., & Garber, H. The Milwaukee Project: A study of the use of family intervention to prevent cultural-familial mental retardation. In B. Friedlander et al. (Eds.), *Exceptional infant, Vol. III: Assessment and intervention*. New York: Brunner/Mazel, 1975.

Heber, R., & Garber, H. Prevention of cultural-familial mental retardation. In A. Jaeger & R. Slotnick (Eds.), *Community mental health: A behavioral-ecological perspective*. New York: Plenum Press, 1980.

Hess, R., & Shipman, V. Early experiences and socialization of cognitive modes in children. *Child Development*, 1965, *36*, 869–886.

Hess, R., & Shipman, V. Maternal influences upon early learning: The cognitive environment of urban preschool children. In R. D. Hess & R. M. Ball (Eds.), *Early education*. Chicago: Aldine, 1968.

McCall, R., Appelbaum, M., & Hogarty, P. Developmental changes in mental performance. *Monographs of the Society for Research in Child Development*, 1973, *38*(3, Serial No. 150).

Palmer, F. An overview of various models for intervention. In M. J. Begab, H. C. Haywood, & H. L. Garber (Eds.), *Psychosocial influences in retarded performance. Volume II: Strategies for improving competence*. Baltimore: University Park Press, 1981.

Thorndike, R. Causation of Binet IQ decrements. *Journal of Educational Measurement*, 1978, *15*, 197–202.

Zigler, E. Familial mental retardation: A continuing dilemma. *Science*, 1967, *155*, 292–298.

# II

## *Modifying Cognitive Skills*

# Introduction:
# Some Common Themes in Contemporary Approaches to the Training of Intelligent Performance

ROBERT J. STERNBERG

*Yale University*

This second section of the book contains presentations of five contemporary approaches to the training of intelligent performance. The approaches deal with a rather wide range of content: learning of and memory for lists of words (Belmont, Butterfield, & Ferretti), reading comprehension and vocabulary acquisition (Sternberg, Ketron, & Powell; Collins & Smith), use of mnemonics (Messick & Sigel), deductive reasoning (Sternberg, Ketron, & Powell), and inductive reasoning (Sternberg, Ketron, & Powell; Messick & Sigel; Glaser & Pellegrino). Despite the differences in content areas to which the approaches have been applied, the approaches have in common their view of intelligence as an information-processing construct that can be modified through training in information-processing skills. The approaches also have in common certain views regarding the prerequisites for training of intelligent performance. I consider in this introduction to the second section of the book what these prerequisites seem to be. The three prerequisites to be discussed constitute neither an exhaustive nor mutually exclusive list, but they provide a basis for understanding some of the common themes that run through contemporary approaches to improving intelligent functioning.

## EXECUTIVE PROCESSING

During the 1970's, we witnessed a spurt of research guided by an information-processing conception of intelligence and how to train it. Much of this research was characterized by an effort to identify the performance components and strategies that typify intelligent behavior (e.g., Hunt, Lunneborg, & Lewis, 1975; Kotovsky & Simon, 1973; Sternberg, 1977; Whitely, 1976). Some investigators realized early on, however, the critical importance of identifying and training the executive processes that control execution of performance components and strategies, as well as of identifying and training the performance components and strategies themselves. Among these prescient investigators were Butterfield and Belmont (1977). In their contribution to the present book, Belmont, Butterfield, and Ferretti argue that meaningful transfer can be attained in learning of new strategies for intelligent performance, only if executive processes such as goal-setting, strategy planning, and self-monitoring are trained in addition to the specific skills from which transfer is being sought. The authors note that whereas six of seven studies they review achieved generalization in training, presumably through the training of executive processes, none of 114 other studies they reviewed earlier (Belmont & Butterfield, 1977) achieved generalization, presumably because none of these studies involved training of executive processes.

Sternberg, Ketron, and Powell also believe that an understanding of executive processes is prerequisite for an understanding of intelligent performance and how to train it. Whereas Sternberg's earlier research on analogical reasoning, for example, focused upon the performance components and strategies people use in solving analogies (Sternberg, 1977), the experiment on analogical reasoning described in the present chapter focuses upon the question of why people select the performance components and strategies they actually end up using. Why, for example, do people tend to be largely self-terminating in their strategies for solving analogies, and even more so for analogies with separable attributes than for analogies with integral attributes?

Collins and Smith clearly take a "top-down" view in their instructional program for teaching reading comprehension. They contend that there are two aspects of reading comprehension that are particularly important to teach— comprehension monitoring and hypothesis formation and evaluation. Comprehension monitoring may be viewed as falling within the domain of executive processing. It concerns a person's ability both to evaluate ongoing comprehension processes while reading through a text and to plan remedial action when one's comprehension processes are seen to be failing (see also Markman, 1979). Collins and Smith review the various kinds of comprehension failure that can take place, and then suggest six strategies that people can use when such failures occur, e.g., suspending judgment, forming a tentative hypothesis, and rereading previous context.

Messick and Sigel's concern with executive processing is evidenced in their conceptualization of *distancing,* whereby an individual is stimulated to reconstruct the past, anticipate the future, and take different perspectives on the present. In distancing, the individual breaks away at least momentarily from the specific context in which a specific task is being performed, and attempts to put his or her task performance into a broader perspective. The authors believe that training children to distance themselves from tasks at hand can greatly stimulate the children's cognitive development.

Finally, Glaser and Pellegrino illustrate the importance of executive processing in analogical reasoning by showing that low-ability children often fail to solve analogies successfully in part because they do not construct a strategy for "analogical" solution of analogies, but rather construct stategies that are essentially non-analogical in nature. Such children may not even have the opportunity to err in the execution of performance components and strategies of analogical reasoning, because they do not set up the problems for solution by analogical methods.

To summarize, current views on the understanding and training of intelligent performance place considerable emphasis upon the importance of executive processing. Such processing seems to play a key role in task performance, probably without regard to the particular task being studied. At least some of the tasks used in the assessment of intelligence may be good measures of intelligence at least as much for the executive processing that they require as for the execution of performance components and strategies that they involve.

## THE ROLES OF KNOWLEDGE IN INFORMATION PROCESSING AND OF INFORMATION PROCESSING IN KNOWLEDGE ACQUISITION

During the spurt of research on the information a processing analysis of intelligence, the emphasis was definitely upon the "processing," rather than the "information" part of "information processing." The approaches described in this section go at least part of the way toward rectifying this imbalance.

Belmont, Butterfield, and Ferretti point out that there is little doubt that retarded individuals are deficient in their knowledge about their own thought processes. According to these authors, the more information an individual has about his or her own cognitive functions and the ways that they can be combined, the more powerful his or her approach to new situations is likely to become. The ability of the retarded individual to process new problems is limited by the individual's restricted knowledge about his or her own processing capabilities.

Sternberg, Ketron, and Powell present a view of the development of verbal ability as deriving in large part from the use of skills for incidentally acquiring the meanings of unfamiliar words presented in everyday contexts. On this view, there is a direct connection between the knowledge base and the processes used in acquiring it. This view is contrasted with that of Hunt (1978), who emphasizes the importance of "mechanistic" processes in the development and manifestation of verbal ability. Whereas Hunt believes that *speed* of access to lexical information stored in memory is a critical determinant of verbal ability, Sternberg, Ketron, and Powell believe that *power* to acquire this information through a specifiable set of knowledge-acquisition skills is a critical determinant of verbal ability. It is quite possible that the two views actually are complementary, and deal with different aspects of verbal ability; but the present view seems more to emphasize interactions between information processing and the knowledge base upon which processes operate.

Collins and Smith's view of verbal abilities seems to be quite similar to that of Sternberg, Ketron, and Powell. Like these latter authors, Collins and Smith stress the importance of decontextualization skills in reading comprehension and verbal comprehension in general. Both sets of authors seem to agree that improvement in verbal ability is to be sought through the direct training of comprehension and comprehension monitoring skills, rather than through training of lexical-access skills (see Hunt et al., 1975). On Collins and Smith's view, one's comprehension processes become an object of knowledge, and one's knowledge of these processes in turn guides the future processes one should use to optimize subsequent comprehension.

The viewpoint of Messick and Sigel also emphasizes the importance of interactions between processes and knowledge. These authors point out that certain kinds of questions, such as "What is the color of this shoe?" demand no reorganization, integration, or transformation of information. Such questions can be answered directly. But, a question such as "What can you tell me about this shoe?" requires much more than simple fact retrieval; and a successful response to such a question entails considerable reorganization and integration of information in one's knowledge base. More optimal representation of information facilitates reorganization and integration of this information. The distancing strategy that the authors propose can be viewed as a way of encouraging individuals to store knowledge in a form that will later be more accessible for a variety of different kinds of uses.

The importance of one's knowledge base, even in the solution of analogies seeming to require only rudimentary knowledge, is shown by Glaser and Pellegrino. These investigators have found that knowledge representation affects solution strategies by defining the limits of the problem domain. In solving numerical analogies, high ability subjects limit their analogical hypotheses to a few plausible mathematical relationships. Low-ability subjects seem much less often to solve the analogies using systematic, mathematically-based rules.

To summarize, the knowledge base and the processes that operate upon it seem to interact closely, and it is difficult on some current views to understand either the knowledge base or the processes that operate upon it in the absence of the other. A belief in "mechanistic processes" that are understandable largely in the absence of an understanding of any particular knowledge base can lead to quite different views on the nature of intelligent performance, and how it might be trained.

## THE CONTEXT OF INTELLIGENT PERFORMANCE

Because information-processing psychologists conduct most of their research in laboratories, there is often an understandable tendency on their part to give short shrift to the context in which intelligent behavior takes place. Many information-processing investigations of intelligence conducted in the 1970's simply ignored the context of intelligent behavior. The present viewpoints, however, show considerable concern with contexts of behavior.

Belmont, Butterfield, and Ferretti point out that it is not particularly difficult to achieve success in a particular instructional manipulation to improve intelligent performance in a particular task context; what is difficult is to achieve generalization to other task contexts that differ in non-trivial ways from the original task context. Only a small proportion of studies in the literature on training retarded individuals show such transfer. These tend to be the studies in which executive processes were taught, so that the authors conclude that the way to get generalization across contexts is to train executive processing.

Sternberg, Ketron, and Powell show some concern for the context of intelligent performance in the design of the experiment they describe on verbal comprehension. The experiment was conducted in a school, a context in which a great deal of intelligent performance takes place during childhood and early adulthood. Their theory of verbal comprehension is tested via texts that are close simulations of those that students actually encounter, and the texts cover a range of types that students encounter, e.g., newspaper articles, magazine articles, novels, textbooks, and the like. The context of this research seems somewhat more likely to encourage normal reading than do, say, laboratory contexts using tachistoscopic procedures to present sometimes unusual forms of reading material.

The Collins and Smith procedures for training reading comprehension are being prepared for use in a large-scale project for improving the intellectual performance of Venezuelan school children functioning in actual school settings. These investigators thus find themselves in the position of having to devise and test a theory that is applicable cross-culturally. The context in which the theory will be tested will without doubt be quite different from that in which most current theories are tested, namely, that of college undergraduates taking psychology courses.

Messick and Sigel state that their distancing model is based on Piaget's notion that the development of cognitive competence stems from the interaction of specific classes of social experience and the child's developmental status. Thus, their notion is motivated by the interaction of the child with his or her social context. On this view, cognition cannot meaningfully be understood acontextually, or in a context radically different from that in which it developed. Distancing, in effect, broadens the context within which problems are perceived.

Pellegrino and Glaser make clear that their interest is not especially in analogies or in any other particular inductive-reasoning task, but rather in what they believe to be a basic and general set of information-processing components that occur in a variety of tasks and task contexts. Thus, their claim is that processes such as encoding, identification and generation of relational features, rule assembly or rule monitoring, and comparison or matching are general across induction tasks and the contexts in which these tasks are presented. In this respect, their approach represents a departure from the kind of particularistic task analysis that characterized much earlier information-processing research, in which it was often not made clear to what extent, if any, the task analysis applied or was meant to apply beyond the particular task being analyzed.

To summarize, the approaches to the training of intelligent performance presented in this section of the book share a concern with the context of intelligent behavior, as well as with the behavior itself. The prevailing view seems to be that intelligent behavior cannot be understood acontextually, and that it is important to investigate the extent to which it can be understood cross-contextually.

In conclusion, at least three themes—executive processing; interaction between knowledge base and the processes that operate upon it, and the context of intelligent behavior—seem to run through all of the chapters in this section of the volume. Many other themes emerge as well in various subsets of the chapters. These themes, as well as some of the general ones, will be discussed in the final commentary by Brown and Campione.

## REFERENCES

Belmont, J. M., & Buttefield, E. C. The instructional approach to developmental cognitive research. In R. Kail & J. Hagen (Eds.), *Perspectives on the development of memory and cognition*. Hillsdale, NJ: Lawrence Erlbaum Associates, 1977.

Butterfield, E. C., & Belmont, J.M. Assessing and improving the executive cognitive functions of mentally retarded people. In I. Bialer & M. Sternlicht (Eds.), *Psychological issues in mental retardation*. New York: Psychological Dimensions, 1977.

Hunt, E. B. Mechanics of verbal ability. *Psychological Review*, 1978, *85*, 109–130.

Hunt, E., Lunneborg, C., & Lewis, J. What does it mean to be high verbal? *Cognitive Psychology*, 1975, *7*, 194–227.

Kotovsky, K., & Simon, H.A. Empirical tests of a theory of human acquisition of concepts for sequential events. *Cognitive Psychology*, 1973, *4*, 399–424.

Markman, E. M. Realizing that you don't understand: Elementary school children's awareness of inconsistencies. *Child Development*, 1979, *50*, 643–655.

Sternberg, R. J. *Intelligence, information processing, and analogical reasoning: The componential analysis of human abilities*. Hillsdale, NJ: Lawrence Erlbaum Associates, 1977.

Whitely, S. E. Solving verbal analogies: Some cognitive components of intelligence test items. *Journal of Educational Psychology*, 1976, *68*, 232–242.

# 5

# *To Secure Transfer of Training Instruct Self-management Skills**

JOHN M. BELMONT,[1] EARL C. BUTTERFIELD AND RALPH P. FERRETTI

*University of Kansas Medical Center*

Adaptation and problem solving are key constructs in the study of the modifiability of intelligence. We propose that transfer of training is a particularly cogent test of cognitive modifiability, and we review seven studies to show that important transfer can be achieved only if general skills such as goal-setting, strategy planning, and self-monitoring are trained, in addition to the specific skills whose transfer is sought. We argue that problem identification and motivation to solve problems are also necessary components of adaptation.

The word "intelligence" derives from the Latin *intelligere,* which means to choose, to decide, to discriminate. These meanings emphasize active evaluation of options, and this emphasis can be seen in the classic psychometric treatises. Binet and Simon (1916) recognized "a fundamental aspect of intelligence, the alteration or lack of which is of the utmost importance for practical life. The faculty is *judgment* . . . practical sense, initiative, the faculty of *adapting one's self to circumstances.* To judge well, to comprehend well, to reason well, these are the essential activities of intelligence." Wechsler likewise viewed intelligence as the "aggregate or global capacity of the individual to act purposefully, to think rationally, and to deal effectively with the environment" (1944, p.3). Binet's and Wechsler's views have far-reaching implications for the measurement of intelligence, yet the tests that bear their names hardly realize those implications. This is formally acknowledged in the decision by the American Association on Mental Deficiency (Grossman, 1973) to define mental retardation not only in terms of "general intellectual functioning," as measured by tests like the Stanford-Binet and the Wechsler, but also in terms of "adaptive behavior," as indexed for example by the AAMD Adaptive Behavior Scale.

*Preparation and presentation of this paper at the American Educational Research Association (Boston, April 10, 1980) was supported by USPHS Grants HD 08911 and HD 00870. The Pacific Cultural Foundation supported the presentation of an expanded version at the 1980 International Workshop on Special Education (Taipei, March 28, 1980). Thanks are due to Rosa Meagher and Wayne Mitchell for their excellent help in preparing the manuscript.

[1]Department of Pediatrics, University of Kansas Medical Center, Kansas City, KS 66103.

In making the distinction between intellectual functioning and adaptive behavior, the AAMD intended *clinicians* to look beyond the IQ for evidence of the client's everyday communication, self-help, academic, reasoning, judgment and social skills, and to characterize the client's relative strengths and weaknesses in these diverse areas. The AAMD was not directly challenging *researchers* to do the same, but it is certainly instructive to consider how, given our current understandings, we might best address the adaptive function inherent in the AAMD's concerns and in the classic definition of intelligence.

To begin with, it is useful to regard adaptation as a matter of choosing among alternatives in problematic situations. Within the framework of developmental cognitive research, adaptive choice might reflect: (1) *mechanisms* by which people choose, (2) *knowledge* on which choice is based, and (3) *conditions* under which choice is necessitated. The concept thus relates the presenting conditions and the thinking that subserves choice. Together, these ideas point to problem solving as a key model for intelligent adaptation (Charlesworth, 1978). By this view, the enquiry as to how intelligence can be modified begins with an analysis of children's failures of problem solving. Do children and retarded people fail because they cannot employ the basic cognitive mechanisms on which good task performance depends (e.g., do they fail on a problem that involves addition because they cannot add)? Or, do they not know that such basic mechanisms are available to them. For example, they may be able to add, but do not recognize that addition is called for in the problem at hand. Or do they not exercise general problem-solving skills that might work regardless of the specific nature of the task currently facing them? For example, they may be able to add, and they may even recognize in a general sense that addition is called for, but they may not work through the problem systematically enough to arrange for a successful addition in that particular case.

The first option is ruled out by experiments which show that retarded children and adults can usefully employ basic cognitive mechanisms. The three studies summarized in Figure 1 make this point very well in the area of memory functioning. Turnure, Buium, and Thurlow (1976) is the Minnesota Study. Brown, Campione, Bray, and Wilcox (1973) is the Illinois Study. Butterfield, Wambold, and Belmont (1973) is the Yale/Kansas Study. Each study involved a group of retarded people who were given a memory problem, without being led to use memory techniques appropriate to the problem. Each study also involved a group who were instructed to use an appropriate technique. The instruction was extremely brief in all three studies, yet in each it was hugely effective, resulting in performance closely similar to that of uninstructed non-retarded adolescents or adults (Figure 1, NORMALS) who were at the same or higher chronological age as the retarded trainees. We are satisfied by these three studies that retarded people do not fail memory problems by reason of inability to perform basic mental calculations in the realm of memory. We assume that similar studies in other cognitive domains would show the same lack of basic disabilities.

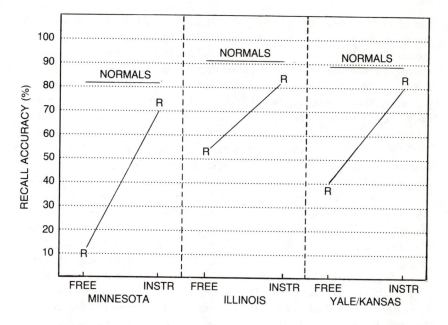

**FIG. 1.** Results of three independent studies showing that task-specific strategy instruction can greatly increase retarded children's memory performance.

The next question is whether children's or retarded people's adaptive failures result from a lack of knowledge about when or in what ways it is appropriate to use the basic information-processing mechanisms which they are clearly capable of using. The question has to do with knowledge about one's own thinking and knowledge about problems. It points to the domain of what Brown (1975) and Flavell and Wellman (1977) have called "meta" knowledge, and there seems little doubt that children and retarded people are deficient throughout this domain. The more experience a person has in dealing with closely similar problems, the greater the likelihood that a new problem will yield to closely similar solutions. The more information he has about his own cognitive functions and the ways they can be combined, the more powerful his approach to new situations may become. Thus, the modifiability of meta-knowledge is a central part of the question of modifiability of intelligence. Meta-knowledge is not sufficient in itself, however, to guarantee full problem solving. A person must also attend to the situation's problematic aspects, and must use his meta-knowledge inventively. There is thus a third level of analysis that cannot be ignored in the study of intelligence and its modifiability.

The third level is the meta-processing counterpart to the meta-knowledge domain. We view meta-processing as a superordinate function by which basic information-processing mechanisms are organized to solve problems. Deficiencies of superordinate processing can lead to adaptive failure in many ways. The one most clearly identifiable in the research literature is also perhaps the one of greatest immediate concern to the classroom teacher: The child fails to transfer recently learned skills to situations other than the one in which initial learning is accomplished. Since there is wide agreement that such transfer is crucial to intelligent adaptation (Belmont & Butterfield, 1977), the question of whether transfer can be experimentally facilitated joins the instructability of meta-knowledge as a central issue in the debate over modifiability of intelligence.

We view the transfer test as an instance of problem solving in which there is no question that the child can do much of the basic information processing. After all, he would not be tested for transfer had he not clearly mastered at least one set of task-appropriate skills. In addition to such specific knowledge, however, the child will need to invent at least one important new process or rearrange those already taught to him. Unless such a novel challenge exists, the test is not a test of transfer, but rather a test of maintenance of an existing skill (Belmont & Butterfield, 1977). Thus, the transfer test is a genuine problem. The child must recognize it as such, must want to solve it, and must manage his efforts to solve it appropriately.

The self-management involved in problem solving can be analyzed into 12 discrete steps (Butterfield, Siladi, & Belmont, 1980). In Figure 2, we have condensed these into six steps, including setting a goal, making a provisional plan to reach the goal, trying out the plan, and evaluating its effectiveness. There are three evaluative steps. First, the child must ask if he was successful. If not, he must ask whether he actually did what he intended to do in his provisional plan. If so, he must ask what was wrong with the plan itself. Decisions of fundamentally different sorts will be made, depending on the results of such self-monitoring.

The experimental literature shows that direct instruction of the superordinate activities illustrated in Figure 2 can induce retarded children to transfer subordinate cognitive skills: Six of the seven experiments that have produced substantial transfer not only delivered specific instruction in subordinate skills, but also led the children to perform, or to see the wisdom of performing activities such as defining goals, designing appropriate plans, and monitoring the implementations and outcomes of those plans.

Brown and her colleagues performed two experiments (Brown & Barclay, 1976; Brown, Campione, & Barclay, 1979) which, taken together, are perhaps the most impressive laboratory demonstration of generalized instructional effects. Their results were achieved by adding a superordinate routine to the training of an effective rehearsal strategy. Training the strategy itself should not have influenced superordinate processing. The additional instruction was designed to induce retarded children to attend to the effects of rehearsal upon their readiness to recall. In terms of the model in Figure 2, the added instruction should have induced children to monitor their rehearsal and decide to respond when the rehearsal proved successful (Steps 3 & 4). The instructions were given for a list-learning problem, and transfer was observed one year later with a prose-recall problem.

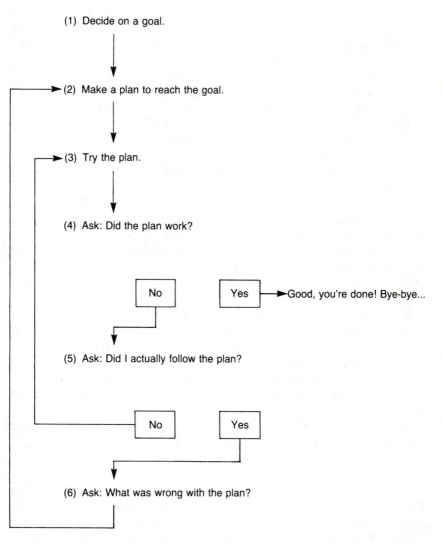

A GENERAL GUIDE TO SELF-MANAGEMENT
(How to Solve a Problem)

(1) Decide on a goal.

(2) Make a plan to reach the goal.

(3) Try the plan.

(4) Ask: Did the plan work?

No    Yes    ►Good, you're done! Bye-bye...

(5) Ask: Did I actually follow the plan?

No    Yes

(6) Ask: What was wrong with the plan?

**FIG. 2.** Flow-diagram model of steps taken by an ideal problem solver who is working out the relationships between plans, actions and outcomes.

151

Like Brown and her colleagues, Kendall, Borkowski, and Cavanaugh (1980) designed a strategy for their subjects and provided them with added instructions that probably induced superordinate processing in Steps 3 & 4. The strategy was to use self-interrogation to produce interactive images between items for a paired-associates task. Superordinate processing was taught indirectly, by providing the retarded subjects with feedback about the effectiveness of their strategic efforts. The instructions were, at first, very detailed and specific, and were then gradually faded. We assume that the fading transfered control over both the self-interrogation strategy and provision of evaluative feedback to the subjects themselves. The instruction was done with a standard paired-associates learning task, and transfer was observed on a triadic-associates task.

Ross and Ross (1978) instructed retarded children to use rehearsal strategies or imagery strategies. Their instructions concentrated on designing strategies and deciding when to use them (Figure 2, Steps 2 & 3). Multiple association memory tests were administered before and five months after training. Compared to a control group that received no strategy instruction, experimental groups showed marked improvement from before to after training, which is to say, they showed good transfer.

Bornstein and Quevillon (1976) produced the farthest transfer of any of the successful experiments. That is, their study established the greatest difference between the situation in which children were trained and that in which transfer was tested. Their subjects were four-year-olds who showed difficult-to-control impulsive behavior. Bornstein and Quevillon taught these children (in a laboratory setting) to ask questions about solving intelligence test items, thereby inducing the children to set goals (Step 1) and helping them to design strategies (Step 2). They instructed them well enough to instruct themselves in strategy implementation and monitoring (Step 3). They also instructed the children to reinforce themselves for good performance (Step 4). Transfer was measured by observing classroom performance. Impressive transfer was obtained. The subjects in this experiment were younger than those in any other cognitive instructional experiment. It is worth noting that Bornstein and Quevillon instructed more superordinate processes than any other investigators.

Belmont, Butterfield, and Borkowski (1978) gave retarded adolescents detailed instruction in the use of a particular rehearsal strategy that could be applied to the training and the transfer tasks, thereby doing an especially detailed job of designing a strategy. They provided full feedback on the results of applying the strategy (Step 4) and related those results to the use of the instructed strategy (Step 5). In addition, half the subjects were trained on only one version of the training task, while the others were trained on two versions. Both groups showed transfer. The doubly-trained group showed more than the singly-trained.

Knapczyk and Livingston (1974) taught junior high school retarded boys to ask questions of their teachers, thereby helping the boys to set performance goals (Step 1) and to design study strategies (Step 2). This instruction increased the amount of time the boys spent doing assignments in class, and it increased their reading comprehension.

In an experiment with pre-linguistic, severely retarded children Kahn (1977) first taught Piagetian sensorimotor skills and then instructed language use, which was facilitated by the previous Piagetian skills training. This looks like transfer (in the context of a learning situation) without the instruction of any superordinate process, though we would need to see a more complete description of Kahn's procedures before being certain that he had not taught any such process. Lacking a fuller description, we conclude that this experiment is an example of teaching prerequisite skills and knowledge, rather than an example of instructing superordinate processes. We take Kahn's experiment as a demonstration that some learning depends upon prior learning, rather than as a contradiction of the utility of instructing superordinate processes.

## CONCLUSION

Six of seven experiments that produced generalized cognition by young and mentally retarded children have instructed some aspect of superordinate processing. Belmont and Butterfield (1977) reviewed 114 other studies on the use of cognitive instruction. None of these involved superordinate processes, nor did any of them report generalized results. These facts suggest that the deliberate training of superordinate processes will result in important gains in the ability of retarded people to think productively, and to solve novel problems. To the extent that productive thinking and novel problem solving signify intelligence, we may be confident that intelligence can be modified by attending to children's superordinate, self-management skills. It is unknown how much improvement can be expected, but we suppose that cognitive researchers have barely scratched the surface. No attempt has yet been made to train all of the self-management steps involved in problem solving, and even when that is done, there will remain two other instructional goals: The child must be taught to know when he is confronted with a problem, and he must be motivated to try to solve problems when he encounters them. Only then will being taught how to solve problems make a substantial difference.

## REFERENCES

Belmont, J.M., & Butterfield, E. C. The instructional approach to developmental cognitive research. In R. Kail & J. Hagen (Eds.), *Perspectives on the Development of Memory and Cognition.* Hillsdale, NJ: Lawrence Erlbaum Associates, 1977.

Belmont, J. M., Butterfield, E. C., & Borkowski, J. G. Training retarded people to generalize memorization methods across memory tasks. In M. M. Gruneberg, P. E. Morris, & R. N. Sykes (Eds.), *Practical Aspects of Memory.* London: Academic Press, 1978.

Binet, A., & Simon, T. *The Development of Intelligence in Children.* Baltimore, MD: Williams and Wilkins, 1916. Quoted by Farber, B. *Mental Retardation: Its Social Context and Social Consequences.* Boston, MA: Houghton Mifflin Co., 1968.

Bornstein, P. H., & Quevillon, R. P. The effects of a self-instructional package on overactive preschool boys. *Journal of Applied Behavior Analysis,* 1976, *9,* 179–188.

Brown, A. L. The development of memory: Knowing, knowing about knowing, and knowing how to know. In H. W. Reese (Ed.), *Advances in Child Development and Behavior* (Vol. 10). New York, NY: Academic Press, 1975.

Brown, A. L., & Barclay, C. R. The effects of training specific mnemonics on the metamnemonic efficiency of retarded children. *Child Development,* 1976, *47,* 70–80.

Brown, A. L., Campione, J. C., Bray, N. W. & Wilcox, B. L. Keeping track of changing variables: Effects of rehearsal training and rehearsal prevention in normal and retarded adolescents. *Journal of Experimental Psychology,* 1973,*101,* 123–131.

Brown, A. L. Campione, J. C., & Barclay, C. R. Training self-checking routines for estimating test readiness: Generalization from list learning to prose recall. *Child Development,* 1979, *50,* 501–512.

Butterfield, E. C., Siladi, D., & Belmont, J. M. Validating theories of intelligence. In H. Reese & L. Lipsitt (Eds.), *Advances in Child Development and Behavior* (Vol. 15). New York, NY: Academic Press, 1980.

Butterfield, E.C., Wambold, C., & Belmont, J. M. On the theory and practice of improving short-term memory. *American Journal of Mental Deficiency,* 1973, *77,* 654–669.

Charlesworth, W. R. Ethology: Its relevance for observational studies of human adaptation. In G. P. Sackett (Ed.), *Observing Behavior, Vol. 1: Theory and Applications in Mental Retardation.* Baltimore, MD: University Park Press, 1978.

Flavell, J. H., & Wellman, H. M. Metamemory. In R. Kail & J. Hagen (Eds.), *Perspectives on the Development of Memory and Cognition.* Hillsdale, NJ: Lawrence Erlbaum Associates, 1977.

Grossman, H. J. (Ed.), *Manual of Terminology and Classification in Mental Retardation, 1973 Revision.* Washington, DC: American Association on Mental Deficiency.

Kahn, J. V. On training generalized thinking. Paper presented at the 85th Annual Convention of the American Psychological Association, San Francisco, August, 1977.

Kendall, C. R., Borkowski, J. G., & Cavanaugh, J. C. Metamemory and the transfer of an interrogative strategy by EMR children. *Intelligence,* 1980, *4,* 255–270.

Knapczyk, D. R., & Livingston, G. The effects of promoting question-asking upon on-task behavior and reading comprehension. *Journal of Applied Behavior Analysis,* 1974, *7,* 115–121.

Ross, D. M., & Ross, S. A. Facilitative effect of mnemonic strategies on multiple associate learning in EMR children. *American Journal of Mental Deficiency,* 1978, *82,* 460–466.

Turnure, J., Buium, N., & Thurlow, M. L. The effectiveness of interrogatives for promoting verbal elaboration productivity in young children. *Child Development,* 1976, *47,* 851–855.

Wechsler, D. *The Measurement of Adult Intelligence. 3rd Edition.* Baltimore, MD: Williams and Wilkins, 1944.

# 6

# Componential Approaches to the Training of Intelligent Performance*

ROBERT J. STERNBERG, JERRY L. KETRON, AND JANET S. POWELL
*Yale University*

This article proposes that ''componential'' approaches to the training of intelligent performance are a useful means for producing and understanding improvements in such performance. We buttress our proposal by citing outcomes (some of them preliminary) from three experiments conducted at Yale. The results of these experiments show that at least some strategies for intelligent performance can be trained; that certain strategies are better, on the average, than others; that the properties of strategies that make them ''better'' or ''worse'' can be isolated through componential means; that certain strategies are preferable for people with certain ability patterns, but that other strategies are preferable for people with other ability patterns; that certain strategies are preferable for use with certain stimulus types, but that other strategies are preferable for use with other stimulus types; and that people may be quite cognizant of the strategy they are trying to employ while at the same time being quite incognizant of the strategy they are actually employing, or of the difference between the two strategies.

The past decade has witnessed a powerful resurgence of interest in the nature and training of intelligent performance. Research conducted during this decade has been largely guided by an information-processing approach to intelligence, rather than by the psychometric (or factorial) approach that guided much earlier research. Facets of intelligence that were formerly studied in terms of structural models based upon patterns of subject variation in task performance have now been studied as well in terms of process models based upon patterns of stimulus variation in task performance. Examples of facets that have been so studied are

---

*Preparation of this article and execution of the research described in this article were supported by Contract N0001478C0025 from the Office of Naval Research to Robert J. Sternberg. Jerry Ketron is supported by a Yale University graduate fellowship; Janet Powell is supported by a National Science Foundation graduate fellowship.

The authors express their appreciation to Evelyn M. Weil for her valuable collaboration in the linear-syllogisms training research (Sternberg & Weil, 1980), and to Barbara E. Conway and Elizabeth Charles for valuable assistance in data analysis in the linear-syllogisms and analogies training research. This article is based upon a presentation at the annual meeting of the American Educational Research Association, Boston, April 1980. Requests for reprints should be sent to Robert J. Sternberg, Department of Psychology, Yale University, Box 11A Yale Station, New Haven, Connecticut 06520.

155

verbal ability (e.g., Hunt, 1978; Hunt, Frost, & Lunneborg, 1973; Hunt, Lunneborg, & Lewis, 1975), reasoning ability (e.g., Pellegrino & Glaser, 1980; Sternberg, 1977; Sternberg, Guyote, & Turner, 1980; Whitely & Barnes, 1979), problem-solving ability (e.g., Newell & Simon, 1972; Siegler, 1978), spatial ability (e.g., Cooper & Shepard, 1973; Egan, 1979; Shepard & Metzler, 1971), and memory ability (e.g., Belmont & Butterfield, 1971; Brown, 1975; Campione & Brown, 1977; Horn, 1980). The psychometric and information-processing approaches to the understanding of intelligence are largely complementary, focusing as they do upon different kinds of variation in task performance. But, the information-processing approach has been particularly fruitful in suggesting directions for training intelligent performance, perhaps because of its emphasis upon the processes and strategies people use in intelligent behavior (Sternberg 1980a, 1980d, 1981a). Impressive training outcomes have been achieved in domains as diverse as reasoning (Feuerstein, 1979, 1980; Holzman, Glaser, & Pellegrino, 1976; Trabasso, Riley, & Wilson, 1975), problem solving (Klahr, 1978; Siegler, 1978), and memory (Belmont & Butterfield, 1971; Butterfield, Wambold, & Belmont, 1973; Brown & Campione, 1977; Wanschura & Borkowski, 1975).

Our own approaches to understanding and training intelligent performance have been guided by an approach characterized by its blend of information-processing and psychometric techniques. Our particular blend of the two techniques, which is only one of many such blends (e.g., Carroll, 1976; Hunt et al., 1973; Jensen, 1979; Mulholland, Pellegrino, & Glaser, 1980; Snow, 1979), has been referred to as "componential analysis" (Sternberg, 1977, 1978, 1979, 1980d, 1981b). A major goal of componential analysis is to isolate information-processing components of intelligent task performance, and to relate these components to each other and to performance on standard psychometric tests and factors of intelligence. We believe the approach has been at least somewhat successful in helping us understand the nature of intelligent performance. During the past few years, we have been asking whether any of this understanding can be translated into a program of action for training intelligent performance. In this article, we list some of the questions we have been asking about training of intelligent performance, and describe some of the research we have done and are currently doing that is addressed to these questions.

The questions that have guided our research are these:

1. Can optimal strategies for intelligent performance be trained?
2. Are certain kinds of strategies better, on the average (over people and stimulus types), than others?
3. What is it about certain strategies that make them better (or worse) than others?
4. Are certain strategies preferable for people with certain ability patterns, and other strategies preferable for people with other ability patterns?

5. Are certain strategies preferable for certain stimulus types, and other strategies preferable for other stimulus types?
6. What information do people have about the strategies they are using and that they should be using?

The remainder of this article describes research we have done and are doing that addresses these questions. We draw in particular upon three training studies, one using deductive problems, namely, linear syllogisms (Sternberg & Weil, 1980); a second using inductive reasoning problems, namely, analogies (Sternberg & Ketron, in press); and a third using verbal comprehension problems, namely, inferring meanings of unfamiliar words presented in familiar kinds of written contexts (Powell & Sternberg, 1982).

## CAN OPTIMAL STRATEGIES FOR INTELLIGENT PERFORMANCE BE TRAINED?

The research of Holzman, Glaser, and Pellegrino (1976) on the training of performance on series extrapolation problems suggested that information-processing strategies can be trained at least to some extent, and our research outcomes are consistent with those of Holzman et al.

In our linear-syllogisms training study (Sternberg & Weil, 1980), college-age subjects were asked to solve problems such as "John is taller than Pete. Pete is taller than Bill. Who is tallest? John, Pete, Bill." Problems were presented to subjects tachistoscopically, and subjects pressed a button indicating their response choice. Subjects were timed as they solved the problems; they were told to solve the problems as quickly as they could without making errors. Subjects were divided into a control group and two experimental groups. Control-group subjects were given no explicit instruction as to how to solve the problems. Experimental-group subjects were told that although there are many ways of solving these problems, they should use the method in which they would be instructed. Subjects in a "visualization" group were told to try to organize the statements into a spatial array or series formation. The important thing, they were told, was to try to visualize the relationships described in the statements. Subjects were shown examples of different pictorial arrays that might correspond to what they would construct in their heads. They were told that they could use any of the pictorial formats, or some other format, so long as they used some pictorial representation to solve the problems. Subjects in an "algorithmic" group were told to read the final question first, then to read the first statement, then to answer the question in terms of the first statement ("John" in the example), and finally to scan the second statement. If the answer to the first statement *was not* contained in the second statement (as in the example, where "Pete " and "Bill," but not "John," appear in the second statement), the answer to the first statement then was also the correct response to the entire problem (hence, "John" is the correct response in this problem). If the answer to the first statement *was* contained in the second statement, then the other answer choice in the second statement was the correct response to the entire problem. This algorithmic strategy, suggested by Quinton and Fellows (1975), works successfully for any linear syllogism in which it is possible to determine the full ordering of all three terms. All linear syllogisms in the experiment did, in fact, have fully determinate orderings of terms. Consider now some basic statistics from the data collected for the linear syllogisms.

Mean solution latency was 7.03 seconds in the untrained group, 7.18 seconds in the visaualization group, but only 4.51 seconds in the algorithmic group. The algorithmic strategy was thus much more time-efficient than the visaualization strategy or the strategy used by the untrained subjects, although the substantial decrease in latency was bought at some expense in accuracy. Mean error rates were 1.7% in the untrained group, 2.0% in the visualization group, and 3.5% in the algorithmic group. Training had some effect, at least in the last group.

These results raised as many questions as they answered. First, what were subjects in the untrained group doing, and did it differ from what subjects in the visualization group were doing? Second, were instructed subjects doing what they were trained to do? Third, if at least some instructed subjects were not doing what they were trained to do, what were they doing? These questions could be answered by analyzing data at the level of individual subjects. Latency data for each subject were mathematically modeled using componential modeling techniques (see Sternberg, 1977, 1980a, 1980b). Four alternative models were fit to each subject's latency data. These models (described in detail in Sternberg, 1980b) asserted that subjects solved the linear syllogisms using either the short-cut algorithmic strategy, which all but bypasses the need for reasoning operations, or that subjects solved the items using reasoning operations working on either a linguistic data base, a spatial (imaginal) data base, or a combination of the two. Subjects were then classified as using the strategy represented by the model best fitting their individual data.

In answer to the first question, that of what subjects in the untrained group were doing and how it differed from what subjects in the visualization group were doing, almost two-thirds of the untrained subjects were using a reasoning strategy operating upon a combination of linguistic and spatial data bases; the remaining subjects were approximately equally split in their use of the other three strategies. The proportions of subjects using each strategy were almost identical in the visualization group, suggesting that when trained to use visualization, subjects do pretty much what they would have done without training.

In answer to the second question, that of whether instructed subjects were doing what they were trained to do, at least three-fourths of the subjects in the visualization group were using a strategy that required visualization (either the strategy acting upon a spatial representation or the one acting upon both a linguistic and a spatial representation). In the algorithmic group, although subjects were about four times as likely to use the algorithmic strategy as were subjects in either of the other two groups, only slightly fewer than half of the 48 subjects actually appear to have used the algorithmic strategy.

In answer to the third question, that of what instructed subjects were doing who were not doing what they were trained to do, about the same number of subjects in the algorithmic group used the reasoning strategy operating upon a linguistic and a spatial representation as used the algorithmic strategy. The few remaining subjects used either the linguistic or the spatial strategy. Thus, the algorithmic training was successful in converting many, but not all subjects to use of the short-cut algorithm. Visualization training was consistent with what most subjects did anyway, and probably had little effect.

In our analogies study (Sternberg & Ketron, in press), data for 96 subjects (half of the target number we shall eventually test for the study) have been collected and analyzed. These college-age subjects were asked to solve analogies of the form A : B :: C : ($D_1$, $D_2$), where analogy terms were schematic pictures of people. These pictures varied on four binary dimensions. The pictures were of two kinds. One kind varied in height (tall-short), shading of clothing (black-white), sex (male-female), and weight (fat-thin). The other kind varied in hat color (black-white), vest pattern (striped-polka-dotted), hand gear (briefcase-umbrella), and footwear (shoes-boots). The critical difference between the two kinds of stimuli was that stimuli of the first kind possessed perceptually integral attributes, which tend to be processed holistically, whereas stimuli of the second kind possessed perceptually separable attributes, which tend to be processed analytically (see Garner, 1974; Sternberg & Rifkin, 1979). No subject saw more than one kind of stimulus attribute. Analogies were presented tachistoscopically, with subjects being told to solve the analogies as quickly as they could without making errors. Subjects receiving each kind of analogy were equally divided among one control group and three experimental groups. Each group received different instructions.

Subjects in the control group were not trained in any particular strategy for analogy solution. They were told simply to solve the analogies in whatever way they wished. Subjects in the experimental groups all received training of the following three kinds.[1]

In a fully "exhaustive" training condition, subjects were trained to infer all four possible relations between the A and B (first and second) analogy terms (e.g., height might change from tall to short, shading remain black in both pictures, sex remain male in both pictures, and weight change from fat to thin), and to apply all four inferred relations from the C (third) analogy term, in order to select the correct D (fourth) analogy term (e.g., height would have to change from tall to short, shading remain the same, sex remain the same, and weight change from

---

[1]We knew when we undertook the analogies training research that most subjects spontaneously use an optimal or near-optimal strategy for analogy solution. The major theoretical question motivating our research was "What general characteristics of certain strategies make them either optimal or non-optimal in reasoning performance?"

fat to thin). In this strategy, then, subjects always inferred and applied all four attributes.

In a fully "self-terminating" training condition, subjects were trained to infer one relation (of their choice) from A to B (e.g., that height changes from tall to short), and immediately to apply this relation from C to D. If that relation distinguished the correct answer option from the incorrect one (e.g., C was tall but only one of the two answer options was short), then subjects were to select the correct option at once. If the attribute did not distinguish between options (e.g., if both options were short), then subjects were to select another attribute (of their choice) and to attempt to choose an answer option on the basis of a distinction between options in their values on that attribute. This procedure was to continue until the correct answer could be distinguished from the incorrect one. In this strategy, then, subjects inferred and applied the minimum possible number of attributes (given their idiosyncratic order of selection of attributes) needed for selecting the correct answer.

In a "mixture" training condition, subjects were trained to infer all four possible relations between the A and B analogy terms, but to apply only as many of those relations as they neeeded to distinguish the correct answer from the incorrect one. In other words, inference was exhaustive, but application was self-terminating: Subjects inferred all possible relations between A and B, but applied only the minimum possible number of relations from C to D. Consider now some mean data from these four conditions.

Mean solution latencies for stimuli with integral attributes were 2.87 seconds for untrained control subjects, 9.02 seconds for exhaustive training subjects, 3.10 seconds for self-terminating training subjects, and 5.46 seconds for mixture training subjects. Error rates were 4%, 4%, 5%, and 3% for the four respective groups. Mean solution latencies for stimuli with separable attributes were 2.78 seconds for untrained control subjects, 7.13 seconds for exhaustive training subjects, 2.77 seconds for self-terminating training subjects, and 4.69 seconds for mixture training subjects. Error rates were 2%, 5%, 3%, and 5% for the four respective groups. Training had some kind of effect.

What were subjects in the various groups actually doing? Although both group and individual data were modeled componentially, the individual data were not of sufficient reliability to allow conclusions to be drawn with confidence; hence, we shall concentrate upon group data. Seven alternative models were fit to the latency data for each group. There were more models than there were training groups because no instruction was given in two components of information processing that appear in a full information-processing model of analogical reasoning (Sternberg, 1977; Sternberg & Rifkin, 1979). These two components are encoding of stimulus terms, which can be either exhaustive or self-terminating with respect to the (four) attributes of each analogy term, and mapping, the perception of the higher-order relations between the first and second halves of the analogy, which can also be either exhaustive or self-terminating. The seven models (see Sternberg & Rifkin, 1979) were:

| *Model I*: | encoding, inference, mapping, and application exhaustive; |
|---|---|
| *Model II*: | encoding, inference, and mapping exhaustive; application self-terminating; |
| *Model III*: | encoding and inference exhaustive; mapping and application self-terminating; |
| *Model IV:* | encoding exhaustive; inference, mapping, and application self-terminating; |
| *Model IM:* | inference and application exhaustive; encoding self-terminating (but mathematically indistinguishable from exhaustive); no mapping; |
| *Model II–IIIM:* | inference exhaustive; encoding and application self-terminating; no mapping; |
| *Model IVM:* | encoding, inference, and application self-terminating; no mapping. |

Consider first model fits for subjects receiving analogies with integral stimulus attributes. Data for subjects in the untrained control group were best fit by Model IV, with Model III a close competitor. In previous experiments (Sternberg, 1977; Sternberg & Rifkin, 1979), data for comparable subjects were best fit by Model III (which differs from Model IV only in inference being exhaustive rather than self-terminating), with Model IV a close competitor, so that these results are close but not identical to previous ones with these stimuli. Data for subjects trained to use full self-termination should be best fit by either Model IV or IVM, in order for these data to be compatible with the kind of training and the subjects received. In fact, the group data were best fit by Model IVM. On the average, therefore, subjects in this group did as they were instructed, that is, they followed a strategy with full self-termination, one that was similar but not identical to the strategy followed by uninstructed subjects. Data for subjects trained to use fully exhaustive processing should be best fit by either Model I or IM, in order for these data to be compatible with the kind of training subjects received. In fact, the data were best fit by Model I, although there were suggestions in the data that some of the subjects used Model II, at least some of the time. In general, though, these data, too, were consistent with the training subjects received; but as could be inferred from the large mean difference between latencies for this group and the untrained group, the strategy followed by subjects in this group differed radically from that followed by untrained subjects. Finally, data for subjects trained to use mixed exhaustive and self-terminating processing should be best fit by any of Models II, III, or II–IIIM, in order for the data to be compatible with the kind of training the subjects received. In fact, the data were best fit by Model III. Thus, these subjects, too, followed instructions, and differed from the untrained subjects only in their use of exhaustive rather than self-terminating inference. To summarize, subjects receiving strategy training for analogies with integral attributes generally followed the strategy they were trained to use.

Consider next model fits for subjects receiving analogies with separable stimulus attributes. Data for subjects in the untrained control group were best fit by Model IVM. In a previous experiment (Sternberg & Rifkin, 1979), data for comparable untrained subjects were also best fit by Model IVM, so that these results were completely consistent with ones obtained in earlier research. Data for subjects trained to use fully self-terminating processing (which should be best fit by Model IV or IVM to be consistent with training) were in fact best fit by Model IVM. Thus, these subjects followed the same strategy as did subjects who were trained to use fully self-terminating information processing for the analogies with integral stimulus attributes. Data for subjects trained to use fully exhaustive processing (which should be best fit by Model I or IM to be consistent with training) were in fact best fit by Model IVM (which is quite different in character from either of Models I or IM), although one parameter (self-terminating encoding) could not be reliably estimated for this group. Thus, it appears likely that subjects in this group did not follow their training instructions, although it is not clear exactly what these subjects did do. Finally, data for subjects trained to use mixed exhaustive and self-terminating processing (which should be best fit by any of Models II, III, or II–IIIM to be consistent with training) were best fit by Model IVM as well, although there was evidence that at least some subjects used Model II–IIIM. Again, strategy usage was not consistent with training. To summarize, subjects receiving strategy training for analogies with separable attributes generally did not follow the strategy they were trained to use, perhaps because Model IVM is so "natural" in some sense for these stimuli: No subjects have been found who use any other model.

In our verbal comprehension study (Powell & Sternberg, 1982), data have been subjected to only the most rudimentary analyses, so our emphasis will be upon describing what we are attempting to accomplish and how we are attempting to accomplish it. A major purpose of the study is to find out how subjects (high school students) learn, retain, and transfer meanings of unfamiliar words presented in familiar kinds of contexts.[2] For our present purposes, however, we shall dwell upon a subsidiary purpose of the study, that of training subjects to learn, retain, and transfer meanings of unfamiliar words presented in context.

All subjects in the study received a set of 33 brief reading passages such as might be found in newspapers, magazines, novels, or textbooks. Embedded within these passages were from one to four very low-frequency words, which could be repeated from zero to four times either within or between passages, but not both. Examples of two such passages, which differ considerably in content, are the following:

> The ultimate goal of those seriously involved in raising livestock is to produce animals with a high percentage of top quality meat and a low percentage of waste. Recently, livestock breeders have successfully developed a new breed of turkey whose *haeccity* is its high proportion of breast meat to dark meat. The most efficient way to improve stock, practiced by many ranches, is to hire a *thremmatologist* to advise in the purchase and mating of different breeds. The *thremmatologist* carefully researches the characteristics of each breed involved and then examines the bloodlines of the specific animals under consideration. The success resulting from this scientific monitoring perhaps

---

[2]A further description of this research can be found in Sternberg (1980d).

justifies the *jactancy* of its proponents, who belittle the old trial-and-error methods and foresee a new age of made-to-order livestock.

Two ill-dressed people—the one a tired woman of middle years and the other a tense young man—sat around a fire where the common meal was almost ready. The mother, Tanith, peered at her son through the *oam* of the bubbling stew. It had been a long time since his last *ceilidh* and Tobar had changed greatly; where once he had seemed all legs and clumsy joints, he now was well-formed and in control of his hard, young body. As they ate, Tobar told of his past year, re-creating for Tanith how he had wandered long and far in his quest to gain the skills he would need to be permitted to rejoin the company. Then all to soon, their brief *ceilidh* over, Tobar walked over to touch his mother's arm and quickly left.

Subjects were divided into three groups. In the first experimental group, subjects were asked to provide ratings regarding the low-frequency words and their surrounding contexts. These ratings were of:

1. how concrete versus abstract each word was,
2. how helpful the part of the passage preceding the occurrence of the low-frequency word was in deciding what the word meant,
3. how helpful the part of the passage following the occurrence of the low-frequency word was in deciding what the word meant,
4. how helpful the passage as a whole was in enabling the subject to decide what the word meant,
5. how important the low-frequency word was to understanding the main idea of the sentence in which it was used, and
6. how important the low-frequency word was to understanding the main idea of the passage in which it occurred.

When a given word occurred more than once in a given passage, subjects were also asked to rate how helpful the part of the passage between occurrences of the word was in deciding what the word meant.[3] In the second experimental group, subjects were asked to define as best they could each of the underlined (low-frequency) words. When a single word appeared twice in a passage, they only needed to define it once, but if a given word appeared again in a later passage, subjects had to redefine the word later on. Subjects were allowed to view the passage they had just read at the time they defined the word, but they were not allowed to look back at previous passages. Subjects in the third (control) group were asked to read each of the passages and to provide a title for it. Thus, subjects in this group had to understand at some level the contents of the passage in order to perform their task, but the attention of these subjects was drawn to aspects of the passage that were less relevant to understanding the low-frequency words.

---

[3]The primary purpose of these ratings was to quantify the independent variables manipulated in the experimental passages.

All subjects received a pretest and a retest that contained passages very much like those in the main part of the study. The subjects' task was to read each passage and define the low-frequency words.

Our major training concern was with the extent to which the two kinds of training exercises would improve subjects' abilities to understand unfamiliar words presented in short passages. The dependent measure was improvement from pretest to retest for each of the experimental groups in comparison to each other and to the control group. Our very preliminary data analyses indicate success for the training procedures in that subjects became more aware of how to define a word presented in context, but we are not yet in a position to evaluate our findings in an informed way.

## ARE CERTAIN KINDS OF STRATEGIES BETTER, ON THE AVERAGE, THAN OTHERS?

The three experiments described above all have implications for answering this question, and on the basis of our observations, we believe the answer is clearly affirmative.

In the linear-syllogisms experiment, the algorithmic strategy resulted in a large decrease in mean solution latency, although at the expense of some increase in error rate. In this particular case, the strategy was one that few subjects adopted spontaneously, but was one that many subjects could be trained to use with just about 10 to 15 minutes of instruction. The strategy does have a disadvantage, namely, its limitation to fully determinate problems (i.e. ones in which the complete ordering of the three terms can be inferred from the problem statement); also, it is not clear how the strategy would be generalized to linear ordering problems with more than three terms, e.g., John is taller than Bill; Bill is taller than Pete; Pete is taller than Mike; who is tallest? The model with the second lowest mean latency, and with a lower error rate, is the mixture model, which involves representations of information both linguistically and spatially. Thus, this model might be the most efficacious one from the standpoint of generality, as well as efficiency of information processing.

In the analogies experiment, the self-terminating Models IV and IVM appear to have been the most efficacious ones for subjects to use. They resulted in the lowest solution latencies, and were not associated with particularly high error rates in this experiment. Most subjects left to their own devices appear to have used either Model IV (analogies with integral attributes) or Model IVM (analogies with separable attributes), and subjects instructed to use a self-terminating model had the lowest solution latencies of any instructed group. For analogies with separable attributes, we had little success in getting subjects to use any model other than IVM, making it difficult to compare results for different strategies. Previous research is consistent with the present research in suggesting that for analogies with separable attributes, subjects as young as seven years of age and as old as adulthood use

Model IVM spontaneously (Sternberg & Rifkin, 1979). This same research found a transition over age in model usage for analogies with integral attributes, however. Second-graders (about 7 years of age) used Model IVM, fourth-graders (about 9 years of age) used Model IV, and sixth-graders through adults used Model III. The empirical data have never distinguished well between Models III and IV, however, and it is quite possible that subjects either alternate over time in their use of one model or the other, or that there are individual differences in which subjects use each of these two models.

We do not yet have sufficient data from the verbal-comprehension study to compare the efficacy of alternative strategies used within the learning-from-context paradigm. We suggest, however, that if one's goal is to improve vocabulary, learning strategies for inferring meanings from context is superior, on the average, to merely memorizing meanings of words from a dictionary or similar source, for reasons to be discussed.

## WHAT IS IT ABOUT CERTAIN STRATEGIES THAT MAKES THEM BETTER OR WORSE THAN OTHER STRATEGIES?

The superiority of the algorithmic strategy for solving linear syllogisms can probably be traced to its mechanistic nature: Subjects essentially bypass the use of transitive inference by using a short cut that provides a solution with minimal information processing. An analogue exists for solving categorical syllogisms (e.g., All B are C. All A are B. Can one conclude that All A are C?): A small set of rules enables one to pick out any of the relatively small subset of categorical syllogisms that is deductively valid (see Copi, 1978). But such short-cut strategies are of less interest than alternative strategies, because they capitalize upon specific features of certain item types and are not generalizable to problems that are even quite similar in structure (e.g., four-term linear syllogisms). The second most efficacious strategy for solving linear syllogisms, that characterized by the mixture model, may be more efficacious than the spatial and linguistic strategies because of its use of that form of representation at each stage of information processing that is most well suited to that particular stage of information processing. The alternative strategies may extend their single representations beyond those stages of information processing where they are most suitable.

The superiority of self-terminating strategies for analogical reasoning can be traced to the reduction in the number of component executions required for analogy solution (which can be substantial for analogies with terms having complex or numerous attributes) and to the reduction in load upon working memory that results from testing one attribute completely, before moving on to consider any other attributes. But, as was the case for linear syllogisms, the user of this highly efficient kind of strategy must beware. Previous research has shown that almost all errors made in analogical reasoning derive from execution of self-terminating (as opposed to exhaustive) information-processing components (within a given strategy) (Sternberg, 1977).

Finally, we would like to state why we speculate that acquiring strategies for inferring meanings of words from context is superior to memorizing lists of words, if one's goal is to improve one's vocabulary. We believe that the former route has at least two advantages. First, our observations of vocabulary-learning in the real world persuade us that learning achieved through rote memorization of words is less durable than meaningful acquisition of words encountered in natural contexts. Unless people see and use the memorized words frequently in everyday contexts, the meanings of the words are forgotten. Almost everyone has had the experience of seeing or hearing words whose meanings one once memorized, but has since forgotten. We believe the meanings of words learned in context are more likely to be durable because the meaning can later be reinstantiated through association with the context, and because even if the meaning of the word is forgotten, if one's skills for learning meanings from context are sufficiently sharp, one can re-infer the meaning of the word from the new context. Second, we suggest that the learning of word meanings in context is more likely to be generalizable than the learning of word meanings in isolation. Words are often used with subtle and multiple shades of meaning that are conveyed in real-world, but not in dictionary, contexts. As one sees a word in multiple contexts, one essentially constructs the meaning of the word, building up a word-meaning representation that mimics in greater or lesser degree some ill-defined and probably not precisely definable "true" meaning. This active construction process results in a representation that is readily usable in everyday life.

## ARE THERE PERSON × STRATEGY INTERACTIONS?

Evidence from our linear-syllogisms research (as well as from the research of others; see, for example, Gavurin, 1967; MacLeod, Hunt, & Mathews, 1978) strongly suggests the existence of person (or aptitude) × strategy interactions. In the linear-syllogisms experiment, we correlated people's scores on orthogonal verbal and spatial ability factors with people's latencies for solving linear syllogisms. The correlations for the original groups were undifferentiated both across groups and across (verbal and spatial) abilities. Latencies were correlated with verbal and spatial abilities in each group, and there were no signs of interactions. Suspecting the possibility of multiple strategies within (as well as between) groups, we modeled each subject's data individually, and discovered that there were indeed strategy differences within each group: Not every trained subject was doing what he or she was trained to do, and untrained subjects showed natural individual differences in strategy selection. We therefore re-sorted subjects into strategy groups on the basis of the individual modeling. We now found that latencies of subjects using the mixture model were significantly correlated with both verbal and spatial ability; latencies of subjects using the linguistic model were significantly correlated with verbal but not spatial ability; latencies of subjects using the spatial model were significantly correlated with spatial but not verbal ability; and latencies of subjects using the algorithmic model were significantly correlated with verbal ability, and marginally correlated with spatial ability. Thus, the efficacy of a given strategy depended upon both the strategy and the subject's pattern of abilities.

In the analogies research, latencies for analogy solution were significantly correlated with an inductive reasoning factor score, but only for analogies with integral stimuli, and only for untrained subjects. Training seems to have removed the correlation for the analogies with integral attributes, and the correlation was not found for analogies with separable attributes. It should be noted that analogies of the kind used in this experiment—ones with simple schematic-picture attributes—tend to yield lower correlations with ability tests than do other kinds of analogies with more complex attributes (Sternberg, 1977).

We have not investigated person × strategy interactions in the verbal-comprehension situation, although we are planning a study to investigate the hypothesis that for some subjects—those who do not have, or have great difficulty acquiring, skills for learning meanings of words from context—rote learning of vocabulary is superior to contextual learning as a means for vocabulary building.

## ARE THERE STIMULUS × STRATEGY INTERACTIONS?

None of several investigations of linear syllogistic reasoning provides any evidence of stimulus × strategy interactions. Subjects were tested with a variety of adjective pairs (taller-shorter, better-worse, older-younger, faster-slower), but strategy usage did not differ across these adjective pairs (Sternberg, 1980d, 1981a; Sternberg & Weil, 1980).

The analogies data show clear signs of a stimulus × strategy interaction. In the Sternberg-Ketron (in press) data, Model IV was preferred for analogies with integral attributes (but Model III was preferred in the Sternberg, 1977, and Sternberg & Rifkin, 1979, data), whereas Model IVM was preferred for analogies with separable attributes (as in the previous Sternberg & Rifkin, 1979, data). The Sternberg-Rifkin data showed an even more complex person × stimulus × strategy interaction: Model IVM was preferred for subjects of all ages when subjects solved analogies with separable attributes; but the preferred model changed with age—from Model IVM to Model IV to Model III—when subjects solved analogies with integral attributes.

The verbal comprehension study did not manipulate stimulus type, and hence contains no suggestions of stimulus × strategy interactions. We would expect, however, that one's purpose, e.g., reading the passages for comprehension versus reading the passages to learn the new words, would, in effect, redefine the task, and therefore would have an effect on which strategy is best.

# WHAT INFORMATION DO PEOPLE HAVE
## ABOUT STRATEGIES?

Our analogies study was conducted in part to explore the question of what impressions people have about various strategies they use. Each subject in each group received a questionnaire asking various questions about the strategy the subject had used in solving the analogies.

Consider first the questionnaire responses for subjects receiving analogies with separable attributes. In previous research, it has been found that subjects were well able to describe their thought processes in solving such analogies (Sternberg & Rifkin, 1979). In the present research, subjects' descriptions were highly consistent with the strategies the subjects were trained to use, but not consistent with the strategies subjects actually did use (at least, according to the mathematical modeling). The data suggest that subjects did in fact try to use the strategy they were trained to use; that their questionnaire descriptions correspond to what they were trying to do (although not, apparently, to what they actually succeeded in doing), and hence that subjects were aware of what they were trying to do; but that subjects were not fully aware of the discrepancy between what they were trying to do and what they actually were doing. These discrepancies were striking. The group trained to use the exhaustive model, for example, showed an $R^2$ of .53 between predicted and observed values for a fully exhaustive model (I or IM), but an $R^2$ of .91 between predicted and observed values for a fully self-terminating model (IVM). Although this patterning of data was quite similar to that for the group trained to use the full self-terminating strategy (where the $R^2$ for the fully self-terminating model was .94), the fact that subjects in the exhaustive training group were trying to do something different from what subjects in the self-terminating group were doing is shown by the fact that the mean solution latency in the exhaustive group was over 7 seconds, compared to less than 3 seconds in the self-terminating group. The former subjects were obviously trying to be exhaustive, although they were apparently less than fully successful in these efforts.

Subjects in the separable-stimuli group described the fully exhaustive strategy as slower (and less accurate) than the mixture strategy, which in turn was perceived as slower than the fully self-terminating strategy. These perceptions were, of course, accurate for the strategies as trained. The exhaustive and mixture strategies were perceived as more difficult both to learn and to maintain (over time), than was the self-terminating strategy. Indeed, subjects reported extreme difficulty in maintaining the exhaustive strategy, and the data indicate that subjects did indeed have extreme difficulty in maintaining this strategy. The exhaustive strategy was also reported correctly as requiring the greatest memory load; the self-terminating strategy was correctly reported as requiring the least memory load. Subjects in the exhaustive group reported having been the most conscious of the strategy they were executing; subjects in the self-terminating group reported having been least conscious of the strategy, with subjects in the mixture group in the middle. Overall, the exhaustive strategy was perceived as the poorest one and the self-terminating strategy as the best one, with the mixture strategy again in the middle. These reports accurately reflected the distribution of mean solution latencies. Almost no subjects in the exhaustive training group reported that they would have used the exhaustive strategy, had they not been trained to use it. Slightly fewer than half of the subjects in the other two groups reported that they would have used the strategy they were trained to use (self-terminating or mixture), had they been untrained. Here, subjects trained to use the self-terminating strategy were inaccurate in their perceptions of what they would have done, since the data from the untrained groups suggest that most subjects left to their own devices will in fact use a self-terminating strategy.

Consider now the questionnaire responses for subjects receiving analogies with integral attributes. In previous research, it has been found that such subjects were not as well able to describe their thought processes, as were subjects solving analogies with separable attributes (Sternberg & Rifkin, 1979). In the present data, the descriptions of the former subjects were slightly less accurate with respect to what they were trained to do, but more accurate with respect to what they were actually doing.

Subjects in the integral-stimuli group correctly described the fully exhaustive strategy as slowest, the self-terminating strategy as fastest, and the mixture strategy as intermediate. The self-terminating strategy was described as easiest to learn and to use, the mixture strategy as hardest to learn and to use (despite the fact that mixture solution latencies were much lower than exhaustive ones). The exhaustive and mixture strategies were described as harder to maintain than the self-terminating strategy. The self-terminating strategy was correctly described as requiring less memory load than the other two strategies. Subjects using the exhaustive strategy were more conscious of their use of this strategy than were subjects using the other two strategies (as was the case for subjects in the separable-stimuli groups). Overall, the mixture strategy was described as worst, followed by the exhaustive strategy; the self-terminating strategy was described as by far the best. About one-fourth of the people in the exhaustive and mixture groups said they would have used the strategies they were trained to use had they been untrained. This estimate was certainly too high for the exhaustive training group.

About two-fifths of the people in the self-terminating group said they would have used the trained strategy, had they been untrained. This estimate was probably too low.

To summarize, subjects' metacognitive knowledge about their strategies differed for separable and integral stimuli. Subjects were probably more aware of what they were trying to do with separable stimuli, but probably less aware of what they were actually doing, at least in the present analogy training paradigm.

## CONCLUSION

We are optimistic that componential approaches to the training of intelligent performance can be successful in improving people's performance. We have shown that strategies for intelligent performance can be trained; that certain strategies are better, on the average, than others; that it is possible to determine why certain kinds of strategies are better or worse than others (at least within the limited domain we explored); that there exist both person × strategy and content × strategy interactions, as well as person × content × strategy interactions; and that people have available good information about what they are trying to do, but perhaps not as good information about what they are actually doing. The goodness of the information may depend upon the type of stimulus, and probably depends upon the type of task as well. We believe that people's quality of metacognitive information might be measurably improved by training the people in a particular strategy, and then pointing out to them how this strategy differs (if at all) from the strategy either that is ideal for the task (on the average) or that people use spontaneously when they are untrained. Such a procedure would give people a base line against which to compare what they are doing, and so make them more aware of the extent to which they are following instructions. It might also provide people with a better basis for perceiving the relative strengths and weaknesses of alternative strategies for problem solution. Ultimately, we hope it will be possible to train people in ways that will make them truly "more intelligent."

## REFERENCES

Belmont, J. M., & Butterfield, E. C. Learning strategies as determinants of memory deficiencies. *Cognitive Psychology*, 1971, *2*, 411–420.

Brown, A. L. The development of memory: Knowing, knowing about knowing, and knowing how to know. In H. W. Reese (Ed.), *Advances in child development* (Vol. 10). New York: Academic Press, 1975.

Brown, A. L., & Campione, J. C. Training strategic study time apportionment in educable retarded children. *Intelligence*, 1977, *1*, 94–107.

Butterfield, E. C., Wambold, C., & Belmont, J. M. On the theory and practice of improving short-term memory. *American Journal of Mental Deficiency*, 1973, *77*, 654–669.

Campione, J. C., & Brown, A. L. Memory and metamemory development in educable retarded children. In R. V. Kail, Jr. & J. W. Hagen (Eds.), *Perspectives on the development of memory and cognition*. Hillsdale, NJ: Lawrence Erlbaum Associates, 1977.

Carroll, J. B. Psychometric tests as cognitive tasks: A new "structure of intellect." In L. B. Resnick (Ed.), *The nature of intelligence*. Hillsdale, NJ: Lawrence Erlbaum Associates, 1976.

Cooper, L. A., & Shepard, R. N. Chronometric studies of the rotation of mental images. In W. Chase (Ed.), *Visual information processing*. New York: Academic Press, 1973.

Copi, I. M. *Introduction to logic* (5th edition). New York: Macmillan, 1978.

Egan, D. E. Testing based on understanding: Implications from studies of spatial ability. *Intelligence*, 1979, *3*, 1–15.

Feuerstein, R. *The dynamic assessment of retarded performers: The learning potential device, theory, instruments, and techniques*. Baltimore, MD: University Park Press, 1979.

Feuerstein, R. *Instrumental enrichment: An intervention program for cognitive modifiability*. Baltimore, MD: University Park Press, 1980.

Garner, W. R. *The processing of information and structure*. Hillsdale, NJ: Lawrence Erlbaum Associates, 1974.

Gavurin, E. I. Anagram solving and spatial ability. *Journal of Psychology*, 1967, *65*, 65–68.

Holzman, T. G., Glaser, R., & Pellegrino, J. W. Process training derived from a computer simulation theory. *Memory and Cognition*, 1976, *4*, 349–356.

Horn, J. L. Concepts of intellect in relation to learning and adult development. *Intelligence*, 1980, *4*, 285–318.

Hunt, E. B. Mechanics of verbal ability. *Psychological Review*, 1978, *85*, 109–130.

Hunt, E. B., Frost, N., & Lunneborg, C. Individual differences in cognition: A new approach to intelligence. In G. Bower (Ed.), *The psychology of learning and motivation* (Vol. 7). New York: Academic Press, 1973.

Hunt, E., Lunneborg, C., & Lewis, J. What does it mean to be high verbal? *Cognitive Psychology*, 1975, *7*, 194–227.

Jensen, A. R. *g*: Outmoded theory or unconquered frontier? *Creative Science and Technology*, 1979, *2*, 16–29.

Klahr, D. Goal formation, planning, and learning by preschool problem solvers or: "My socks are in the dryer." In R. Siegler (Ed.), *Children's thinking: What develops?* Hillsdale, N.J.: Lawrence Erlbaum Associates, 1978.

MacLeod, C. M., Hunt, E. B., & Mathews, N. N. Individual differences in the verification of sentence-picture relationships. *Journal of Verbal Learning and Verbal Behavior*, 1978, *17*, 493–507.

Mulholland, T. M., Pellegrino, J. W., & Glaser, R. Components of geometric analogy solution. *Cognitive Psychology*, 1980, *12*, 252–284.

Newell, A., & Simon, H. A. *Human problem solving.* Englewood Cliffs, NJ: Prentice-Hall, 1972.

Pellegrino, J. W., & Glaser, R. Components of inductive reasoning. In R. E. Snow, P.-A. Federico, & W. Montague (Eds.), *Aptitude, learning, and instruction: Cognitive process analyses of aptitude* (Vol. 1). Hillsdale, NJ: Lawrence Erlbaum Associates, 1980.

Powell, J. S., & Sternberg, R. J. Acquisition of vocabulary from context. Manuscript submitted for publication, 1982.

Quinton, G., & Fellows, B. "Perceptual" strategies in the solving of three-term series problems. *British Journal of Psychology*, 1975, *66*, 69–78.

Siegler, R. S. The origins of scientific reasoning. In R. S. Siegler (Ed.), *Children's thinking: What develops?* Hillsdale, NJ: Lawrence Erlbaum Associates, 1978.

Shepard, R. N., & Metzler, J. Mental rotation of three-dimensional objects. *Science*, 1971, *171*, 701–703.

Snow, R. E. Theory and method for research on aptitude processes. In R. J. Sternberg & D. K. Detterman (Eds.), *Human intelligence: Perspectives on its theory and measurement.* Norwood, NJ: Ablex, 1979.

Sternberg, R. J. *Intelligence, information processing, and analogical reasoning: The componential analysis of human abilities.* Hillsdale, NJ: Lawrence Erlbaum Associates, 1977.

Sternberg, R. J. Componential investigations of human intelligence. In A. Lesgold, J. Pellegrino, S. Fokkema, & R. Glaser (Eds.), *Cognitive psychology and instruction.* New York: Plenum, 1978.

Sternberg, R. J. The nature of mental abilities. *American Psychologist*, 1979, *28*, 469–498.

Sternberg, R. J., The development of linear syllogistic reasoning. *Journal of Experimental Child Psychology*, 1980, *29*, 340–356. (a)

Sternberg, R. J. A proposed resolution of curious conflicts in the literature on linear syllogisms. In R. Nickerson (Ed.), *Attention and performance VIII*. Hillsdale, NJ: Lawrence Erlbaum Associates, 1980. (b)

Sternberg, R. J. Representation and process in linear syllogistic reasoning. *Journal of Experimental Psychology: General*, 1980, *109*, 119–159. (c)

Sternberg, R. J. Sketch of a componential subtheory of human intelligence. *Behavioral and Brain Sciences*, 1980, *3*, 573–584. (d)

Sternberg, R. J. Cognitive-behavioral approaches to the training of intelligence in the retarded. *Journal of Special Education*, 1981, *15*, 165–183. (a)

Sternberg, R. J. Toward a unified componential theory of human intelligence. I. Fluid ability. In M. Friedman, J. Das, & N. O'Connor (Eds.), *Intelligence and learning*. New York: Plenum, 1981. (b)

Sternberg, R. J., Guyote, M. J., & Turner, M. E. Deductive reasoning. In R. E. Snow, P.-A, Federico, & W. Montague (Eds.), *Aptitude, learning, and instruction: Cognitive process analyses of aptitude* (Vol. 1). Hillsdale, NJ: Lawrence Erlbaum Associates, 1980.

Sternberg, R. J., & Ketron, J. L. Selection and implementation of strategies in reasoning by analogy. *Journal of Educational Psychology*, in press.

Sternberg, R. J., Rifkin, B. The development of analogical reasoning processes, *Journal of Experimental Child Psychology*, 1979, *27*, 195–232.

Sternberg, R. J., & Weil, E. M. An aptitude-strategy interaction in linear syllogistic reasoning. *Journal of Educational Psychology*, 1980, *72*, 226–234.

Trabasso, T., Riley, C. A., & Wilson, E. G. The representation of linear order and spatial strategies in reasoning: A developmental study. In R. J. Falmagne (Ed.), *Reasoning: Representation and process*. Hillsdale, NJ: Lawrence Erlbaum Associates, 1975.

Wanschura, P. B., & Borkowski, J. G. Long-term transfer of a mediational strategy by moderately retarded children. *American Journal of Mental Deficiency*, 1975, *80*, 323–333.

Whitely, S. E., & Barnes, G. M. The implications of processing event sequences for theories of analogical reasoning. *Memory and Cognition*, 1979, *7*, 323–331.

# 7

# *Teaching the Process of Reading Comprehension\**

ALLAN COLLINS
EDWARD E. SMITH
*Bolt Beranek and Newman Inc.*

Current methods for teaching comprehension tend to emphasize the *products* of comprehension, and neglect the *processes* of comprehension. There are two sets of processing skills that we think are particularly important to teach. The first set includes comprehension monitoring skills, which involve the reader's monitoring of his or her ongoing processing for possible comprehension failures, and taking remedial action when failures occur. Comprehension failures can occur at various levels, including: particular words, particular sentences, relations between sentences, and relations between larger units. For each kind of failure, we specify possible remedial actions the reader can take. The second set of processing skills that we advocate teaching involve using clues in the text to generate, evaluate, and revise hypotheses about current and future events in the text. We consider hypotheses about: event expectations (often based on the traits and goals of the text characters); text-structure expectations (based, for example on genre); and other interpretive skills, like determining the main points. Finally, we propose that in teaching these processing skills, the teacher first should model the skills, and then gradually turn over the processing responsibilities to the students.

## INTRODUCTION

The cognitive approach to education assumes that if we can specify in enough detail the tacit processes that underlie various thinking skills, then we can find methods to teach students to master these skills. In this paper, we focus on one critical domain—reading comprehension—and attempt to specify the thinking skills required, together with interactive methods for teaching these skills.

Reading comprehension is usually taught in schools in one of two ways. One method is to have students read a text, and then read comments or answer questions about the text. The comments and questions can range over a variety of

---

*This research was supported in part by the National Institute of Education under Contract No. US-NIE-C-400-76-0116 and in part by the Republic of Venezuela under Purchase Order No. M76075. We thank Chip Bruce and Andee Rubin for their comments on a previous draft of the paper. We also thank Marilyn Adams and Tom Anderson for discussions that led to the ideas presented here.

topics, from what particular words mean to the main point of the whole text. This method stresses important components of reading comprehension, but treats them purely as *products* (i.e., interpretations), rather than as *processes* (i.e., constructing interpretations). In particular, it doesn't teach students what to do when they have difficulty comprehending parts of the text; nor does it teach them how to construct and revise hypotheses about what is likely to occur in the text, based on what they have already read. Both of these aspects are important in constructing an interpretation of the text.

The other common method for teaching reading comprehension is the reading group. In a reading group, children take turns reading aloud. The teacher usually helps out when the student has difficulties, and sometimes comments or asks a question about the text. This method goes some way toward teaching the process of reading comprehension, but typically, the teacher deals only with low-level difficulties (word and parsing difficulties), and asks questions only about interpretations. The method that we will propose incorporates aspects of both of the common methods, elaborated to include a much richer set of comments and questions. It is akin to the process-oriented curricula now used, such as the ReQuest and DRT methods (Tierney, Readence, & Dishner, 1980).

There are two aspects of comprehension processes that we think are important to teach: (1) comprehension monitoring, and (2) hypothesis formation and evaluation. The notion of comprehension-monitoring comes out of the recent research on meta-cognition (e.g., Brown, 1978; Flavell, 1978; Markman, 1979). Comprehension monitoring concerns the student's ability both to evaluate his or her ongoing comprehension processes while reading through a text, and to take some sort of remedial action when these processes bog down. In the next section, we will detail the kinds of comprehension difficulties students should learn to look for, and the kinds of remedial actions they should learn to take.

In addition to comprehension-monitoring skills, students also need to be able to use clues in the text to make hypotheses about what is happening or is likely to happen next, to evaluate these hypotheses as new evidence comes in, and to revise them, should evidence accumulate to indicate that they are wrong. The role of hypothesis formation and revision is central to recent artificial intelligence approaches to comprehension processes (Brown, Collins, & Harris, 1978; Bruce & Newman, 1978; Collins, Brown, & Larkin, 1980; Rubin, Bruce, & Brown, 1976; Schank & Abelson, 1977; Wilensky, 1978). We distinguish between two basic kinds of hypothesis formation skills: making interpretations of the text vs. making predictions about what will happen in the text. These two are often intertwined, however. In a subsequent section, we will try to enumerate the kinds of hypotheses and expectations that seem particularly valuable for reading comprehension.

All of the preceding is concerned with *what* readers need to learn, not *how* they should be taught it. As an answer to the *how* issue, in the final section of this paper, we propose a method that starts with the teacher modelling to students the above two aspects of comprehending—comprehension monitoring and hypothesis formation. This modelling can be viewed as running a kind of "slow motion" film of the way comprehending takes place in a sophisticated reader. Gradually, this process should be turned over from the teacher to the students so that they internalize these same reading strategies.

To reiterate, the next two sections of this paper detail the skills involved in comprehension monitoring and hypothesis formation and testing; the final section describes the method we propose for teaching students to develop these skills. One point to keep in mind throughout is that the skills we discuss are those needed when reading for depth and detail. Other kinds of reading—e.g., skimming or just trying to get the main points—may require only a subset of the proposed skills, or conceivably even a different set entirely.

## COMPREHENSION MONITORING

Comprehension-monitoring skills range from handling local word-level failures to global text-level failures. Table 1 shows our taxonomy of possible comprehension failures. There are four basic types. They include failures to understand: (1) particular words, (2) particular sentences, (3) relations between sentences, and (4) how the text fits together as a whole. Each type of failure can, in fact, have ramifications at more global levels. We will discuss each kind of failure along with certain remedies that students should learn to take.

1. *Failure to understand a word.* The simplest kind of problem occurs when the reader doesn't understand a word, either because it is novel, or because its known meaning doesn't make sense in the current context.

TABLE 1
Taxonomy of Comprehension Failures

1. Failure to understand a word
   a. Novel word
   b. Known word that doesn't make sense in the context
2. Failure to understand a sentence
   a. Can find no interpretation
   b. Can only find vague, abstract interpretation
   c. Can find several possible interpretations (ambiguous sentence)
   d. Interpretation conflicts with prior knowledge
3. Failure to understand how one sentence relates to another
   a. Interpretation of one sentence conflicts with another
   b. Can find no connection between the sentences
   c. Can find several possible connections between the sentences
4. Failure to understand how the whole text fits together
   a. Can find no point to whole or part of the text
   b. Cannot understand why certain episodes or sections occurred
   c. Cannot understand the motivations of certain characters

2. *Failure to understand a sentence.* There are several different ways a reader can fail to understand a sentence. One possibility is that he or she fails to find any interpretation at all. Another is that the only interpretation found is so abstract as to seem hopelessly vague. (Somewhat surprisingly, this seems to be a common occurrence in scientific and technical texts.) Alternatively, the reader may find several interpretations, because of some semantic or syntactic ambiguity. A fourth problem occurs if the reader's interpretation conflicts with his or her prior knowledge.

3. *Failure to understand how one sentence relates to another.* One kind of failure that can occur at the intersentence level is when an interpretation of one sentence is inconsistent with that of another. Monitoring for such inconsistencies is clearly an ability that develops with experience. Markman (1979) found that sixth-graders were far better than third-graders in detecting explicit contradictions in text. In this experiment, even the older children were surprisingly poor at detecting inconsistencies; and, experimental work by Baker (1979a) suggests that even college students have trouble monitoring for inconsistencies.

   In addition to inconsistencies, there are two other kinds of failures that can occur at the intersentence level: the reader can find no connection between two sentences that by juxtaposition should be related, and the reader can find several possible connections between two sentences (i.e., there is an ambiguous relation between the two sentences).

4. *Failure to understand how the whole text fits together.* There are a number of failures that can occur at more global levels. These include failures to understand the point of the text or some part of it, failure to understand why certain episodes or sections were included, and failure to understand the motivations of one or more characters in the text. We have analyzed in detail elsewhere the kinds of strategies sophisticated readers use to reinterpret a text (Collins, Brown, & Larkin, 1980).

## Remedies and Their Triggering Conditions.

There are a number of actions readers can take if they fail to understand a word or passage. We have listed possible remedies below, roughly in the order of increasing disruptiveness of the flow of reading. There is a cost to any but the first option: the more drastic the action taken, the more you lose the thread of what you're reading. Therefore, more disruptive actions require more justification in terms of potential benefit. This is captured by the *triggering conditions* for an action, some of which are indicated in the description of each action. The triggering conditions are partially determined by the type of failures and partially by the costs and benefits of taking any action.

1. *Ignore and read on.* If the word or passage is not critical to understanding, then the most effective action is to ignore it. For example, failures within

descriptions and details usually can safely be ignored. If the reader is failing to understand a large proportion of the text, this is evidence that the "ignore and read on" strategy is not working.

2. *Suspend judgment.* This is a wait and see strategy that should be applied when the reader thinks the failure will be clarified later. For example, new words or general principles are often explained in subsequent text. The structure of the text should tell the reader when an idea is likely to be clarified later. If it is not, it may be necessary to go back and reread.

3. *Form a tentative hypothesis.* Here, the reader tries to figure out from context what a word, sentence, or passage means. The hypothesis may be a partial hypothesis or a quite specific hypothesis. It acts as a *pending question* (Collins, Brown, Morgan, & Brewer, 1977) that the reader tests as he or she continues reading. This is a particularly useful strategy to apply if a statement is abstract or vague, or if an unknown word is fairly central and there are clues to its meaning.

4. *Reread the current sentence(s).* If the reader cannot form a tentative hypothesis, then it often helps to reread the current sentence or sentences, looking for a revised interpretation that would clarify the problem. This is especially useful if the reader perceives some contradiction or several possible interpretations. But, it is a fairly disruptive remedy.

5. *Reread the previous context.* Jumping back to the previous context is even more disruptive to the flow of reading. But, if there is a contradiction with some earlier piece of the text, or the reader is overloaded with too many pending questions, then jumping back and rereading is the most effective strategy.

6. *Going to an expert source.* The most disruptive action the reader can take is to go to an outside source, such as a teacher, parent, dictionary, or other book. But this is sometimes required, for example when a word is repeatedly used and the reader cannot figure out what it means, or when a whole section of text does not make sense.

Several points are worth emphasizing about these remedies. First, some of these remedies correspond to strategies that college students report they use when they run into comprehension problems (Baker, 1979a). So we have some evidence that our remedies are indeed useful to skilled readers. Second, the order in which the remedies are listed, roughly corresponds to the order in which we think they should be tried. In particular, the latter strategies are quite disruptive (you have to stop reading for at least a few seconds), so they should usually be the last remedies tried. Third, it is important to teach the triggering conditions that can clue the reader when to give up on one remedy and try another. Finally, we should point out that applying these remedies is anything but trivial. Using a sentence context to form a hypothesis about a novel word, for example, may be an instance of a general ability for extracting meaning from linguistic context, and this could be one of the things that separates good readers from poor ones.

### Some General Comments About
### Comprehension Monitoring

One common reaction to proposals like the above is that too much comprehension monitoring can actually interfere with reading. Thus, in *A guide to effective study,* Locke (1975) writes:

> In short, you need to monitor your mental processes while studying. This does not mean you should monitor every second; this would obviously make it impossible to learn the material. (p. 126)

We have two reactions to this kind of argument. First, when it comes to reading deeply and analytically, we hold that monitoring is in fact needed all the time. Contrary to claims like Locke's, such constant monitoring will not interfere with learning, once the monitoring is sufficiently well practiced so that it is automated and unconscious (see Adams, 1980). That is, the fallacy in the above claim lies in the hidden assumption that monitoring must go on consciously and hence usurp limited processing resources; in fact, it seems that some kinds of mental process that are practiced enough can become unconscious and automated, thereby not requiring resources that are in short supply (e.g., Schneider & Shiffrin, 1977). Comprehension monitoring may well be this kind of process.

But, while we take issue with the claim that constant monitoring can impede learning, we recognize that there are numerous reading situations that do not require constant monitoring. Thus, if one is reading a text just to get the main points, one can probably safely ignore a novel word that occurs in an unimportant sentence. More generally, different kinds of reading situations carry with them different criteria for comprehension, and the weaker the criterion (e.g., "just get the main point" vs. "be able to reproduce the arguments exposited"), the less the monitoring that may be needed (Baker, 1979b).

## HYPOTHESIS GENERATION, EVALUATION,
## AND REVISION

In discussing comprehension monitoring, we mentioned the need to form tentative hypotheses about the meaning of a word or sentence. As they center on specific words and sentences, such hypotheses are very local. In the present section, we are concerned with far more general hypotheses: ones that are based on the characters' intentions and other global aspects of the text rather than on words and sentences.

As mentioned earlier, we distinguish between two basic kinds of hypotheses: predictions and interpretations. Predictions are hypotheses about what will happen, and interpretations are hypotheses about what is happening. Sometimes, as in character attributions described below, an interpretation is made (e.g., the hero is jealous) in order to make some prediction (e.g., he will try to outdo his rival).

TABLE 2
Types of Hypotheses

1. Event Expectations
   a. Character attributions (permanent and temporary)
   b. Situational attributions
   c. Goal interaction between characters (competition and cooperation)
   d. Goal interactions within a character (conflict)
   e. Termination of a goal-subsumption state
2. Text Structure Expectations
   a. Structure of the genre
   b. Predictions from headings and titles
3. Interpretations
   a. Determining the main points
   b. Determining story themes
   c. Determining devices used by authors

Both predictions and interpretations are often wrong, so the reader must look for further evidence and revise any predictions or interpretations that prove wrong.

Another way in which the hypotheses of present concern differ from those mentioned earlier is that the present ones are not triggered by comprehension failures. There is, however, an interplay between what was covered in the preceding section and the general hypotheses we consider here: to the extent students generate and test general hypotheses while reading, they may confront fewer comprehension failures. In some sense, then, the present section is concerned with *preventing* the kinds of problems that the prior section tried to *remedy*.

Table 2 shows our initial taxonomy of the kinds of general hypotheses students should learn to make as they read a text. We discuss each kind in turn.

1. *Event expectations*. Expectations about future events occur mainly in fiction. We distinguish five major kinds of event expectation, the last three of which derive from Wilensky's (1978) analysis of stories.
   a) *Character attributions*. Very commonly, authors create a set of expectations about what a particular character will do, based on some attribution of a permanent character type (e.g., evil, jealous, impatient) or of a temporary state (e.g., grief or happiness). One of the most common character types with predictive expectations is the "bad guy." If someone is referred to as having a "curling lip" or a "jagged tooth," these are clues that the character plays the role of villain in the story, and therefore is likely to take some action against the central character.
   b) *Situational attributions*. Another source of expectations about future events is the specific situations that characters find themselves in. Regardless of their personality traits, we can expect most characters to be sad at a loved one's funeral, elated upon winning a valuable prize or award, conforming when confronted by a powerful authority, and so

on. Recent experiments on story memory suggests that adult readers make extensive use of situational attributions (e.g., Bower, 1978).

c) *Goal interactions between characters*. When two characters' goals come into conflict, or when they come to share a common goal, this creates expectations about how the characters will interact (Bruce & Newman, 1978; Wilensky, 1978). Conflict predicts various attempts to undermine the other character's ability to reach the goal, or attempts to outdo the other character. Sharing goals predicts various kinds of helping.

d) *Goal interactions within a character*. Often, a character wants to pursue several goals that come into conflict, such as studying for an exam vs. having fun with the gang (Wilensky, 1978). Such goal interactions lead to expectations about characters giving up something they want to do or ought to do, together with expectations about the consequences that flow from the particular choice (not studying can lead to failing a course, not getting into a good school or job, etc.).

e) *Termination of a goal-subsumption state*. Wilensky (1978) also points out that termination of a goal-subsumption state often leads to expectations about a character's actions. A goal-subsumption state occurs when a person is in a state where a number of goals are satisfied automatically (e.g., the state of having a job can satisfy goals having to do with eating, recreation, and travel). When such a state terminates, the character has to find a way to satisfy the goals that are no longer subsumed. Thus, being married is a goal-subsumption state, and if a woman leaves her husband, we expect her to take actions to deal with whatever goals are no longer subsumed (e.g., finding a source of extra money, babysitting, companionship, etc.).

2. *Text Structure Expectations*. There are a number of expectations that derive from text structure *per se*, rather than from the content of the text. We haven't tried to enumerate all these structural expectations systematically, but we can give a few examples of the kinds of predictions from text structure that students should learn to make.

a) *Structure of the genre*. Both in stories and expository texts, there are standard structures that should create expectations in the reader. For example, a mystery story should lead one to look for clues as to who committed or will commit a crime. The clues often come in the form of extraneous details or discrepancies between what a character says and what one can infer must have been the case. To give an example from expository literature, a standard form for presenting new material is what Armbruster & Anderson (1980) call the ''Compare and Contrast'' structure. When a new object is introduced by comparison to a known object, the reader should expect a point by point comparison of the similarities and differences between the two objects.

b) *Titles and headings*. The titles and headings in a text usually provide a clue as to what will come next, particularly with respect to the main point of the succeeding text. Readers often ignore headings, and by doing so they lose one of the main clues as to the high-level structure of the text. It is therefore important for teachers to stress the predictive and interpretive power of headings, even though they are sometimes misleading (Anderson, Armbruster, & Kantor, 1980).

3. *Other Interpretive Skills.* There are a number of other high-level interpretive skills that are currently emphasized in most reading curricula, which should be emphasized in any process-oriented curriculum as well. The difference between our approach and that of most product-oriented curricula is that we emphasize the specific clues a reader can use to make interpretations. We will discuss three kinds of skills and their triggering cues as examples of what we have in mind.

   a) *Determining the main points.* There are a number of cues that signal when a particular idea is the main point of a paragraph or expository text. For example, if an idea is mentioned in a heading or opening sentence, it is likely to be a main point. Main points are also likely to be reiterated or marked by some verbal cue such as "Therefore," "The point is," or even "This is exemplified by" where the idea expanded upon is the main point. Students should learn to recognize these and other cues that authors use to signal main points.

   b) *Determining story themes.* Extracting the theme of a story is an important skill that is rarely taught directly. One aspect of it is to recognize the kinds of ideas that can function as story themes, e.g., that "persistence pays off," or that "revenge may be sweet momentarily, but is costly in the long run." Then, students must learn to extract the clues from the text that enable them to identify what the theme of a particular story is. Themes usually derive from the salient characteristics of the main characters and the central events they are involved in (Brown, Collins, & Harris, 1978).

   c) *Determining devices used by authors.* One of the important aspects of writing is the devices authors use to create different effects on the reader: to catch their interest, create suspense, create a sense of danger or villainy, etc. (Collins & Gentner, 1980). Students need to be able to recognize the clues for the various devices. For example, a sense of danger can be created by eerie sounds, unexplained events, etc. Detailed knowledge about how effects on readers are created is useful to the students both as readers and as writers.

## TEACHING STRATEGIES

Our ultimate goals are to have students be vigilant for the various comprehension failures they might encounter during silent reading and to know how to remedy them, to actively hypothesize about what will happen next, and to recognize cues in the text that signal main points, themes, and narrative devices. It seems best, though, to approach these goals in stages. Accordingly, the first stage will consist of the teacher modelling comprehension, and commenting on his or her monitoring and hypotheses, while reading aloud to a student. The next stage will consist of encouraging students to practice these techniques themselves while reading aloud. The third and final stage will be to have students use these skills while reading silently.

### The Modelling Stage

The basic idea in the modelling stage is that the teacher reads a story or other text aloud, making comments while reading. In this stage it is easiest if the teacher uses a longer text that is unfamiliar. As the text is being read, the teacher interrupts maybe once or twice a paragraph to make comments about all the different aspects of the comprehension processes discussed above. For example:

1. *Generating hypotheses about the text.* The teacher should generate any hypothesis that comes to mind. The more wrong hypotheses (up to some point) the better, because the students must learn about hypothesis revision, and that initial hypotheses are not always correct. It is also important for students to realize that it is okay to verbalize wrong hypotheses.
2. *Evidence Supporting Hypotheses.* When a prediction is made, then the teacher should mention the reasons for the prediction. It is particularly important to point out any evidence occurring later in the text that supports the hypothesis.
3. *Evidence Against Any Hypothesis.* When something happens in the text that disconfirms any hypothesis, the teacher should point this out. If it causes the teacher to revise the hypothesis, any revisions should be explained.
4. *Confusion or doubts on the part of the teacher.* If the teacher doesn't understand a word, or how two events are related, etc., he or she should point out the confusion and explain the source of it. If it is a word or concept, then he or she might suggest any of the remedies we described earlier. If the teacher thinks the author is deliberately trying to mislead the reader (a narrative device used in numerous stories), this too should be pointed out. If the teacher thinks the confusion will be clarified later, he or she should point that out as well.
5. *Critical comments on text.* If the teacher has any insights as to what the author is trying to do and how effectively he is doing it, he or she should point that out. Both favorable and unfavorable comments should be made.

Even in this first stage, the teacher should encourage the student's active participation as early as possible. Thus, the teacher can ask the student to generate hypotheses, e.g., "If Bill is really going swimming, what do you think he'll do next?", or "Does that sentence make sense to you?" The extent of the student's participation should gradually increase, thereby making the transition to the second stage a gradual one.

### The Student Participation Stage

This stage can start out with questions suggesting hypotheses, "Do you think X is a bad guy?" or "Do you think X will do Y?", and move to more open-ended questions, "What do you think will happen to X?" or "How do you think the story will end?". It is particularly important to reward students for generating their own hypotheses. One way to do this is to cite the evidence supporting their hypotheses. When evidence comes in that bears on any of the students' hypotheses, the teacher should always point that out.

With respect to comprehension monitoring, the teacher should gradually shift the major responsibility for spotting failures and generating remedies to the students. Initially, the teacher asks the students about things they may find confusing. Later, the teacher should serve mainly a corrective function, pointing out problems the student may have missed, suggesting possible remedies when none are forthcoming from the students, etc.

If the teacher encourages the students enough, they should be offering their predictions as freely as the teacher, after a little while. It is important to get the dynamic going so that everyone has different ideas as to what may happen. Then, reading becomes a game for the students, where they get to see who guessed right. Everybody in the group should make their own guesses. Then, they have a stake in how the story turns out. It effectively enhances the motivation in reading, as well as stressing the hypothesis formation and revision process.

### The Read-Silently Stage

What we want to do here is encourage students to monitor comprehension and make predictions while reading silently. But of course, we need some kind of output from students to see how they are doing. One procedure for accomplishing this is to tell students there is something "wrong" with a piece of text, and that they are to read it silently and then tell the tutor what the problem is. Though this procedure seems adequate for assessing students' ability to detect problems, it does not assess their use of remedies. To get at the latter, one can give students comprehension questions on texts (read silently) that are constructed to be difficult in various ways, where correct answers are likely only if the right remedies have been applied to problems inserted in the text.

In order to get at the students' ability to make predictions while reading silently, we can insert various questions at different points in a text that require predictions about what will happen next. The correctness of the answers will not be determined by what actually happens in the text, but by the reasonableness of the prediction at the point at which the prediction is made. If a multiple-choice format is used, the alternatives should not always include what actually happens, so that the hypothesis-revision process can be tapped with later questions. The texts involved can be constructed so as to provide examples of all the types of hypotheses we have discussed. Furthermore, each type of hypothesis should be used with very different texts—stories, instructions, and descriptions. This diversity of learning contexts is needed to insure that whatever skills are acquired will generalize to as wide a domain as possible.

## CONCLUSION

Many reading curricula used in the schools do not try to teach the kind of comprehension monitoring and predictive skills that we have discussed. Instead, the curricula emphasize the final interpretations a reader ends up with, from word and sentence meaning to author intentions and main points. This particular emphasis comes from trying to teach the product of reading (i.e., the interpretation), rather than the process of reading (i.e., the construction of an interpretation).

We do not argue that reading curricula shouldn't stress interpretations. We argue only that a reading curriculum should also try to teach how to construct interpretations: that comprehension monitoring and hypothesis testing are necessary to the development of skilled reading. If we do not teach these skills, then the better students will develop them on their own, and the worse students will find reading very frustrating.

## REFERENCES

Adams, M. J. Failures to comprehend and levels of processing in reading. In R. Spiro, B. C. Bruce, & W. Brewer (Eds.), *Theoretical issues in reading comprehension.* Hillsdale, NJ: Lawrence Erlbaum Associates, 1980.

Anderson, T. H., Armbruster, B. B., & Kantor, R. N. *How clearly written are children's textbooks? Or, of bladderworts and alfa.* (Reading Education Rep. No. 16). Urbana, IL: University of Illinois, Center for the Study of Reading, August 1980.

Armbruster, B. B., & Anderson T. H. *The effects of mapping on the free recall of expository text* (Tech. Rep. No. 160). Urbana, IL: University of Illinois, Center for the Study of Reading, February 1980.

Baker, L. *Comprehension monitoring: Identifying and coping with text confusions* (Tech. Rep. No. 145). Urbana, IL: University of Illinois, Center for the Study of Reading, 1979a.

Baker, L. *Do I understand or do I not understand: That is the question* (Tech. Rep. No. 10). Urbana, IL: University of Illinois, Center for the Study of Reading, 1979b.

Bower, G. H. Experiments on story comprehension and recall. *Discourse Processes,* 1978, *1,* 211–231.

Brown, A. L. Knowing when, where, and how to remember: A problem of metacognition. In R. Glaser (Ed.), *Advances in instructional psychology* (Vol. 1). Hillsdale, NJ: Lawrence Erlbaum Associates, 1978.

Brown, J. S., Collins, A., & Harris, G.  Artificial intelligence and learning strategies. In H. F. O'Neil (Ed.), *Learning strategies*. New York: Academic Press, 1978.

Bruce, B. C., & Newman, D.  Interacting plans. *Cognitive Science, 1978, 2,* 195–233.

Collins, A., Brown, J. S., & Larkin, K. M.  Inference in text understanding. In R. J. Spiro, B. C. Bruce, & W. F. Brewer (Eds.), *Theoretical issues in reading comprehension*. Hillsdale, NJ: Lawrence Erlbaum Associates, 1980.

Collins, A., Brown, A. L., Morgan, J. L., & Brewer, W. F.  *The analysis of reading tasks and texts* (Tech. Rep. No. 43). Urbana, IL: University of Illinois, Center for the Study of Reading, April 1977.

Collins, A. & Gentner, D. G.  A framework for a cognitive theory of writing. In L. W. Gregg & E. R. Steinberg (Eds.), *Cognitive processes in writing*. Hillsdale, NJ: Lawrence Erlbaum Associates, 1980.

Flavell, J. H.  Metacognitive development. In J. M. Scandura & C. J. Brainerd (Eds.), *Structural/process theories of complex human behavior*. Alphen a.d. Rijn, The Netherlands: Sijthoff and Nordhoff, 1978.

Locke, E. Q.  *A guide to effective study*. New York: Springer, 1975.

Markman, E. M.  Realizing that you don't understand: Elementary school children's awareness of inconsistencies. *Child Development, 1979, 50,* 643–655.

Rubin, A. D., Bruce, B., & Brown, J. S.  *A process-oriented language for describing aspects of reading comprehension* (Tech. Rep. No. 13). Urbana, IL: University of Illinois, Center for the Study of Reading, October 1976. (ERIC Document Reproduction Service No. 136 188)

Schank, R., & Abelson, R.  *Scripts, plans, goals, and understanding*. Hillsdale, NJ: Lawrence Erlbaum Associates, 1977.

Schneider, W., & Shiffrin, R. M.  Controlled and automatic human information processing: I. Detection, search and attention. *Psychological Review, 1977, 84,* 1–66.

Tierney, R. J., Readence, J. E., & Dishner, E. K.  *Reading strategies and practices: A guide for improving instruction*. Boston, MA: Allyn and Bacon, Inc., 1980.

Wilensky, R.  Why John married Mary: Understanding stories involving recurring goals. *Cognitive Science, 1978, 2,* 235–266.

# 8

# *Conceptual and Methodological Issues in Facilitating Growth in Intelligence**

SAMUEL MESSICK AND IRVING SIGEL

*Educational Testing Service*

Particular theories of intelligence—whether monolithic, hierarchical, morphological, componential, or functional—have different implications for facilitating growth in intellective skill. Such theories are embedded in different concepts and attitudes about the sources and development of intelligence and, more broadly, about the nature of the human being and of human perfectibility. They vary profoundly in their emphasis on different determinants of performance, ranging from a heavy hereditarian perspective to an exigent environmental one. Of particular moment is the degree to which modifications in the course of growth are deemed to be possible. Thus, theories of intelligence shape the nature of intervention strategies, while their value overtones influence the intensity of intervention efforts and the commitment to change.

Particular theories of intelligence—whether monolithic, hierarchical, morphological, componential, or functional—have different implications for facilitating growth in intellective skills. Such theories are embedded in different concepts and attitudes about the sources and development of intelligence and, more broadly, about the nature of the human being and of human perfectibility. While theories of intelligence shape the nature of intervention strategies, their ideological underpinnings influence the scope and intensity of intervention efforts and the commitment to change. Various approaches to the study of intelligence differ in a number of ways ostensibly reflecting theoretical or methodological predilections, but tacitly conveying subtle value overtones. We will attempt to illuminate some of these differences through a series of nonpolar contrasts which are admittedly interconnected and somewhat overlapping but which highlight distinctive features of various theoretical orientations that have implications for educational practice. By means of these contrasts, we will consider whether a theoretical approach emphasizes the *limits* or the *potentialities* of mental functioning, whether it stresses *structure* or *process*, the *general* or the *specific*, the *task* or the *person*, and *development* or *learning*.

---

*Paper presented as part of symposium, ''How, and How Much, Can Intelligence Be Modified,'' at the meeting of the American Educational Research Association, Boston, April 1980.

The first contrast between the limits and the potentialities of intellectual growth distinguishes theories in terms of their stance on the nature-nurture controversy and their views about the crystallization, stabilization, and eventual decline of intellectual powers. Positions on heredity versus environment and on stabilization and decline of intellectual functioning are orthogonal, however, rather than coordinate, although they may share some common implications for educational practice. For example, an hereditarian like Jensen (1972), noting that some individuals and social groups operate at the level of rote learning while others operate at a higher level of abstract learning, proposes to tailor educational programs to match those functional skills in order to capitalize on their respective strengths in subsequent school learning (Jensen, 1969). But an environmentalist like Ferguson (1954, 1956), holding that intellectual abilities are learned proficiencies that attain a crude limit of stability through overlearning, would also find such a capitalization matching strategy congenial because these developed abilities facilitate subsequent learning through transfer effects. However, for Ferguson, existing abilities also facilitate the differentiation and development of new abilities through transfer, so he should be more prone than Jensen to favor as well a corrective matching strategy that focuses learning experiences on the remediation of ability weaknesses, or a challenge matching strategy that attempts to stimulate new development by confronting new problems (Messick, 1976; Salomon, 1972). In the case of Jensen's two levels of learning, a concerted effort would then be made, through strategies of remediation or confrontation, to stimulate and develop abstract reasoning processes in those students currently relying on rote processes. Thus, the educational implications of an aptitude $\times$ treatment interaction can shift from capitalization on existing strengths to correction of intellective weaknesses to stimulation of ability development, depending on whether a distinction is made between fixity and stability and between stable abilities as products of development or as facilitators of development.

The second contrast distinguishes theories of intelligence in terms of their relative emphasis on structure as opposed to process. The main contrast here is between theories that focus on the structure of individual differences in intellectual functioning and those that focus on information-processing operations in the performance of intellective tasks. The former are usually factor analytic, and the dimensions of individual differences are ability factors; the latter are usually task analytic, and the components of task performance are elementary information processes. The distinction is not clean, however, since information processes are often highly structured into hierarchies, feedback loops, and organized sequences, while the dimensions of individual differences or ability factors represent constellations of intellective processes. Sternberg's (1977) componential theory of human abilities, by virtue of being equally cognizant of both information-processing components and individual differences, offers a potential bridge between the contrasting approaches. In Sternberg's terms, task performances are constellations of information-processing components that form task solutions or otherwise satisfy specific task requirements. Ability factors are constellations of information-processing components that form stable patterns of individual differences across multiple tasks. To further obscure the distinction between structure and process, ability factors may play a role in the selection and organization of information-processing components, since individual students may prefer task strategies that exploit their abilities or compensate for their weaknesses (Frederiksen, 1969). Moreover, ability factors, as organized constellations of information processes, may serve as components or subroutines in still more complex or temporally extended sequential processes such as problem solving or concept formation (Dunham, Guilford, & Hoepfner, 1968; Messick, 1972). Although cognitive styles are more likely candidates to serve as organizers of such complex sequential processes, higher-order abilities may also serve that role as well (Messick, 1973). An emphasis on the structure of individual differences carries with it into educational practice an emphasis on *variety* in human performance, thereby highlighting the possibility that individuals with different levels and patterns of abilities might perform the same tasks in different ways. This leads naturally to concepts like aptitude × treatment interaction and S-R-R or R-S-R paradigms (Glanzer, 1967; Snow, Note 1). An emphasis on the processes underlying task performance carries with it into educational practice an emphasis on *optimal* task performance. This leads naturally to concepts like mastery learning and S-R paradigms (Bloom, 1976; Messick, 1981).

The third contrast, that between the general and the specific, distinguishes among theoretical approaches in terms of whether the most promising lever for effecting growth is seen in the training of general processes common to many tasks or in the training of specific processes limited to particular classes of tasks. In this regard, a central issue is the priority given to the mastery of key tasks, as opposed to generalizability in coping with a variety of tasks. In hierarchical theories of intelligence, such as those derived from successive factor analyses of correlated factors, one often has a choice between working with the generalities at the top to influence the specifics at the bottom or vice versa. One could also start in the middle, of course, and work in either or both directions. The choice might depend, however, on whether the theory in question conceptualized higher-order factors as organizing and controlling source traits, as Cattell (1957, 1971) does, or as descriptive categories for classifying related abilities, as Burt (1940) does. Some theories, such as Garrett's (1946) differentiation hypothesis, hold that the higher-order factors, starting with g at the pinnacle, are the more basic processes, which differentiate over time into ever more specific lower-order processes. Other conceptions, such as Ferguson's (1954, 1956) transfer theory, hold that specific abilities are primary and that higher-order factors derive from positive transfer effects reflected in correlated abilities. In these cases, the choice of specific versus general intervention strategies would presumably follow the developmental flow of the theory. In a morphological model like Guilford's (1967), which deals with a three-way 5 × 4 × 6 cross-classification of uncorrelated factors rather than with a nested hierarchy of correlated factors, one would appear to have no choice but to focus on the 120 specific factors separately. However, according to Guilford's theory, these 120 factors evolve from the application of the five information-processing operations of comprehension, memory, convergent production, divergent production, and evaluation to the processing of 24 types of information in the environment, which in turn are generated by the crossing of four kinds of content (figural, symbolic, semantic, and behavioral) with six kinds of product (units, classes, relations, systems, transformations, and implications). There is thus a logical hierarchy implicit in Guilford's three-way model (Guttman, 1958; Messick, 1973) and a psychological primacy among the higher-order factors for the five information-processing operations. A choice between specific and general intervention strategies carries with it a natural preference for criteria of success, namely *degree of mastery* for specific strategies and *degree of generalizability* for general strategies, but both criteria should be employed in evaluating any intervention designed to facilitate growth in intelligence.

The fourth contrast between theories that are task-centered and those that are person-centered is a variation on previous themes. Here the concern is not with the relative emphasis on task processes as opposed to individual differences, but with task processes as opposed to intraindividual consistencies. These intraindividual consistencies include both ipsative patterns of the relative strength or level of abilities and traits within the person and idiographic patterns of their relative centrality or personal importance to the individual (Allport, 1961). Regardless of their normative levels, if certain abilities stand out for the individual because they are relatively higher or more developed than others or because they are more highly valued by that person, those abilities may influence the choice and organization of components in task performance. Cognitive styles are also patterns of intraindividual consistency that may serve to organize and regulate the course of information processing in intellective functioning, particularly in regard to the control of competing responses, motivational disturbances, and anxiety over error (Messick, 1972, 1973). Person-centered intervention strategies would tend to gear the intervention to the individual's current level and mode of functioning as a starting point. This is done, especially by theorists in the Piagetian orbit like Hunt (1961), not so much to obtain a match as to obtain an optimal mismatch. Environmental demands are contrived that are sufficiently beyond current competence to be challenging yet close enough to be manageable with some effort.

The final contrast is between theories stressing development and theories stressing learning. A key issue here is the nature of mediating processes. Mediating processes in theories emphasizing learning tend to be direct links between the stimulus conditions or task requirements and the response properties of task performance, whether these are conceptualized as internal chains of encoded stimuli and transformational responses organized into habit family hierarchies (Berlyne, 1965) or as elementary information-processing components organized into plans or production systems (Miller, Galanter, & Pribram, 1960; Newell & Simon, 1972). Mediating processes in theories emphasizing development tend to be facilitators and vehicles for task performance rather than components of task performance. The structure of cognitive operations available to the learner—whether concrete or formal in Piaget's terms—is an example of such a mediating vehicle. Another example is the level at which such cognitive modes as representational thinking are readily available to the individual. From this developmental perspective, an effective intervention strategy attempts to enhance the facilitating mediators that would in turn enhance a variety of cognitive performances, as opposed to direct attempts to enhance the components of cognitive performance per se, which would be a strategy more consistent with the learning perspective. An important instance of this developmental approach is Sigel's (1970) *distancing* strategy that attempts to create cognitive environments in which the child is constantly stimulated to reconstruct the past, anticipate the future, and take different perspectives on the present as a means of fostering representational thinking. Representational thinking as a mode of cognition could then facilitate the development of a panoply of cognitive processes, including the acquisition processes whereby new experiences are assimilated and accommodated and new cognitive structures are formed.

Within this context of alternative theoretical approaches and contrasting implications for educational practice, we will next consider this distancing hypothesis in more detail and examine some of its empirical ramifications. The distancing model derives from Piaget's conception of cognitive development, in which self-regulating processes function in and interact with a social context. The critical cognitive dependent variable in the distancing model is representational thinking. Since every experience has to be transformed into some symbolic system that mediates between experience and action, the first assumption is that representational thinking, as a central mode of cognitive functioning, establishes a basic set of processes necessary for general intellective functioning. The second assumption is that experience is not processed in its totality, but rather is abstracted and then transformed into an appropriate symbolic mode. Hence, what is assimilated in this process is in essence not experience but a representation of experience.

Because experience is multidimensional, its abstraction, assimilation, and subsequent accommodation in some representational mode may vary on at least two major dimensions—conventional and idiosyncratic. For example, while Western culture provides basic shared conventional knowledge, each of us has also had unique experiences. The conventional representation of an automobile, for instance, may relate to its function or structure, while idiosyncratic representation may reflect aesthetics or utility. One of the key implications of this perspective concerns the use of multiple-choice test formats in psychological assessment. Most correct responses can be considered to be in the domain of conventional or shared representation, while some errors may reflect idiosyncratic representation and interpretation. Thus, errors on multiple-choice items may not universally be attributed to ignorance or misinformation but sometimes to idiosyncratic applications of different representational symbols (Sigel, 1963).

Representational thinking and the ability to re-present experience into a symbolic mode such as language is inherent in the human condition. The development of substantive representations, both conventional and idiosyncratic, is a function of particular social interactions as they in turn interact with the level of maturity of the child. The content of the symbolic expression therefore varies with the type of social interactions experienced and the child's maturity level. Consistencies in these interactions culminate in characteristic patterns of transformation of experience.

The critical social interactions for facilitating cognitive development are distancing strategies: those external social behaviors that require an individual to transcend the present in time or space to satisfy the cognitive demand—by recreating the past, speculating about the future, or taking another's perspective on the present (Sigel, 1970; Sigel & Cocking, 1977). Inquiry has been found to be a particularly effective distancing strategy. Answering a question requires understanding of the message or directive, retrieving relevant information from storage, and transforming the retrieved constructions to represent them in an appropriate form of communication such as language, pictures, or gestures. However, if the question tends to focus on associative knowledge or is otherwise mundane—e.g., "What is the color of this shoe?"—there is no demand for reorganization or for integrating various elements and, therefore, little opportunity to develop and enhance representational thinking. If, on the other hand, the answer to the question requires reorganization, integration, and transformation—e.g., "What can you tell me about this shoe?"—such inquiry will stimulate and foster representational thinking. Open-ended inquiry places greater cognitive demands on a child than does closed inquiry and, further, allows for increased interaction and follow-up. This follow-up can provide feedback that in turn yields additional opportunities for reorganizing, restructuring, representing, and re-presenting experience (Sigel & Saunders, 1979).

This distancing model, integrating social interaction with cognitive development, provided the primary teaching strategy for two educational intervention programs implemented with preschool children from low- and middle-income families (Sigel, 1979). In both instances, when teachers systematically employed distancing strategies, the pupils developed more effective mnemonic, classification, and predictive skills than did children exposed to more typical preschool program approaches (Cocking & Sigel, 1979; Sigel & Cocking, 1977; Sigel, Secrist, & Forman, 1973).

Additional evidence of the functional value of distancing strategies was obtained in an investigation of parental use of such strategies with their preschool children (Sigel, McGillicuddy-DeLisi, & Johnson, Note 2). Again, systematic use of distancing strategies yielded increased mnemonic, classificatory, and predictive skills, suggesting that distancing strategies are potent sources for stimulating cognitive development irrespective of the agents employing them (parents or teachers) and the context in which they are used (home or school).

The distancing model is thus based on Piaget's fundamental proposition that development of cognitive competence stems from the interaction of specific classes of social experience and the child's developmental status. This interactive paradigm implies an interactive form of educational intervention that stimulates the child to *represent* experience internally as a means of achieving a variety of cognitive outcomes, which culminate in the development of symbolic representational thinking. This representational thinking is hypothesized to provide the cognitive base for subsequent skill development in reading, mathematics, and knowledge acquisition. The approach also implies an appropriate mode of assessment of cognitive competence, namely the use of measures which tap process as well as product (Sigel & Cocking, 1977; Sigel & Gallas, 1979). Moreover, a particular perspective on the role of affect or motivation is inherent in the distancing model. Piaget holds that affect and cognition are indissoluble, leading to a conception in which affect (feelings, interest, motivation) is embedded in each cognitive act. The distancing model does not isolate these affects, but recognizes that intellective functioning cannot be separated from the affective context. Inquiry may activate both a stimulating and a demanding cognitive environment. This helps to maintain interest and involvement, to be sure, but it may also produce stress and anxiety through frequency or difficulty of the questions. The teacher or parent has to accommodate to this affect, whether positive or negative, if the goals of the inquiry are to be optimally achieved.

In summary, the various conceptions of intelligence derive from different theoretical forebears and from different ideological assumptions about the nature of the human being. In an effort to illuminate some of the differences among these conceptions, a set of five nonpolar contrasts were formulated to highlight distinctive features of various theories of intelligence that have implications for educational practice. By means of these contrasts, we considered whether a theoretical approach emphasized the *limits* or the *potentialities* of mental functioning, whether it stressed *structure* or *process,* the *general* or the *specific,* the *task* or the *person,* and *development* or *learning.* Sigel's (1970) distancing strategy was discussed in some detail as an example of a pedagogical intervention deriving from the developmental as opposed to the learning perspective. Although distancing falls at one extreme of the development vs. learning contrast, this strategy is variously intermediate with respect to the other four contrasts: Deriving from the interactive theory of Jean Piaget, it stresses growth potentialities through social interaction, but as limited by the child's developmental level; it stresses cognitive structures, but also the processes of structuring and restructuring; it uses specific questions to stimulate general representational processes which in turn facilitate the development of specific cognitive skills; and, it highlights both the task and the person by virtue of stressing the optimality of the match between task demands and the individual's level and mode of cognitive functioning. This type of conceptual analysis of the theoretical roots of pedagogical strategies is intended to illuminate not only the theoretical implications but the value implications tacit in each approach.

## REFERENCE NOTES

1. Snow, R. E. *Theory and method for research on aptitude processes: A prospectus.* (Technical Report No. 2, Aptitude Research Project). Stanford, CA: School of Education, Stanford University, 1976.
2. Sigel, I. E., McGillicuddy-DeLisi, A., & Johnson, J. E. *The effects of spacing and birth order on problem-solving competence of preschool children* (Final Report, Grant No. R01 H1686. Prepared for the Office of Population Research, National Institute of Health). Princeton, NJ: Educational Testing Service, 1980.

## REFERENCES

Allport, G. W. *Pattern and growth in personality.* New York: Holt, Rinehart and Winston, 1961.
Berlyne, D. E. *Structure and direction in thinking.* New York: Wiley, 1965.
Bloom, B. S. *Human characteristics and school learning.* New York: McGraw-Hill, 1976.
Burt, C. *Factors of the mind.* London: University of London Press, 1940.
Cattell, R. B. *Personality and motivation structure and measurement.* Yonkers, NY: World Book, 1957.
Cattell, R. B. *Abilities: Their structure, growth, and action.* Boston, MA: Houghton-Mifflin, 1971.
Cocking, R. R., & Sigel, I. E. The concept of décalage as it applies to representational thinking. In N. R. Smith & M. E. Franklin (Eds.), *Symbolic functioning in young children.* Hillsdale, NJ: Lawrence Erlbaum Associates, 1979.
Dunham, J. L., Guilford, J. P., & Hoepfner, R. Multivariate approaches to discovering the intellectual components of concept learning. *Psychological Review,* 1968, *75,* 206–221.
Ferguson, G. A. On learning and human ability. *Canadian Journal of psychology,* 1954, *8,* 95–111.
Ferguson, G. A. On transfer and the abilities of man. *Canadian Journal of Psychology,* 1956, *10,* 121–131.
Frederiksen, C. H. Abilities, transfer, and information retrieval in verbal learning. *Multivariate Behavioral Research Monograph 69-2,* 1969.
Garrett, H. E. A developmental theory of intelligence. *American Psychologist,* 1946, *1,* 372–378.
Glanzer, M. Individual performances, R-R theory, and perception. In R. M. Gagne (Ed.), *Learning and individual differences.* Columbus, OH: Merrill, 1967.
Guilford, J. P. *The nature of human intelligence.* New York: McGraw-Hill, 1967.
Guttman, L. What lies ahead for factor analysis? *Educational and Psychological Measurement,* 1958, *18,* 497–515.
Hunt, J. McV. *Intelligence and experience.* New York: Ronald Press, 1961.
Jensen, A. R. How much can we boost IQ and scholastic achievement? *Harvard Educational Review,* 1969, *39,* 1–123.
Jensen, A. R. *Genetics and education.* New York: Harper & Row, 1972.
Messick, S. Beyond structure: In search of functional models of psychological process. *Psychometrika,* 1972, *37,* 357–375.
Messick, S. Multivariate models of cognition and personality: The need for both process and structure in psychological theory and measurement. In J. R. Royce (Ed.), *Multivariate analysis and psychological theory.* New York: Academic Press, 1973.
Messick, S. Personal styles and educational options. In S. Messick (Ed.), *Individuality in learning: Implications of cognitive styles and creativity for human development.* San Francisco, CA: Jossey-Bass, 1976.

Messick, S. Constructs and their vicissitudes in educational and psychological measurement. *Psychological Bulletin*, 1981, *89*, 575–588.

Miller, G. A., Galanter, E., & Pribram, K. H. *Plans and the structure of behavior*. New York: Holt, 1960.

Newell, A., & Simon, H. A. *Human problem solving*. Englewood Cliffs, NJ: Prentice-Hall, 1972.

Salomon, G. Heuristic models for the generation of aptitude-treatment interaction hypotheses. *Review of Educational Research*, 1972, *42*, 327–343.

Sigel, I. E. How intelligence tests limit understanding of intelligence. *Merrill-Palmer Quarterly*, 1963, *9*, 39–56. (Also in: Ira J. Gordon (Eds.), *Readings in research in developmental psychology*. Glenview, IL: Scott, Foresman, 1971.)

Sigel, I. E. The distancing hypothesis: A causal hypothesis for the acquisition of representational thought. In M. R. Jones (Ed.), *Miami Symposium on the Prediction of Behavior, 1968: Effect of early experiences*. Coral Gables, FL: University of Miami Press, 1970.

Sigel, I. E. On becoming a thinker: A psychoeducational model. *Educational Psychologist*, 1979, *14*, 70–78.

Sigel, I. E., & Cocking, R. R. Cognition and communication: A dialectic paradigm for development. In M. Lewis & L. A. Rosenblum (Eds.), *Interaction, conversation, and the development of language*. New York: Wiley, 1977.

Sigel, I. E., & Gallas, H. B. Cognitive-developmental assessment in children: Application of a cybernetic model. In M. N. Ozer (Ed.), *A cybernetic approach to the assessment of children: Toward a more humane use of human beings*. Boulder, CO: Westview Press, 1979.

Sigel, I. E., & Saunders, R. An inquiry into inquiry: Question asking as an instructional model. In L. G. Katz (Ed.), *Current topics in early childhood education* (Vol. 2). Norwood, NJ: Ablex, 1979.

Sigel, I. E., Secrist, A., & Forman, G. Psycho-educational intervention beginning at age two: Reflections and outcomes. In J. C. Stanley (Ed.), *Compensatory education for children, ages two to eight: Recent studies of educational intervention*. Baltimore, MD: Johns Hopkins University Press, 1973.

Sternberg, R. J. *Intelligence, information processing, and analogical reasoning: The componential analysis of human abilities*. Hillsdale, NJ: Lawrence Erlbaum Associates, 1977.

# 9

# *Improving the Skills of Learning*

ROBERT GLASER AND JAMES PELLEGRINO*

*University of Pittsburgh*
*University of California, Santa Barbara*

Reported here is a summary of research that attempts to identify and understand the processes and knowledge critical to abilities for learning in school. Solution strategies for inductive reasoning tasks, central to aptitude and intelligence tests, indicate three interrelated factors that differentiate high- and low-skill individuals. Analysis of performance on figural analogies indicates the importance of managing memory load: Young children and less proficient solvers appear to be particularly inefficient in allocating enough processing resources to reduce or avoid information loss. Studies of verbal analogy solutions reveal that skilled analogy solvers have more knowledge of task constraints; an appropriate understanding of rule structure is maintained despite problem complexity. Analysis of protocols of numerical-analogy solution highlights the necessity for accurate knowledge representation: Low-ability children, who have lower-order number concepts, do not solve analogies with systematic, mathematically-based rules. The implications of these findings for instruction in academic learning skills are discussed.

An individual begins a course of learning with initial knowledge and skills that facilitate or retard the learning of subject matters taught in school. While these initial competencies are comprised of specific knowledge and skills that will be modified by teaching, they also consist of general skills for learning that affect the extent of that modification. This initial competence of the learner has been considered in educational practice in several ways. One way considers the diagnostic assessment of a student's strengths and weaknesses in a subject matter—weaknesses that could be attended to in remedial programs. A second, used particularly with young children, is the assessment and training of necessary readiness skills (e.g., sound and symbol discriminations) that involve perceptual and language competencies required for beginning instruction in elementary school subjects. A third involves assessment through aptitude and intelligence test scores which are predictive of scholastic achievement. These three approaches refer to interrelated characteristics of an individual's performance; but in general, they emphasize dif-

*Our colleague Mary Beth Curtis contributed substantial revisions to the final form of this paper.
Preparation of this paper was supported by funds provided by the Learning Research and Development Center, University of Pittsburgh, which is supported in part by the National Institute of Education, U.S. Department of Education.

ferent aspects, namely, subject matter prerequisites, developmental level, and general and specific intelligence.

This paper summarizes our initial attempts to gain theoretical, and eventually practical understanding of the last of these approaches. It is now quite clear that commonly used tests of general intelligence and of verbal and quantitative aptitude measure the kind of intellectual performance that is most accurately called "general scholastic ability." The abilities of individuals tested by these methods are those that correlational evidence has shown to be predictive of success in school learning. That these tests measure certain abilities helpful in most school work has been reemphasized recently by Carroll (1978).

> The performances required on many types of mental ability tests—tests of language competence, of ability to manipulate abstract concepts and relationships, of ability to apply knowledge to the solution of problems, and even of the ability to make simple and rapid comparisons of stimuli (as in a test of perceptual speed)—have great and obvious resemblances to performances required in school learning, and indeed in many other fields of human activity. If these performances are seen as based on learned, developed abilities of a rather generalized character, it would frequently be useful to assess the extent to which an individual had acquired these abilities. This could be for the purpose of determining the extent to which these abilities would need to be improved to prepare the individual for further experiences or learning activities, or of determining what kinds and amounts of intervention might be required to effect such improvements. These determinations, however, would have to be based on more exact information than we now have concerning the effects of different types of learning experiences, including observation, practice, instruction, and so forth, on the improvement of these abilities. As matters stand now, we know very little about the parameters governing the growth of such individual attributes as language competence, reasoning ability and speed of cognitive operations. (pp. 93–94)

With the above in mind, the program of research described here overviews a continuing attempt to analyze the intellectual functions that are assessed in measures of scholastic aptitude. Our goal is to understand the development and organization of the constituent processes and content that lead to individual differences in the ability to learn and to show how these might be influenced through instruction. Over the long term, this goal will be achieved if we can relate abilities to learn to concepts drawn from modern cognitive theory, and then develop procedures, based on these interpretations, to identify sources of strengths and weaknesses in the skills that facilitate academic achievement.

## A GENERAL ANALYTIC SCHEME

The general analytic scheme that has guided our research efforts has evolved from our own work and that of others (Pellegrino & Glaser, 1978), and consists of a series of stages of analysis.

Our first step has been to identify a domain of tasks associated with an aptitude factor. By this we mean identifying a core set of tasks that frequently occur across widely used tests and have demonstrated consistent interrelationships in factor-analytic studies. Thus, a particular task or set of tasks chosen for analysis must have both a history of reliable association with an aptitude construct of reasonable generality and consistent predictive validity with respect to a criterion performance of academic achievement.

Having defined the domain of tasks associated with an aptitude construct of interest, the second step is to develop and validate information-processing models for the different tasks. These models must differentiate among multiple levels of cognitive processing—from estimates of molecular-basic processes to more molar and higher-level strategies controlling process integration and sequencing. This flexibility is necessary because individual differences may be manifested at different levels as a function of the range and distribution of ability being considered. The processes specified as the component processes of performance must also be accompanied by a level of analysis sufficient to explain individual item characteristics, individual subject performance, and the interaction of the two.

The third step in the analysis is to use the models of task performance as the basis for individual-differences analyses. Part of this analysis involves the investigation of the sources of inter-age and intra-age individual differences within tasks. A combined developmental and individual differences approach is important because it is necessary to map out the relationship between overall developmental change in mental ability and sources of individual differences within separate age groups. There may be no reason to assume that the sources of individual differences within one age group are necessarily applicable to individuals at a higher or lower maturational level.

The next step is the examination of cross-task consistency in sources of individual differences, resulting in a distinction between cognitive components that are general across all task forms representative of the aptitude construct and those that are specific to a given form or content area.

Once individual and developmental differences in cognitive processes are identified, work can then proceed on the analysis of criterion tasks similar to those used to establish aptitude test validities. In this way, the process and knowledge-structure characteristics of the cognitive performances accounting for the correlations of the aptitude measure with criterion performance can be identified. This sets the stage for investigation of the instructability of these characteristics and investigation of the influence of this instruction on learning.

## INDUCTIVE REASONING AND GENERAL ABILITY

Our work thus far has been concerned with the analysis of performance on tasks that represent the inductive reasoning factor. We have focused on these tasks because they have high scores on any general factor and the task forms cut across major content dimensions. Thus, while many forms of symbolic input serve to assess inductive reasoning skill, all inductive reasoning tasks have the same basic form or generic property requiring that the individual induce a rule governing a set of elements. Figure 1 provides an illustration of the various task forms associated with inductive reasoning and the different content dimensions that are typically utilized for a given form. For verbal and figural classification problems, the task is to determine the relationship(s), semantic, logical, geometric, etc., governing the base set and then to select the alternative that is consistent with the inferred rule. For the letter and number series problems, the task is to determine the relational and periodic structure of the element string and use it to complete the blank spaces. The verbal and figural analogy items require the individual to choose the alternative that relates to the third term in the same way that the second term relates to the first.

The numerical analogy is a similar form of this task, but uses two initial item pairs to reduce any ambiguity in specifying the appropriate type of relationship governing the problem. Finally, the figural matrix problem requires the individual to select the alternative that completes the matrix and that is consistent with the relationship governing the column and row structure. One or more of these task forms can be found on virtually any standardized aptitude or intelligence test at any age level.

## GENERAL COMPONENTS OF INDUCTION TASKS

The different inductive reasoning tasks described above have been the subject of various empirical and theoretical studies.[1] A synthesis of these efforts provides a general framework for our discussion of the general abilities assessed by these tasks.

Inductive reasoning tasks can be said to require the following general set of processes:

1. encoding or representational processes that depend on information stored in permanent memory,
2. inference processes that can identify and/or generate relational features shared by two or more encoded elements,
3. rule assembly or rule monitoring processes that organize individual relational features into simple or complex relational structures,
4. comparison or match processes that can evaluate the similarities among relational structures,

---

[1]For example, serial pattern problems have been studied by Holzman, Glaser, and Pellegrino (1976), Kotovsky and Simon (1973), Restle (1970), Simon and Kotovsky (1963), and Vitz and Todd (1969); analogy problems by Evans (1968), Mulholland, Pellegrino, and Glaser (1980), Pellegrino and Glaser (1980), Reitman (1965), Sternberg (1977), and Whitely (1976); figural matrix problems (of the type found on the Raven's test) by Hunt (1974), and Jacobs and Vanderventer (1976).

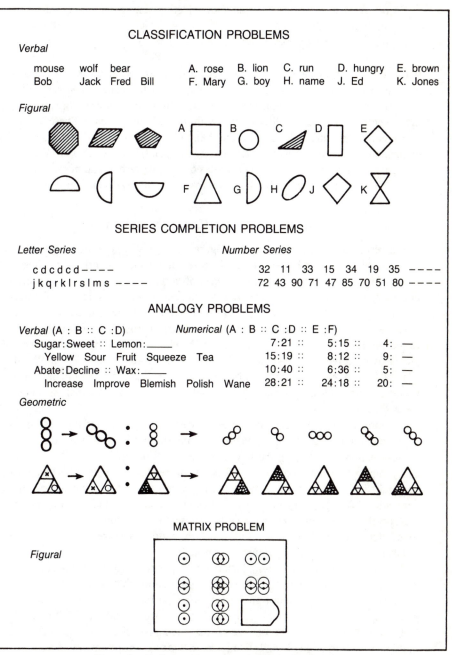

Figure 1. Task forms associated with inductive reasoning.

5. discrimination processes capable of selecting among competing relational structures, and
6. decision and response processes.

Published work provides extensive theoretical and empirical analysis of the details of these processes (see footnote 1). For the purposes of this paper, however, and at the expense of much oversimplification, we infer from our own work three interrelated factors that appear to differentiate high-low skill individuals. These are the management of memory load, procedural knowledge of task constraints, and organization of an appropriate declarative (or conceptual) knowledge base. We discuss each with reference to relevant studies of figural, verbal, and numeric analogy tasks, and then suggest implications for improving skills of learning.

## MEMORY LOAD (FIGURAL ANALOGIES)

In our research, we first investigated figural analogies because item features in these problems seemed easier to analyze (Mulholland, Pellegrino, & Glaser, 1980). In contrast to the symbolic aspects of verbal analogies, the information necessary for item solution is externally represented in the physical-problem array. The specific aspects of item content are the figural elements used to construct the separate analogy terms, and the spatial and logical transformations are applied to the elements to construct overall rules. The elements that comprise the terms are easily perceived, plane geometric figures—lines, circles, triangles, and quadrilaterals. The basic transformations include removing or adding elements; rotating, reflecting, and displacing elements; size changes; and variations in element shading.

A simplified model of the relationship between item content and processing assumes an initial pattern comparison and decomposition process which yields units of information representing the individual elements of a pair of analogy terms. The complexity of such a process is a function of the number of elements that must be isolated. The second stage of processing is transformation analysis and rule generation. This phase of processing attempts to determine the transformations that specify the rule for changing the A stimulus into the B stimulus. The complexity of identifying and ordering a set of transformations is a direct function of the number of transformations required in an item.

Each operation associated with pattern decomposition and transformation analysis of an A-B pair of terms yields a unit of information that is stored in working memory, and each element-transformation proposition requires an individual placekeeper or slot in working memory (e.g., Rumelhart, 1977; Simon & Kotovsky, 1963). As a consequence of this, the largest single source of error is multiple transformation of single elements. In this case, the intermediate results of the C-D rule-generation inference process must be retained in memory, and the entire transformation sequence inferred before the truth values of the D terms can be judged. Thus, it is possible for some of the original element-transformation information to be lost or degraded, due to such additional demands on working memory.

As the number of transformations in a figural analogy problem increases, the load of working memory can become substantial and give rise to errors. Increases in memory load may also require the individual to allocate substantial processing resources to avoiding or reducing information loss. In the processing of figural analogies, young children and less proficient solvers appear to be particularly inefficient in these aspects of performance.

The memory-load influence upon performance has been verified by empirical studies of other test-item forms, such as series extrapolation problems, where individual letter series problems, which theoretically involve several placekeepers in working memory, show the highest error rates (e.g., Holzman, Glaser, & Pellegrino, 1976; Kotovsky & Simon, 1973). A similar set of processing and working-memory assumptions may also be applicable to performance differences across items on figural matrix problems, such as those in the Raven's Progressive Matrices Test (see Hunt's, 1974, analysis of this task). In all the work of this kind, what has not been carefully studied is the strategies that individuals use to manage memory load, and the extent to which different individuals represent figural elements in memory in different ways to reduce memory load.

## PROCEDURAL CONSTRAINTS (VERBAL ANALOGIES)

The notion of differential procedural task constraints for high- and low-aptitude individuals has been developed in our studies of verbal analogy test tasks. On the basis of an extensive protocol analysis study of multiple-choice verbal analogy items, Heller (1979) has proposed a general model of analogical reasoning performance that attempts to describe the information-processing differences between individuals of varying skill in terms of behaviors that conform to or violate analogy task constraints. Effective problem solution is characterized as a series of steps directed toward the satisfaction of specific goals; and, the more constraints a solver is aware of, the more highly constrained will be the goals pursued.

By considering the "syntax" or rules for interpreting the structure of analogy items, solution episodes can be examined to determine whether they include behaviors that violate task constraints. When this is done, three categories of solutions emerge: analogical, nonanalogical, and "buggy" solutions. Solutions that contain no violations of task constraints are categorized as *analogical*. These analogical solutions are characterized by: (1) consistent attention to the relations contained in two allowable word pairs, and (2) consistent attention to the match between these pairs of relations.

Solutions that contain major violations of task constraints throughout a solution episode are categorized as *nonanalogical*. Nonanalogical solutions are characterized by: (1) attention only to relations between "illegal" pairs of elements, and/or (2) consistent attention to the match between inappropriately selected pairs of relations in two word pairs, and/or (3) a consistent disregard for the match between relations contained in two-word pairs.

The category called "buggy" solutions involves some behavior that violates task constraints, but is otherwise analogical. (The term "buggy" is borrowed from the computer programming notion of program "bugs" corresponding essentially to analogical procedures with "subroutines" that "misfire" under certain conditions, or analogical procedures with missing or faulty subroutines that manifest themselves under certain conditions.) "Buggy" analogical solutions contained both of the types of behavior described for analogical and nonanalogical solutions. Sample solution protocols for analogical and nonanalogical solution types are shown in Table 1, protocols one through five (Heller, 1979).

### Analogical solutions

When the performance of individuals who did solve items analogically is examined, a major distinction among analogical solutions is apparent in the development of the solvers' understanding of the analogical rule in an item—i.e., solutions can be "conceptually driven" or "interactive." In the conceptually-driven solutions, the solver's initial understanding of the A-B rule drives evaluation of the optional completion terms and is sufficient for discrimination among the options. However, in interactive solutions, the A-B relation is either inaccessible initially, or does not permit identification of a unique completion term from the option set. The rule is therefore identified or modified with reference to C-D relations. Interactive solutions require more extensive processing than conceptually-driven solutions, since they involve increasingly detailed specification of the analogical rule and/or consideration of alternative conceptualizations of the rule.

Individual differences in analogical reasoning ability appear to correspond to the differential availability or utilization of these additional processes. Low-ability solvers show an increased reliance upon conceptually-driven solutions—i.e., when low-ability individuals use the analogical solution procedure, they tend, more often than high-ability solvers, to evoke a sequence of processes corresponding to initial identification of the analogical rule. They do not subsequently modify that rule. Although low-ability solvers are also capable of solving items interactively, they do so less often than higher-ability solvers. On more difficult items, which are less likely to be solvable in the conceptually-driven mode, low-ability solvers exhibit performance that violates task constraints. This observation is further apparent in examination of nonanalogical solutions.

### Nonanalogical solutions

Three types of nonanalogical solutions were identified: one type represented solutions in which no attempt was made to identify the A-B relation—attention was paid only to the presence or absence of C-D relations. A second type repre-

TABLE 1
Sample Solution Protocols
(from Heller 1979)

| Analogy Elements Presented | | Solver's Response |
| --- | --- | --- |
| | Analogical Solution: Protocol 1 | |
| | Conceptually driven; one option matches initial specifications | |
| TEA:COFFEE :: BREAD: | | Tea is to coffee as bread is to . . . rolls because tea and coffee, they're both drinks, and they're about the same thing, just two different names for two different drinks, and a bread and a roll would be about the same—two different names for the same thing. |
| MILK | (Reject) | That doesn't fit, it's a drink. |
| BUTTER | (Reject) | Butter is something you put on bread, that doesn't fit. |
| ROLLS | (Accept) | That's good. |
| JAM | (Reject) | It's like butter, something you put on bread. It wouldn't fit because you don't put coffee on tea or in tea. |
| | Analogical Solution: Protocol 2: | |
| | Interactive; initial failure to identify A-B relation—analogical rule identified during option verification | |
| ABATE:DECLINE :: WAX: | | This is a good one, Oh Christ, I don't know—I can't say anything yet because I don't know what "abate" means. |
| POLISH | (Accept) | Well, wax and polish mean almost—well they're very close, and maybe abate and decline are very close. I don't know, I'm just gonna put true. |
| INCREASE | (Reject) | I just don't know. |
| WANE | (Reject) | To me, decline seems to have something to do with abate, even though I don't know what it means, but wane doesn't have anything to do with wax. |
| IMPROVE | (Reject) | I was thinking, maybe abate means "to decline" because wax may mean "to improve." And like before, it means "to polish." I like polish better, though. |
| | Non-Analogical Solution: Protocol 3 | |
| | Consideration of C-D relations only | |
| LINE:RULER :: CIRCLE: | | Ball. Because a ball is a circle, it's round. |
| ROUND | (Accept) | Yeah, a circle is round. |
| DRAW | (Accept) | No, because draw can't be a circle. Oh! Yes, it could be because you draw a circle. |
| RADIUS | (Accept) | Radius is the numbers in the circle, that's good. |
| COMPASS | (Accept) | Compass you use to go around—like you put your pencil and it's a circle. |
| (Which of these do you think best completes the analogy?) | | Round, because a circle is round. |
| | Nonanalogical Solution: Protocol 4 | |
| | Identification of A-B and C-D relations; no relational cmparison | |
| TELL:LISTEN :: GIVE: | | Take. If you tell something, they're like taking it in. If you give something, they take it. |

*(continued)*

(Table 1 continued)

| Analogy Elements Presented | Solver's Response |
|---|---|
| *PRESENT* (Accept) | Tell is to listen as give is to present? Yeah, I'd go with that! You give presents? |
| *LOSE* (Reject) | No. Most people find something, they ain't gonna give it back. |
| *GET* (Accept) | Yeah. If you get something, somebody gave it to you. |
| *HAVE* (Accept) | When they give it to you, you have it. Yeah. |
| (Which of these do you think is best?) | Present. Because you give presents. |

Nonanalogical Solution: Protocol 5
Consideration of A-B-C-D interrelations only

| | |
|---|---|
| *SUBJECT:CITIZEN ::* *KING:* | King—king—queen. |
| (Could you explain how you got that?) | Well, subject to citizen—like the king is married to a queen so I figured king and queen. They stay together. |
| (What about subject and citizen made you think you'd need something that went with a king?) | Well, citizen is a person and is like a subject. So I figured that king and queen ought to fit into it. Same as subject and citizen. If I hear you talking about a subject, then it's probably the queen. |
| *RULE* (Accept) | This one is a good one here because you're describing the rules. The king and rule is almost like the citizens and rule and I think that, I guess this is a pretty good one. It's kinda hard. |
| (Could you explain a little bit more what subject has to do with citizen and king and has to do with rule?) | Well, the subject is a type of one thing and a citizen is like a person. So the king is a man who's higher and the rule is—the king rules the citizen. |
| *KNIGHT* (Reject) | I don't think so. Because knight—I can't really say why. |
| (What is a knight?) | A knight is a man that guards the king. That's all I can really say. |
| *PRESIDENT* (Accept) | This one's all right. President—king's almost the same thing, and both of them are citizens and they're subjects. |
| (What do you mean "They are subjects?") | Well, it's something—subject to something, I can't explain. King and president are citizens and they're subjects to another person—they're the subject of what other people are talking about. |
| *KINGDOM* (Accept) | This one's all right because the kingdom's where the king lives. I guess it's all right—I can't go against it. |
| (You said that president, kingdom, and rule are possible. Which of those three do you like the best?) | President, I like the king and the president because they're almost the same persons, they both rule in different places. |
| (And how do they connect with subject and citizen?) | Because they're both citizens and are subjects to a person. |

sented solutions in which an attempt was made (either successful or unsuccessful) to identify both A-B and C-D relations, but no apparent attempts were made to determine whether any two relations matched. A third type represented solutions in which all four analogy terms were considered, but attention was paid to the interrelations among three of four terms, rather than to the match between two distinct relations within element pairs. All three of these types of nonanalogical solutions include, by definition, violation of the central constraints of the analogy task—essentially that behavior should be directed toward identifying two distinct relations that are analogous or matching. However, the three conform with task constraints to different extents, and individual differences were reflected in the ability to solve analogies in accordance with task constraints. Nonanalogical solutions by the low-ability solvers were primarily of the types where no attempt is made to identify the A-B relation, or to refer to two distinct relations. Higher-ability solvers, on the other hand, considered all four terms in most of their nonanalogical solutions, and attended to two allowable relations.

In general, this research suggests that skilled analogy solvers are characterized by more knowledge of task constraints and by the ability to develop an understanding of the analogical rule in response to the item stem and response options. This is accomplished by suspending the top analogical goal momentarily and working on subgoals of the problem structure while maintaining overall task constraints. Conversely, less skilled solvers proceed analogically when they can easily identify an analogical rule, but if that rule is initially inaccessible, or no C-D relation can be found to match the initially specified rule, they violate task constraints of appropriate analogical syntax.

## KNOWLEDGE BASE INFLUENCES
## (NUMERICAL ANALOGIES)

Thus far in our discussion, we have essentially ignored the issue of the declarative or conceptual knowledge base necessary for solving analogies. We now turn to our work on numerical analogies where the influence of knowledge structure on solutions has been the focus of several studies (Corsale & Gitomer, 1979; Pellegrino, Chi, & Majetic, 1978). While such knowledge is relatively circumscribed for problems using numbers in the typical range of 0 – 1,000, it is nevertheless variable across individuals, depending on their background and experiences, and differentially affects performance.

The study by Corsale and Gitomer (1979) attempted to characterize the differences in the knowledge bases of high- and low-ability individuals, and then to indicate how these knowledge differences influence subjects' strategies. Two kinds of data were collected: an initial set that was used to characterize the knowledge representations of the elementary school children participating in the study and a second set of protocol data taken from their problem solutions.

Two tasks were designed to tap the representations of the children's knowledge of numerical relationships. The first task was a grouping task in which the child was given a matrix of numbers from 0 – 32, and asked to select groups of numbers that went together and to justify his or her groupings. On the basis of these justifications, the kinds of groups children made were classified into four types:

1. abstract concepts, representing mathematically-based groupings with superordinate labels, such as the set of primes and multiplicative or exponential relationships,
2. operational concepts, which involved the stringing together of numbers into number sentences,
3. non-mathematical concepts, which were idiosyncratic groupings or groups based on orthographic similarities, and
4. digit-based groupings, involving numbers that shared common digits, the set of single-digit numbers, etc.

In the second knowledge-representation task, children were presented with 20 pairs of numbers, and asked to state as many relationships as they could for each pair.

Data from the grouping and pairs tasks were reduced by means of a factor analysis. Three factor scores were derived for each child. The first factor was readily interpretable as an estimate of the degree of "abstractness" found in the children's groupings and pair relationships. The second was a non-mathematical factor seeming to estimate the number of groupings and relations generated. The third factor represented a preference factor in which operational or computation-based groups and relations were preferred or were more salient than abstract groupings. Multiple regression analyses on these factor scores, using analogy test performance as the criterion variable, indicated that the degree of abstractness in number knowledge is an important predictor of success in analogical problem solving.

Having demonstrated that the form of knowledge representation is an influential variable, the interactions of knowledge representation and strategy usage for children of different abilities were then examined. The highest and the lowest scorers on the standardized analogy test were selected and engaged individually in a session of oral problem solving.

Analysis of these protocols indicates that knowledge representation drives solution strategies by defining the limits of the problem domain. Thus, high-ability individuals who have clear, high-level number concepts that are abstract in nature limit their analogical hypotheses to a few plausible mathematical relationships. Low-ability children, in contrast, have lower-order number concepts, and their analogical solutions indicate that they do not solve analogies with systematic, mathematically-based rules.

There were two categories of errors in analogy solution. The first, mathematical errors, were of two types:

1. computation errors, or
2. digit errors, in which the subject treated a number not as a total number concept, but as a set of isolated digits (e.g., "64 and 16 go together because they both have a 6 in them").

The second category of errors, analogical ones, were a variety of types:

1. nonrestrictive errors, where the relationship between the numbers in a pair was not specific enough to allow distinguishing among the options,
2. series errors, where analogy problems were turned into series problems,
3. single-pair errors, where the subject adopted a rule to apply to E that was true only of AB or of CD, but not both,
4. AC-BD errors, where children looked for relationships across pairs rather than within pairs,
5. nonanalogical computation errors, where computations were analogically inappropriate,
6. errors where an individual applied the correct rule, but in the wrong direction.

Low-ability children committed more analogically inappropriate computation, nonrestrictive, and digit errors. The kinds of errors they make indicate that they do not restrict their hypotheses concerning an analogical rule to mathematical concepts (as noted by the digit errors) or to analogical concepts (as noted by analogically inappropriate computation). Apparently, low-skill subjects have more diffuse, less-structured knowledge representations of numbers. This is manifested in the kinds of errors they make.

The lack of solution power, based on the less structured knowledge of low-skill children, is seen particularly in the probability of success in interactive solution procedure. This occurs in the course of solving an analogy when an individual does not initially infer the AB relationship and uses a backward inference strategy when presented with the CD pair. Both low- and high-skill individuals use an interactive strategy with equal frequency. Its successful use, however, is significantly higher in high-aptitude individuals.

The parallel between knowledge representation and solution strategy can also be seen in errors of the high-ability individuals. Analogies were turned into series problems more frequently by highly-skilled children in contrast to low-ability children. This is a sophisticated kind of error involving the detection of mathematical relationships across pairs that follow a constrained rule. In general, the errors made by skilled individuals show that the knowledge representation data, which indicated constrained mathematical concepts for these individuals, parallels their use of that knowledge. High-ability children, when they could not detect a rule, would "give up" and not select a multiple-choice answer, whereas low-ability children would select an answer—usually a wrong one—and justify it post hoc. High-ability children operate within both mathematical and analogical constraints, in order to achieve an analogically correct answer. They know when they are wrong and give up rather than choose an answer that they know is wrong. Not only do low-ability children choose the wrong answer rather than give up, but the protocol evidence suggests that they can justify their choices on nonanalogical and/or non-mathematical grounds.

Considering both the knowledge representation data and the protocol data, the study by Corsale and Gitomer suggests first that high-aptitude individuals have a greater degree of abstract mathematical knowledge and a greater salience of abstract over operational concepts. This knowledge correlates with and predicts analogy performance. High-ability subjects use their knowledge of abstract number relationships to constrain the domain of permissible operations, and this knowledge base determines the appropriate use of strategies. Low-skill children, in contrast, often engaged in analogically inappropriate computation and nonrestrictive errors. They apparently have not developed the highly constrained organizational structure of knowledge that would provide them with constrained rules of operation.

## DISCUSSION

As is apparent from the work reported here, we are in the early stages of our effort to understand and assess the instructability of learning skills. The bare outlines of our findings thus far as described here, permit some speculation. Three interrelated factors emerge that appear to differentiate high- and low-skill individuals. One is the management of memory as reflected by speed of performance and the handling of demands on working memory. Second, are the individual differences in the knowledge of the constraints of problem-solving procedures—what we have called the syntax of analogical problem solving. Effective problem solution is characterized by problem-solving steps directed toward the satisfaction of particular goals that are determined by problem-solving constraints. The more constraints the solver is aware of, the more highly constrained will be the goals pursued. Faced with a difficult problem, a skilled individual generates subgoals that enable a return to higher-level goals. For the low-skilled individual, solution difficulty results in violations of problem-solving constraints, the imposition of procedural bugs, and the inability to recover higher-level goals when subgoals need to be pursued. Third, the structure of the declarative-conceptual knowledge base and the level of representation of this knowledge differ as a function of ability. High-skill individuals employ conceptual forms of knowledge that constrain their induction of relations, whereas low-skill individuals encode their knowledge at more surface levels; this is manifested by their limited inferential power.

What are the implications of these findings of the experimental analysis of prototypical test tasks for a conception of academic learning skills? Of the three differentiating aspects mentioned above, the memory management component might suggest some sort of processing facility and process training, such as the employment of rehearsal and organizational strategies of the kind studied in memory experiments. The other two components, however, concerned with knowledge representation and problem-solving procedures, suggest a different emphasis. Overemphasis on memory management puts us in the position of considering the possibility of influencing a mental processing skill, such as better methods for searching memory and elaborating connections, so as to facilitate storage and retrieval. For example, could an individual be taught to see fewer single elements and more holistic features in figural analogy problems?

In contrast, an emphasis on the knowledge base and its representation, and an emphasis on the knowledge of problem-solving constraints suggest that we consider a knowledge strategy. In a knowledge strategy, progress is seen in terms of improving the ways in which a knowledge base is recognized and manipulated. When highly-skilled individuals learn something new or undertake a new problem of induction, they engage a highly organized structure of appropriate facts and relationships and associated procedures and goals constraints. Skilled individuals are skilled because of their knowledge of the content involved in a problem and their knowledge of the procedural constraints of a particular problem form, such as inductive or analogical reasoning. These two kinds of knowledge interact so that procedural constraints are exercised in the content knowledge base, and the knowledge base enables procedural goals to be attained.

This kind of analysis leads us to suggest that the improvement of the skills of learning will take place through the exercise and development of procedural (problem-solving) knowledge in the context of specific knowledge domains. The suggestion is that learning skills are developed when we teach more than mechanisms of recall and recognition for a body of knowledge. Learning skill is acquired as the content and concepts of a knowledge domain are attained in learning situations that constrain that knowledge in the service of certain purposes and goals. The goals are defined by uses of that knowledge in procedural schemes, such as those required in analogical reasoning and inductive inference.

How this facility could actually be taught is difficult to say at this point. One might teach more of the knowledge base and its high-level concepts, or one might teach procedural knowledge, such as planning ahead and recognizing when procedural constraints are violated. However, teaching either separately would probably be unsuccessful because each kind of knowledge facilitates the development of the other. Learning skills are probably developed through graded sequences of experience that combine conceptual and procedural knowledge. This is what must take place when a good instructor develops a series of examples that stimulate thinking.

Finally, there is the problem of diagnosing the weaknesses in individuals who are unskilled in academic learning. When this is done, we generally find that their knowledge base is not rich and that their skill in maintaining directed use of this knowledge is not developed. Perhaps a reasonable tactic is to identify some attained knowledge base where instruction can begin. Knowledge developed in the course of prior cultural experience can provide knowledge representations and goal-directed behavior that can be exploited. These exist in varying degrees in individuals as a result of prior experiences, and they can be transferred to domains of related knowledge which approximate more and more closely the formal abstractions and procedural requirements necessary for school learning.

## REFERENCES

Carroll, J. B. On the theory-practice interface in the measurement of intellectual abilities. In P. Suppes (Ed.), *Impact of research on education: Some case studies.* Washington, DC: National Academy of Education, 1978.

Corsale, K., & Gitomer, D. *Developmental and individual differences in mathematical aptitude.* Paper presented at the meeting of the Psychonomic Society, Phoenix, November 1979.

Evans, T. G. Program for the solution of a class of geometric-analogy intelligence-test questions. In M. Minsky (Ed.), *Semantic information processing.* Cambridge, MA: MIT Press, 1968.

Heller, J. T. *Cognitive processing in verbal analogy solution.* Unpublished doctoral dissertation, University of Pittsburgh, 1979.

Holzman, T. G., Glaser, R., & Pellegrino, J. W. Process training derived from a computer simulation theory. *Memory & Cognition, 1976, 4,* 349–356.

Hunt, E. Quote the Raven? Nevermore! In L. W. Gregg (Ed.), *Knowledge and cognition.* Potomac, MD: Erlbaum, 1974.

Jacobs, P. I., & Vanderventer, M. Evaluating the teaching of intelligence. *Educational and Psychological Measurement, 1976, 32,* 235–248.

Kotovsky, K., & Simon, H. A. Empirical tests of a theory of human acquisition of concepts for sequential events. *Cognitive Psychology, 1973, 4,* 399–424.

Mulholland, T. M., Pellegrino, J. W., & Glaser, R. Components of geometric analogy solution. *Cognitive Psychology, 1980, 12,* 252–284.

Pellegrino, J. W., Chi, M. T. H., & Majetic, D. *Ability differences and the processing of quantitative information.* Paper presented at the meeting of the Psychonomic Society, San Antonio, November 1978.

Pellegrino, J. W., & Glaser, R. Cognitive process analysis of aptitude: The nature of inductive reasoning tasks. *Bulletin de Psychologie, 1978–1979, 32,* 603–615.

Pellegrino, J. W., & Glaser, R. Components of inductive reasoning. In R.E. Snow, P-A. Federico, & W. E. Montague (Eds.), *Aptitude, learning, and instruction: Cognitive process analyses of aptitude* (Vol. 1) Hillsdale, NJ: Lawrence Erlbaum Associates, 1980.

Reitman, W. *Cognition and thought.* New York: Wiley, 1965.

Restle, F. Theory of serial pattern learning: Structural trees. *Psychological Review, 1970, 77,* 481–495.

Rumelhart, D. E. *Introduction to human information processing.* New York: Wiley, 1977.

Simon, H. A., & Kotovsky, K. Human acquisition of concepts for sequential patterns. *Psychological Review, 1963, 70,* 534–546.

Sternberg, R. Component processes in analogical reasoning. *Psychological Review, 1977, 84,* 353–378.

Vitz, P. C., & Todd, T. C. A coded element model of the perceptual processing of sequential stimuli. *Psychological Review, 1969, 76,* 433–449.

Whitely, S. E. Solving verbal analogies: Some cognitive components of intelligence test items. *Journal of Educational Psychology, 1976, 68,* 232–242.

# III

## *Discussion*

# 10

# *Modifying Intelligence or Modifying Cognitive Skills: More Than a Semantic Quibble?**

ANN L. BROWN AND JOSEPH C. CAMPIONE
*Center for the Study of Reading*
*University of Illinois*

The title of this volume: How, and How Much, Can Intelligence be Increased invites the inference that we know what intelligence is and we agree that it can be modified—thus, we are left with the trivial problem of the degree to which we can modify the beast. There are many who would quibble with these assumptions, who hold fast to one or more of the following awkward ideas: (1) we don't know what intelligence is, or at least we deal only with a very restricted range of intelligent activities, (2) it is essentially not modifiable, in the sense that intelligence is a relative term, referring to rank orderings of individuals within an age group, and the prognosis for changing those rank orders is not good, and (3) it is not clear we would agree on an outcome measure that would signify that intelligence in any real sense has been modified—tricky problems! Luckily, the papers presented in this symposium, with the exception of that of Garber and Heber, tend to be delightfully vague concerning the relation of their work to the title and in general, refreshingly modest in their claim to be at the modifying stage of anything. We agree, then, with Glaser and Pellegrino, that it is "the understatement of the decade" (we might even raise them a decade or so) to say we are in the early stages of our effort to understand and assess the instructability of intelligence. But the papers presented here do provide excellent insights into how far we have advanced and also serve to highlight some of the very thorny problems we still face.

First, we will solve the problem of what intelligence is, for the purpose of this discussion, by adopting Neisser's (1979) approach of seeking a consensus—here from the symposium participants. Sternberg, Ketron, and Powell and Glaser and Pellegrino are dealing with performance on IQ or aptitude test items, specifically a general class of inductive reasoning problems. Collins and Smith are planning to

---

*The preparation of this paper was supported by Grants HD 06864, HD 05951 and a Research Career Development Award HD 00011 from the National Institutes of Child Health and Human Development.

215

look at the possibility of inculcating comprehension monitoring skills in the context of classroom-like reading tasks. Belmont, Butterfield, and Ferretti are concerned with the possibility of training general strategies, relatively free of context; and Garber and Heber are interested in the extent to which large-scale and long-term intervention can lead to improvement in (or at least maintenance of) IQ scores which they believe to be indicative of general learning ability. Thus, by consensus, intelligence is the ability to perform well on school- and test-like tasks (i.e., the skills of academic intelligence). The main theme of the general enterprise is to diagnose the cognitive processes underlying familiar academic tasks with the potential goal of instigating training. This approach serves to translate the problem from one of training intelligence per se to training specific school-like cognitive skills. Although the difference may appear to be no more than a minor semantic quibble, we are much more comfortable talking about the feasibility of modifying a specified subset of cognitive skills than talking about modifying intelligence. We will return to this point at the end of the paper. But first, we will make a few specific points about the different approaches taken in some selected papers before returning to the general theme of intelligence and its modifiability.

The first distinguishing feature of the participants' chosen approaches is their initial choice of tasks and subjects. Some researchers in this area (e.g., Belmont & Butterfield, 1977; Brown & Campione, 1981; Feuerstein, 1979, 1980) select classes cf subjects as their main focus, while others (Sternberg, 1977; Mulholland, Pellegrino, & Glaser, 1980) start with the selection of tasks. Both then introduce variations in the other class. This initial choice has some interesting sequalae.

For example, in this symposium Sternberg et al., and Glaser and Pellegrino focus on IQ test-type items (analogies, syllogisms) and then look for sources of individual differences within those tasks, i.e., look at a range of subjects. Belmont and Butterfield choose to work with retarded children and then work within areas where these subjects are known to experience difficulty (e.g., memory problems). While in either case, the research must involve variations in both tasks and subjects, the choice of focus does influence the kind of research done and the kinds of questions asked. Sternberg et al., and Glaser and Pellegrino, beginning with a theoretical analysis of a class of tasks, then search for individual differences. The choice of subjects seems immaterial; Sternberg et al. work with college-age students who perform virtually errorlessly and rather quickly, making training efforts of questionable interest practically, although theoretically useful; and Glaser and Pellegrino do not always feel it necessary to mention who the subjects in the cited studies are. But the choice of subjects does seriously affect the kinds of inferences one makes about intelligence. Investigators who have worked primarily with college students (e.g., Hunt, 1978; Sternberg, 1977) have relied heavily on chronometric analyses and have emphasized speed of processing differences. Others, such as Brown and Campione (1981), and Belmont and Butterfield (1977), working with more extreme comparison groups, have emphasized the development and use of various problem-solving strategies and the understanding and control of them, i.e., the popular area of metacognition, which are well established in the developmental literature and now becoming more attractive to those working with adult subjects. Quite simply, the choice of tasks and subjects is not a trivial determinant of the theory of intelligence one works with and the relative importance attributed to various cognitive components.

The second general point concerns the stage in the cognitive modifiability game at which the symposium participants are working. All the participants have undertaken the first step; they have selected a task and subject population with which to work. All of the participants gave cogent reasons why the tasks they selected are related to the general topic of the symposium, and we found them quite convincing. No one here is concentrating on some obscure skills practiced in even stranger settings, and bearing a dubious relation at best to intelligence, although there have been many examples of such enterprises during the long history of this topic.

The second step is to compare experts and novices, or successful and unsuccessful performers, to see how they differ on the target task. The most detailed treatment of this stage at this symposium is provided by Glaser and Pellegrino. They map out differences between good and poor analogy problem solvers, both in terms of strategies and knowledge base components. This is an essential prerequisite for designing adequate training, given the increasing evidence to support the familiar notion of readiness. Quite simply, if you want to effect cognitive improvement, begin by diagnosing starting competence and then tailor instruction accordingly (Brown, 1982; Brown & Campione, 1981).

The third stage is to actually design training, hopefully in keeping with both the starting level of the subject and the purposes of training. Belmont et al., and Collins and Smith are both at this stage of the game, although neither has yet actually instigated any training, or at least any training following their grand design. The only paper of the four where anything approaching training was attempted is that of Sternberg et al., but this was a very specialized form of training—a point to which we shall return.

Finally, it is necessary to design outcome measures, or tests of transfer to see what it is that one's training has actually accomplished. None of the participants have taken this last step, although the theme of the Belmont et al. paper is on how one might achieve transfer of training. We will also return to this point later, but will first make a few general comments on some of the papers.

Sternberg, Ketron, and Powell situate their work within a domain, syllogistic and analogic reasoning, where a considerable amount of theoretical analysis has already been done. Sternberg (1977) has developed the implications of a number of alternative models which could be applied to these tasks. These models correspond to alternative ways of approaching the problem and thus permit inferences about how the problems might be solved, and how individuals might be taught to solve them. Using the models as a guide, it is possible to identify the approach taken by the expert and then to try to teach this to the novice.

We will begin with a few quibbles, or differences in interpretation. Sternberg et al. are interested initially in the tasks chosen and the specific models being tested. The choice of subjects is secondary, and they end up working with college students who perform extremely well and quickly on these inductive reasoning tasks. The very high levels of unaided performance makes these subjects less interesting trainees in the context of a discussion on what intelligence is and how it can be modified, and it forces a particular research strategy of which Sternberg et al. are certainly aware (see their footnote 1). They are concerned not with improving performance but with the question of "what general characteristics of certain strategies make them either optimal or nonoptimal in reasoning performance?" This is fine, but it raises two issues. The first is that the authors make this comment about the analogies research but not about the syllogism experiment, presumably because in the latter case, one training program was deemed effective in improving performance. This finding leads to the second point, alluded to by Sternberg et al., and one we would particularly like to emphasize here. When dealing with attempts to train or describe intelligent behavior, we wonder whether it is possible to talk about the "relative optimality" or a strategy without appending, (optimal for what?) which in turn requires a specification of what intelligent behavior (or intelligence) is presumed to be.

For example, consider the successful attempt to teach subjects an algorithmic strategy for dealing with syllogisms such as the problem, "John is taller than Pete. Pete is taller than Bill. Who is tallest?" As Sternberg et al. describe it, "Subjects in an 'algorithmic' group were told to read the final question first, then to read the first statement, then to answer the question in terms of the first statement ('John' in the example), and finally to scan the second statement. If the answer to the first statement *was not* contained in the second statement (as in the example, where 'Pete' and 'Bill', but not 'John', appear in the second statement), the answer to the first statement then was also the correct response to the entire problem (hence 'John' is the correct response in this problem). If the answer to the first statement *was* contained in the second statement, then the other answer choice in the second statement was the correct answer to the entire problem." Training here is "effective" in that it reduces solution time by 36% (from 7.03 sec. to 4.51 sec.). Sternberg et al. argue that the superiority of this strategy can be traced to its mechanistic (non-intelligent?) nature; it requires less thought. They do express some second thoughts about this strategy's optimality. We would like to emphasize their second thoughts. Note first that this algorithm works only with fully-determinate problems. We argue that the effects of teaching such a rule would be to enhance performance on the experimental problems (all of which are fully determinate) but to interfere with an intelligent approach to a greater variety of syllogism problems. That is, we would use transfer performance as a criterion measure, and transfer of this specific rule would seem to lead only to errors, for example, on indeterminate problems (John is taller than Pete. Bill is taller than Pete. Who is tallest?). An analogue would be to teach children that when confronted with a verbal arithmetic problem involving two numbers, the solution rule is to add those numbers (i.e., get them to ignore all aspects of the problem except the two numbers). We then give them a series of problems where this rule works; our prediction is that they will perform more quickly and accurately than an untrained control group. When subsequent verbal problems, some requiring subtraction, are presented, however, continued application of the instructed rule would lead to errors. Intelligence is generally assumed to refer to the ability to select the solution plan corresponding to the problem type, not the propensity to apply a blind rule. In the situation where individuals are taught to apply a rule which works for each of a series of problems, beneficial results of that instruction do not imply that there has been an increase in intelligent behavior, rather than the situation having been arranged in such a way that intelligence is no longer required. We will return to this contrast at the end of the paper.

The strengths of the Sternberg et al. approach are both clear and illuminating. The theoretical analyses are detailed and explicit, bringing out that which might otherwise remain tacit. Their analyses highlight both the advantages and liabilities of different strategies. In the analogies area, for example, self-terminating strategies require less time (as they involve fewer component executions) and place less demand on working memory; however, they run the risk of producing more errors. This detailed picture of the strategy can tie in well with attempts to match strategies to subjects. For example, young or retarded children have more severe functional limitations in working memory than older or brighter ones; hence, the use of a self-terminating routine may be even more advantageous for them and, therefore, an obvious candidate for training. The increased error rate introduced by the failure to search exhaustively could be more than offset by the reduced load on working memory. We have found in our own work that there are occasions on which retarded children benefit more from theoretically less powerful approaches to memory tasks, as they appear to lack some of the abilities necessary to carry out the more powerful strategy (Brown & Campione, 1977).

Another clear virtue of the Sternberg et al. work stems from their ability to make accurate determinations of what subjects in the various conditions are actually doing. If we want to know what the effects of strategy training are, we need to know what people do when left to their own devices, and what they do in response to training. An implicit assumption in training research is that subjects do what they are told to do, and experiments involving independent checks on that assumption are somewhat rare (see Belmont & Butterfield, 1977; Campione, Brown, & Ferrara, in press). Even less attention is typically devoted to what it is that the control groups are doing. In this regard, the Sternberg et al. studies represent a model against which others can be evaluated. It is possible for Sternberg et al. to make reasonable estimates of what individual subjects are doing (i.e., what strategy they are using).

Sternberg et al. also provide data that illustrate some of the problems associated with interview-based attempts to determine the kinds of strategies individual subjects may be using. For example, in their analogies study, Sternberg et al. report, ''. . . subjects' descriptions were highly consistent with the strategies subjects were trained to use, but not consistent with the strategies subjects actually did use . . .'' We do not necessarily agree with the further comment that this discrepancy indicates a lack of awareness on the part of the subjects of what it is that they were doing. The subjects may well know what they are doing but they may also realize that this is different from what the experimenter told them to do; in this bind, college-age subjects may well respond to the demand characteristics of the situation, and tell the experimenter that they are conforming. This minor disagreement merely emphasizes the strength of the Sternberg et al. approach and the importance of having some method for determining exactly what the learner is doing in our tasks. For, while there may be a variety of alternative explanations of the ''metacognitive'' data, the explanations agree in one important way—they question the extent to which introspective reports provide unambiguous data concerning the actual thought processes of the learners. This in turn makes it even more necessary to have independent ways of estimating strategy use while sidestepping these problems.

Glaser and Pellegrino, also working with inductive reasoning tasks, are concerned with both the strategic and factual knowledge necessary to solve a variety of analogy problems. Their approach differs somewhat from that of Sternberg et al. in that they use more difficult problems, thereby increasing the likelihood of errors. As a result, they must be concerned not only with the sequencing of component executions and the efficiency with which they can be carried out, but also with the factors that may affect the subjects' likelihood or ability to carry out the components correctly. Glaser and Pellegrino share with Sternberg et al. the approach of carefully delineating various potential methods of dealing with the items. Whereas Sternberg et al. begin with a set of analytic models, their approach is somewhat more data-driven. Glaser and Pellegrino are guided by the various solutions attempted by their subjects. These observations are then used to construct a theoretical framework within which to view individual differences. Armed with such a theoretical framework, it is possible to design instruction based on areas of particular difficulty for problem learners. Thus, the framework not only provides a description of individual differences, it also suggests the potential form and focus of remediation.

The Glaser and Pellegrino paper is then an excellent example of the technique of mapping the differences between experts and novices as a preliminary step to training. If one does not fully understand the extent of a novice's problems, training must be inadequate. While it may be axiomatic in instructional work that training should be aimed at the level of the trainee, this is not possible unless we have a fairly detailed account of different levels of sophistication possible within the task. The type of analysis undertaken by Glaser and Pellegrino takes us a long way in that direction.

While acknowledging the importance of strategic factors, Glaser and Pellegrino also emphasize knowledge-base factors that have tended to be overlooked in recent years. Although most theorists in this area pay lip service to knowledge-base components of performance, until recently the principal theoretical and empirical emphasis has been on either the design, selection and control of strategies by children (due to the obvious problems immature learners have with such activities) or on speed-of-processing differences shown by adults. But, it is also clear that the state of the learner's knowledge affects both speed of processing and strategy selection; thus, the call for an interactive model (Brown, 1982) is timely, and the emphasis on the knowledge base important.

Our only caveat with this approach in general concerns the current tendency to overemphasize the knowledge-base components—a tendency not indulged in by Glaser and Pellegrino, and a problem of which we are sure they are fully aware. Speed or strategic elements may have been overstated in the past, and there is an obvious need to redress the balance, but in so doing, we should avoid going too far in the other direction. Two potential problems of overemphasizing the knowledge base are: (1) the tendency to engage in suspiciously *circular arguments,* and (2) the tendency to confuse *stupidity* and *ignorance.* Consider the Corsale and Gitomer study quoted by Glaser and Pellegrino. They intended to show that a measure of numerical sophistication or knowledge is a prime determinant of performance on number analogy problems. The main measure of the knowledge base is the number of relations individual subjects can identify from given pairs or sets of numbers. This does in fact predict analogy performance, but as analogy performance requires the identification of (the same) relations, is this surprising? High ability subjects (both in the knowledge measure and in analogy performance) do show interesting and very neat processing differences—e.g., their flexibility when in trouble and their ability to see that they cannot solve some problems. But again, are these results very surprising? A learner cannot be flexible when he has little information available; flexibility requires a fair amount of knowledge. And, do the differences reflect ignorance or stupidity? From our perspective, an interesting question would be the extent to which analogy performance would differ across subjects who were "equated" in terms of their knowledge about number relations. For example, we might expect that individuals equated on knowledge would still differ in terms of their ability to access and use that knowledge when it was required. Knowledge is necessary, but not sufficient, for performance. Subjects vary not only in what they know, but in what they do with what they know and, therefore, what is needed is some measure of the efficiency with which a subject uses whatever is available (Brown, 1982; Brown, Bransford, Ferrara, & Campione, in press; Brown & Campione, 1981; Campione, Brown, & Ferrara, in press).

Belmont, Butterfield and Ferretti are engaged in designing a training package that would result in transfer of that training. To achieve this end, they advocate concentrating on executive control, metacomponents, general strategies, etc. We obviously agree with this emphasis. Our only caveat here is again to warn against overemphasis, in this case on the *generality* of the skills that are trained and the degree to which such skills can be *context free*. Belmont et al. are obviously aware that it is impossible to train executive control in the absence of the skills to be controlled (Belmont & Butterfield, 1977), and their own empirical work has been conducted within a readily definable domain—memory strategies. But, the current emphasis on training executive processes that are very general invites the inference that lateral transfer (Gagné, 1962) across quite diverse domains is to be expected. One might consider, in this light, the difficulty experienced by even college students in recognizing what are (to the experimenter) obvious problem isomorphs (Gick & Holyoak, 1980; Simon & Hayes, 1976). A great deal of learning is context-bound, and broad general transfer may be a chimera (Brown, 1982). In addition, although we agree that it might be possible to instigate a general *set* to be strategic, to troubleshoot, etc., one can only expect this attitude to be fully manifested in areas where the trainee has some expertise.

We are also somewhat uncomfortable with classifying as alike the six successful training studies merely because they all concentrate on self-control. Although, at some level, these studies are similar, they differ distinctly in their approach to what is being controlled or managed. We see a distinct difference between cognitive behavior modification, self-control packages (Meichenbaum, 1977) and cognitive skills training approaches, such as our own (Brown & Campione, 1981) and that of Belmont and Butterfield. The majority of clinical self-control programs are aimed at overcoming impulsive behavior; the desired outcome measure is transfer of self-control from the clinical (or laboratory) setting into the classroom. Training is usually aimed at improving "on-task" behavior, and success is measured by maintenance of "on-task" behavior in the classroom. It is often assumed that the skills needed to perform "on-task" are already within the child's repertoire; training is then aimed at overcoming emotional impediments to good performance. To oversimplify, perhaps to the point of distortion, far transfer in these programs has a decidedly physical ring. It is far transfer if the subject can carry the desired behavior with him from the clinic to the classroom.

In the cognitive skills training programs, the cognitive components of the skills in question are primary, not secondary, and it is usually assumed, and sometimes even demonstrated, that the trainee requires instruction in the basic processes needed to perform effectively, in addition to instructions in self-control. Success is also measured in terms of maintenance and transfer where maintenance refers to the continued use of the trained skill on the training task, and transfer refers to intelligent use of the trained skill on a class of tasks deemed to be "similar" to the training vehicle (Brown & Campione, 1978). Note that for it to be judged successful transfer, the learner must show appropriate application of trained *processes*, rather than self-control of emotional reactions. Here, far transfer is across conceptual distance, not physical space.

The assumed equivalence of the two approaches suggested by the six studies comparison tends to gloss over some real differences. And, this concentration on similarity, rather than difference, is particularly dangerous when comparing studies in terms of breadth of transfer, when one study might be concerned with "physical" distance and another with conceptual similarity. Under such circumstances, how can one meaningfully make a comparison of who transferred farther?

We argue that, although the two approaches share some common features, the cognitive skills training and cognitive behavior modification programs, as they currently exist, are very different enterprises, and what one would regard as transfer reflects these differences. Although the evidence is, in general, weak, we would expect that generality would be more likely in the impulsivity-control programs because of the complex interaction of subordinate processes, executive control, and knowledge factors involved in cognitive transfer. Again, the point is that it is very difficult to be strategic or planful in totally novel domains. And, recognizing the transfer context as an instance of the training domain is not a simple matter. In general, though, we welcome the research program outlined by Belmont et al., and look forward to discussing its fruits.

*Collins and Smith* also concentrate on metacognitive skills, such as predicting, monitoring, and evaluating one's own performance, but they hope to situate this training in the context of reading comprehension tasks common in the classroom. This practice has a great many advantages, not least of which is that it could serve to alleviate somewhat the problems of generality—their aim is to instill self-regulation in a context that is instructionally relevant. The main disadvantage to their approach is that we may not be ready yet to specify completely how comprehension-monitoring activities are used by experts—thus leaving somewhat vague their instructions to students (Baker & Brown, in press-a,b; Brown, 1980, 1981, in press-a).

In order to affect improvement in immature thinkers, it is usually necessary to be quite explicit about what they are required to do; the point where a decision is left open to the subjects' interpretation is usually the point where the training program breaks down. In reading Collins and Smith's proposal, we were repeatedly struck by the number of individual decisions the trainees must make and the imprecision of the criteria against which they must evaluate their understanding. Given the degree of latitude open to the subject, we were somewhat skeptical concerning the prognosis for instilling cognitive monitoring techniques readily in the young learner.

A recent training study from our laboratory (Palincsar, Note 1), however, was remarkably successful at improving the comprehension skills of problem learners. Palincsar set out to instruct her students in the use of more appropriate self-questioning strategies. The subjects were four seventh graders with adequate decoding skills (fifth-grade) but poor comprehension skills (second-grade). The form of comprehension strategy she trained was influenced by Collins and Smith's taxonomy, the main emphasis was on inference making and hypothesis testing.

The design of the study was influenced by the technology of applied behavior analysis. Each subject served as his or her own control. Palincsar had two interventions that she referred to as corrective feedback and reciprocal questioning. *Corrective feedback* consisted of asking children questions about a story they had read, and providing explicit information concerning the correct answer, the location of the answer in the text, and whether or not the material was implicitly (needed to be inferred) or explicitly stated. *Reciprocal questioning* was based on the *Re Quest* procedure developed by Manzo (1968). The student and the instructor took turns asking each other questions concerning the text. In this section, the instructor modelled two of the comprehension question types suggested by Collins and Smith: hypothesis testing and prediction making.

The children were tested for approximately 40–50 days (as it was a multiple-base line study the exact number of days varied slightly across subjects). Consider the optimal sequence where the children received first the directive feedback training in making inferences, and then the reciprocal questioning sessions where the primary focus was on hypothesis testing. During the base line, the students read grade appropriate stories, and answered 10 comprehension questions on each. They performed poorly, achieving a level of approximately 10% correct. Base line was followed by directive feedback where the level of performance increased to 50%—a level that was maintained during the return to base line, or maintenance phase. During the reciprocal questioning sessions, the level of correct question-answering rose to 90%, again a level maintained when the training sessions ceased. Note that these levels of correct responding were taken, *not* from the training session, but from performance on a novel text that the students read unaided, immediately after the interaction with the instructor was completed each day. Having appropriate questions modelled for them greatly increased the students' *independent* comprehension scores; in other words, the students internalized the activities that they had engaged in during social interaction as part of their own cognitive repertoire.

It is clear that Collins and Smith's training package also rests heavily on the ability of students to internalize the fruits of initially interactive learning sessions. In fact, the Collins and Smith training package is essentially similar to interactive learning studies inspired by the Vygotsky theory of internalization (Brown & French, 1979; Brown & Ferrara, in press; Vygotsky, 1978; Wertsch, 1978). The common feature of these programs is an emphasis on instilling self-control with the help of a supportive, knowledgeable other: a teacher, the mother, a peer, a master craftsman, etc. The passage is from other-regulation, with the supportive other modelling the questioning and monitoring behavior, to self-regulation where the expert cedes control to the novice. With time and experience, the regulatory functions exhibited (modelled) by the expert become internalized as part of the students' self-regulatory functions.

A very similar mechanism could be responsible for the success of the inquiry training programs described by Messick and Siegel. They contrast open-ended and closed inquiry techniques. For example, questions that force the child to focus on mundane details (i.e., ''What is the color of this shoe?'') create no demands for cognitive restructuring or growth. Open-ended inquiry (''What can you tell me about shoes?''), however, places ''greater cognitive demands on a child than does closed inquiry and, further, allows for increased interaction and follow-up. This follow-up can provide feedback that in turn yields additional opportunities for reorganizing, restructuring, representing, and re-presenting experience.'' In a series of training studies where the teacher employed the open-ended inquiry techniques, pupils were said to have developed more effective ''mnemonic, classification, and predictive skills.'' Although insufficient detail is given to enable a real comparison, the similarity with the Collins and Smith model and the Palincsar study is on the surface quite striking. Modelling appropriate questioning techniques provides an appropriate context for cognitive growth, the catalyst being the internalization of originally other-directed questioning that evolves on self-questioning.

A clear problem with all these theories is that the nature of this internalization mechanism is more than somewhat mystical and we are a long way from knowing how to ''turn it on'' on command. But, on the positive side, this is the essence of naturally occurring mother-child problem-solving interactions, and master craftsman and apprenticeship dyads. Furthermore, the Feuerstein Instrumental Enrichment program (Feuerstein, 1980), Collins' work with e xpert teachers, and recent experimental work in our laboratory (Brown, in 1981; Brown & Ferrara, in press) all depend on the internalization principle, and it does seem to work. We believe such training procedures mimic ''naturally-occurring'' learning situations. We argue strongly that the more we come to understand the mechanisms that promote the internalization process, the better manipulators of childrens' learning we will become.

Garber and Heber report the results of the most ambitious program of intervention of anyone in this symposium and make the strongest claim. In the abstract of their paper, they state that ''a differential of 20 points in Wechsler IQ found at the end of a preschool program was maintained at the end of fourth grade, indicating that a treatment program for high-risk children can prevent mental retardation.'' While we cannot in a few pages critique any effort as massive as the Milwaukee Project, we will make a few comments about some selected aspects of their presentation.

One concern is with the reliance upon changes in IQ scores as the major index of increases in intelligence, particularly in the context of a large-scale intervention program. If we accept the definition of retardation as an IQ below some cutoff point, then a program which raises the IQ score of its subjects above that point has in fact demonstrated that in some cases ''retardation'' can be prevented. The obvious problem here is that the intervention may involve a considerable amount of ''teaching to the test.'' Garber and Heber address this possibility by providing data on a number of other learning/performance measures which differentiate their experimental and control groups. One important set of comparisons involves school performance, although the fourth-grade data are somewhat disappointing in this respect. Thus, with a straight IQ-based definition of intelligence, their strong statement that retardation can be prevented does receive some support from their data; but if we include other indicators available, such as academic performance, the claim appears to be weakened.

For the purposes of this paper, however, we would like to avoid any further quibbling about their data base, and address a different point. Suppose we could be convinced that IQ scores, some measures of academic success, and other related aspects of performance were in fact elevated in the experimental group. Such results would be of clear and obvious practical importance. There would, however, remain the theoretical question: Would we be willing to conclude that the intelligence of the experimental group had been raised? Again, the answer depends upon the answerer's view of intelligence. If an individual's intelligence were regarded as an indication of his or her relative standing, all other things being equal, in terms of performance in some domain, we would argue that the data presented by Garber and Heber are not sufficient to allow any conclusion. For example, suppose the samples had included risk and non-risk children and suppose that all children showed equal increases in performance (i.e., the mean increased but the rank ordering remained unchanged). If intelligence is indexed by level of performance, then everyone's intelligence would have increased. In contrast, if relative standing were the essential defining feature, no one's would have. Given this outcome, we might conclude that important cognitive skills had been taught but that intelligence had remained unchanged. We will return to the distinction between improving cognitive skills and increasing intelligence later.

## GENERAL DISCUSSION

We now return to the contrast made in the title between training cognitive skills and raising intelligence. We would argue that although the participants may eventually be quite successful at training cognitive skills, their present papers are silent on the issue of intelligence and its modifiability.

First, the papers in this symposium do not address the issue. Theories of intelligence are noticeably absent, even though several of the participants have broached the larger issue in other contexts. The theories that are promoted in these papers are theories of learning within highly specified domains. How these domains relate to a global theory of intelligence is left unspecified.

For the sake of argument, suppose that the participants were further along in the modifiability game and had succeeded in training students to perform well on problems they previously could not solve. Again, for the sake of argument, let us suppose that the class of problems is the formal analogies. What would a successful training attempt of this kind mean? It would mean, of course, that the students would now be better able to cope with the type of formal analogy problem that occurs on IQ tests. It could also mean that the IQ scores of the trained students would go up as a direct result of their improved performance on the analogies subset of the test. But does this mean that intelligence has been modified in any serious sense?

We would argue that improvement on an intelligence test alone would not constitute proof of improvement in intelligence. Furthermore, we would argue that (within some obvious limitations) it is easy to raise scores on the IQ test. The trick is to adopt the tried and true ploy of "training to the test" (Campione & Armbruster, in press).

The technique of training to the test often results in an improvement in subtest scores, but again we would argue that this tells us nothing about intelligence unless something else accrues from training.[1] Improving everyone's scores merely destroys the predictive validity of that item by wiping out the range of individual scores, and hence, providing no information about rank ordering. It is only in a trivial sense that rank orderings are obliterated by, for example, "mastery learning" procedures or training-to-the-test (Campione & Armbruster, in press). They can very easily be recaptured by using, as a measure of efficiency, the extent of training needed to bring a student to mastery; this is the procedure adopted by researchers who are concerned with the "zone of proximal development" or the "region of sensitivity to instruction" as indices of intellectual functioning (Brown & Ferrara, in press; Brown & French, 1979; Vygotsky, 1978).

To illustrate, compare a hypothetical initially poor and initially superior student in the analogy training program. The initially poor student who has been brought to the level of the initially superior student through instruction may still differ considerably from the superior student. The superior student arrived at mastery with minimal instruction and, presumably, has arrived at, and will continue to arrive at, levels of mastery in many other situations with minimal help. The question is whether the poorer student will demonstrate improved learning as a result of training to mastery on a particular class of problem. If not, we would conclude that the student had acquired specific skills but had not acquired (to paraphrase Glaser and Pellegrino's title) "improved skills of learning." Our own theoretical bias creeps in here (indeed, it saturates the whole discussion), for we regard the traditional definitions of intelligence as valid. Intelligence is the efficiency of new learning and the breadth of transfer. Improving intelligence, therefore, must in-

---

[1]We would like to point out that Glaser and Pellegrino and Sternberg, the analogy buffs in this session, are *not* proposing only to train analogy problem solving to a level of mastery. They would argue that their interest is in understanding the processes that underlie successful performance on such problems for the cogent reason that intelligent people do well on analogy problems. An understanding of the *processes* that lead to successful performance will inform our theories of what processes underlie intelligence. We assume that if they undertake training, it will concentrate on the identified processes, not merely on achieving mastery on analogies problems. They could (as we all could) run into trouble if it should turn out that the processes underlying inductive reasoning performance are of limited generality, or are themselves indirect measures of "true" intelligence.

volve improving learning-to-learn skills (Brown, Bransford, Ferrara, & Campione, in press; Brown & Ferrara, in press; Campione, Brown, & Ferrara, in press).

Returning to our analogy training example, we would argue that in order to say anything about whether successful training tells us anything about modifying intelligence, we would need to know if anything else improved (i.e., what transfer of training accrued). We believe that transfer criteria are not just nice but necessary, but only because transfer is an integral part of our theory about what intelligence is, but also because considering transfer, one is forced to ask: transfer of what? mastery of what? . . . hence one is forced to make explicit what one is trying to train, what one is attempting to modify—and hence, by extension, just what one thinks intelligence is. For example, analyses of the success of existing cognitive skills training programs concentrate on the thorny problem of outcome measures (Bransford, Stein, Arbitman-Smith, & Vye, in press; Campione & Armbruster, in press). For example, how would one set about examining whether the Feuerstein Instrumental Enrichment Program (1980) "works?" Improvement in IQ scores might be nice but, as the contents of the training program are very similar to the contents of IQ tests, such a criteria is open to the criticism raised above, that one has trained to the test. Improvement in school achievement would certainly be a welcomed and encouraging outcome, but from a theoretical point of view, one would like to know exactly what improved and what were the mechanisms of change. What does the Feuerstein program claim to teach? Mainly learning to learn. If this is so, then a suitable outcome test would surely be some index of increased learning-to-learn ability. The point of this example is to emphasize that the choice of a "transfer task" or "outcome measure" is not trivial; it represents one's theory of what is being modified, of how much one can expect training to accomplish (the extent and domain of transfer), and, indeed, it represents one's theory of intelligence.

In the first part of their paper, Messick and Siegel argue cogently that the theory of intelligence that one adopts has powerful consequences on how one would design intervention and how one would decide if intervention has worked. We strongly endorse their argument.

These discussions concerning the nature of intelligence and the potential for modifying it through instruction or otherwise are certainly not new (Binet, 1909), nor are they without theoretical problems. As mentioned in the beginning of this paper, we are much happier talking about the modification of cognitive skills. The major criterion for successful cognitive skills training seems to be instructional relevance, and a desirable outcome measure seems to be significant improvement in a domain that has clear relevance for schooling (at least this seems to be the consensus). Some might quibble about the degree of instructional relevance of a particular activity or the importance for "everyday life," "job satisfaction," etc. But in general the nature of the enterprise is clear and a successful outcome would be readily recognized . . . if the child writes better, reads more fluently, progresses to word problems in arithmetic, etc., most people would be satisfied with the cognitive skills training program that accomplished these results. Issues of rank ordering, prediction, and selections are not of concern here; they belong to the "raising intelligence" argument. Indeed, an argument could be made that if one can engineer improved creative writing (see, for example, Scardamalia & Bereiter, in press) or summary writing (see Brown & Day, in press), the need for transfer is not pressing. Maintenance of the trained strategy on those occasions when called upon to write and summarize would be a significant, school-relevant gain.

The currently fashionable enterprise of cognitive skills training has two major advantages, the theoretical and the practical. Theoretically, if one has a model of the processes underlying success on a particular academic task, and one trains those processes and improvement accrues, this contributes a validation of the theory. Manipulative experiments of this type are an important complement to the descriptive and correlational studies which may represent a necessary first step in the overall scheme. The practical benefits of choosing to analyze an academically relevant task and situating training within that task are obvious. Issues of intelligence and its modifiability need not enter.

## REFERENCE NOTES

1. Palincsar, A. *Corrective feedback and strategy training to improve the comprehension of poor readers*. Unpublished manuscript, University of Illinois, 1980.

## REFERENCES

Baker, L., & Brown, A. L. Metacognition and the reading process. In P. D. Pearson (Ed.), *Handbook of reading research*. New York: Longman Inc., in press (a).

Baker, L., & Brown, A. L. Cognitive monitoring in reading. In J. Flood (Ed.), *Understanding reading comprehension*. Newark, DE: International Reading Association, in press (b).

Belmont, J. M. & Butterfield, E. C. The instructional approach to developmental cognitive research. In R. V. Kail, Jr., & J. W. Hagen (Eds.), *Perspectives on the development of memory and cognition*. Hillsdale, NJ: Lawrence Erlbaum Associates, 1977.

Binet, A. *Les idees modernes sur les infants*. Paris: Ernest Flamarion, 1909.

Bransford, J. D., Stein, B. S., Arbitman-Smith, R., & Vye, N. J. Three approaches to improving thinking and learning skills. In S. Chipman, J. Segal, & R. Glaser (Eds.), *Cognitive skills and instruction*. Hillsdale, NJ: Lawrence Erlbaum Associates, in press.

Brown, A. L. Metacognitive development and reading. In R. J. Spiro, B. C. Bruce, & W. F. Brewer (Eds.), *Theoretical issues in reading comprehension*. Hillsdale, NJ: Lawrence Erlbaum Associates, 1980.

Brown, A. L. Learning and development: The problems of compatability, access and induction. *Human Development*, 1982, *25,* 89–115.

Brown, A. L. Learning to learn how to read. In J. Langer & T. Smith-Burke (Eds.), *Reader meets author, bridging the gap: A psycholinguistic and social linguistic perspective*. Newark, DE: Dell Publishing, in press.

Brown, A. L. Metacognition and reading and writing: The development and facilitation of selective attention strategies for learning from texts. In M. L. Kamil (Ed.), *Directions in Reading: Research and instruction*. Washington DC: The National Reading Conference, 1981.

Brown, A. L., Bransford, J. D., & Ferrara, R. A., & Campione, J. C. Learning, remembering and understanding. In J. H. Flavell & E. M. Markman (Eds.), *Carmichael's manual of child psychology* (Vol. 1). New York: John Wiley & Sons, Inc., in press.

Brown, A. L., & Campione, J. C. Training strategic study time apportionment in educable retarded children. *Intelligence*, 1977, *1*, 94–107.

Brown, A. L., & Campione, J. C. Permissible inferences from the outcome of training studies in cognitive development research. In W. S. Hall & M. Cole (Eds.), *Quarterly Newsletter of the Institute for Comparative Human Development*, 1978, *2*, 46–53.

Brown, A. L., & Campione, J. C. Inducing flexible thinking: A problem of access. In M. Friedman, J. P. Das, & N. O'Connor (Eds.), *Intelligence and learning*. New York: Plenum Press, 1981.

Brown, A. L., & Ferrara, R. A. Diagnosing zones of proximal development. In J. V. Wertsch (Ed.), *Culture, communication, and cognition: Vygotskian perspective*. New York: Cambridge University Press, in press.

Brown, A. L., & French, L. A. The zone of potential development: Implications for intelligence testing in the year 2000. *Intelligence*, 1979, *3*, 255–277.

Campione, J. C., & Armbruster, B. B. Acquiring information from texts: An analysis of four approaches. In S. Chipman, J. Segal, & R. Glaser (Eds.) *Cognitive skills and instruction*. Hillsdale, NJ: Lawrence Erlbaum Associates, in press.

Campione, J. C., Brown, A. L., & Ferrara, R. A. Mental retardation and intelligence. In R. J. Sternberg (Ed.), *Handbook of human intelligence*. New York: Cambridge University Press, in press.

Feuerstein, R. *The dynamic assessment of retarded performers: The learning potential assessment device, theory, instruments, and techniques*. Baltimore, MD: University Park Press, 1979.

Feuerstein, R. *Instrumental enrichment: An intervention program for cognitive modifiability*. Baltimore, MD: University Park Press, 1980.

Gagné, R. M. The acquisition of knowledge. *Psychological Review*, 1962, *4*, 355–365.

Gick, M. L., & Holyoak, K. J. Analogical problem solving. *Cognitive Psychology*, 1980, *12*, 306–355.

Hunt, E. B. Mechanics of verbal ability. *Psychological Review*, 1978, *85*, 109–130.

Manzo, A. V. Improving reading comprehension through reciprocal questioning. Unpublished doctoral dissertation, Syracuse University, 1968.

Meichenbaum, D. *Cognitive-behavior modification: An integrative approach*. New York: Plenum Press, 1977.

Mulholland, T. M., Pellegrino, J. W., & Glaser, R. Components of geometric analogy solution. *Cognitive Psychology*, 1980, *12*, 252–284.

Neisser, U. The concept of intelligence. *Intelligence*, 1979, *3*, 187–214.

Scardamalia, M., & Bereiter, C. Fostering the development of self-regulation in children's knowledge processing. In S. Chipman, J. Segal, & R. Glaser (Eds.) *Cognitive skills and instruction*. Hillsdale, NJ: Lawrence Erlbaum Associates, in press.

Simon, H. A., & Hayes, J. R. The understanding process: Problem isomorphs. *Cognitive Psychology*, 1976, *8*, 165–190.

Sternberg, R. J. *Intelligence, information processing, and analogical reasoning: The componential analysis of human ability*. Hillsdale, NJ: Lawrence Erlbaum Associates, 1977.

Vygotsky, L. S. *Mind in society: The development of higher psychological processes*. M. Cole, V. John-Steiner, S. Scribner, & E. Souberman (Eds.) Cambridge, MA: Harvard University Press, 1978.

Wertsch, J. W. Adult-child interaction and the roots of metacognition. *Quarterly Newsletter of the Institute for Comparative Human Development*, 1978, *1*, 15–18.

# Author Index

**Y**

Yachel, E. R., 89,
114
Yarrow, L., 75, *118*
York, R. L., *33*

**Z**

Zelazo, P. R., 90, 99, *115*
Zeskind, P. S., 78, 93, 109, *119*
Zigler, E. F., 14, 15, *37, 57, 65,* 71, 74, 75,
110, 111, *119,* 131, *137*

# Subject Index